# LOVE IN THE AGE OF THE INTERNET

# LOVE IN THE AGE OF THE INTERNET

## Attachment in the Digital Era

Edited by

*Linda Cundy*

KARNAC

First published in 2015 by
Karnac Books Ltd
118 Finchley Road, London NW3 5HT



British Library Cataloguing in Publication Data

A C.I.P. for this book is available from the British Library

ISBN 978 1 78220 146 5

Edited, designed and produced by The Studio Publishing Services Ltd

www.publishingservicesuk.co.uk

e-mail: studio@publishingservicesuk.co.uk

www.karnacbooks.com

*CONTENTS*

# *ACKNOWLEDGEMENTS*

I extend my gratitude to Dr Maggie Turp for her guidance throughout the sometimes stressful process of writing and editing, and to Judy Davies for her very skilful proof reading of my work. Also to Iro Tsavala for the lovely, evocative cover image that so elegantly conveys the potential of technology to both connect people and to alienate.

Thanks, too, to John Priestley, Paula Stone, and Joanna Benfield at the Wimbledon Guild Counselling Service for their enthusiasm for attachment over many years: they have given me opportunities and an environment in which to develop my ideas through the training courses we have evolved there. The original idea for this book was sparked while running a training day on attachment at the Wimbledon Guild, and it was Toni Rodgers, who was present that day, who invited me to write a paper to present for the Counselling Centre, Tunbridge Wells conference in 2012; a version of that paper is included here as chapter one.

This, my first attempt at writing for publication and at editing, was made easier by the staff at Karnac, in particular, Rod Tweedy and Constance Govindin, who responded reliably to all of my queries and guided me through each step, and Oliver Rathbone.

I thank all the authors who have contributed work to this book: finding time to think creatively, research, and write numerous proofs alongside full schedules as psychotherapists, supervisors, and teachers, demands great commitment. I really appreciate all the effort made to meet various deadlines, and your gracious acceptance of my editing and feedback. I extend special appreciation to Anne Power, who has encouraged me to write, often meeting my stubborn resistance, throughout our long friendship.

Finally, many thanks to close friends and families of each contributor, and my own nearest and dearest, for tolerating the preoccupation and absence of your attachment figures for so many months. I imagine that you have felt abandoned or, at least, short-changed on many occasions when your loved one had little time or energy to share with you. I hope you feel proud of their achievements and enjoy the book.

## *ABOUT THE EDITOR AND CONTRIBUTORS*

**John Beveridge** is a UKCP registered, attachment-based psychoanalytic psychotherapist, supervisor, and trainer working in private practice in Central London. His thirty-four years in recovery from addiction, and further training in the treatment of sex addiction and trauma reduction with Pia Melody at The Meadows, Arizona and at The Sensorimotor Institute, informs his work with people in recovery from trauma, chemical dependency, sex and relationship addiction, emotional anorexia, and co-dependency. He enjoys public speaking and sharing his clinical expertise on the connections between attachment, trauma and addiction. John is a trustee with ATSAC—a non-profit-making professional association dedicated to providing education and information about sex addiction and compulsivity.

**Linda Cundy** is an attachment-based psychoanalytic psychotherapist with a private practice in North London. She has taught for two decades on counselling and psychotherapy courses and is also an independent trainer specialising in attachment, human development, and clinical practice. She is Course Director and lead tutor of the Post-Graduate Diploma in Attachment-based Therapy, and consultant to the Foundation Diploma in Attachment-based Counselling, both at the Wimbledon Guild. She is Chair of Hackney Bereavement Service, which offers face-to-face and real-time online bereavement counselling to residents of the London Borough of Hackney aged fifty and over. Trained as a counsellor in the 1980s, Linda worked for a number of years for ChildLine and for mental health services until retraining at the Bowlby Centre in the 1990s.

**Lindsay Hamilton** is a psychotherapist in private practice and has worked with clients with a range of difficulties for eleven years. She is the Vice Chair of the Bowlby Centre. Lindsay teaches psychotherapy seminars, is a course tutor, the convenor of the Bowlby Centre Curriculum Development Group, active on the Clinical Training Committee (formerly Vice Chair), the line manager for the referrals committee, and is overseeing the redevelopment of the Bowlby Centre website and publicity. Alongside her training in psychotherapy, initially with the Minster Centre and subsequently with the Bowlby Centre, Lindsay worked with the Citizens Advice Bureau in management and staff training, and as an advice worker. She read Social Anthropology, Sociology, Social and Developmental Psychology, and Women's Studies at Cambridge University, graduating with honours in 1987. Besides her deep interest in psychotherapy, Lindsay enjoys writing, sculpture, painting, yoga, and raising three teenagers.

**Anthony Hanford** is a UKCP registered attachment-based psychoanalytic psychotherapist and an associate member of the BACP. He maintains a small private practice in Abingdon, Oxfordshire, and works part-time for Oxfordshire Mind as a group work facilitator. He also teaches on the Post Graduate Diploma in Attachment-Based Therapy at the Wimbledon Guild. Before becoming a psychotherapist, Tony worked for many years in supported housing and community resource projects with clients with severe and enduring mental health problems.

**Anne Power** qualified as a psychoanalytic psychotherapist at The Bowlby Centre after a preliminary group work training in the humanistic tradition. Her subsequent training with Relate introduced her to systemic therapy, and in her work with couples she draws on this in combination with attachment theory and psychodynamic understanding. She has an MA in Supervision from WPF/Roehampton

University. Most recently, she has completed studies in psychosexual work at Tavistock Centre for Couple Relationships and with Pink Therapy. She worked for some years in the NHS and for voluntary agencies, including Terrence Higgins Trust, and now has a private practice in central London. Since 2000, she has taught on various psychotherapy and supervision courses and is currently a visiting lecturer at Regent's University. Anne has published papers with an attachment perspective on supervision, couple work, and boarding schools, and is currently writing a book about therapists' retirement.

**Niki Reeves** has worked in clinical practice for almost twenty years, having trained as a psychodynamic counsellor in the early 1990s and then as an attachment-based psychoanalytic psychotherapist at The Bowlby Centre in London, where she is a member of the Ethics Committee. Niki has a full private practice in Southampton, working with individuals, couples, and families, is a qualified supervisor, and has tutored counsellors to diploma level. Niki has recently ended a term as Head of Counselling at Southampton Counselling in order to devote her time to writing and to running workshops on attachment.

**Jenny Riddell** is a psychoanalytic psychotherapist working with individuals and couples. She is a registered member of The Bowlby Centre and British Society of Couple Psychotherapists and Counsellors. Her specialist interests are in how a couple grieve, infertility, affairs, and working with couples in later life. She has a private practice and supervises, trains, teaches, and is academic supervisor for Master's dissertations on a variety of psychotherapy trainings. She has worked with Relate, WPF, TCCR, and is a member of BPC, UKCP, BAPPS, COSRT, and BACP.

*INTRODUCTION*

# Looking back and looking forward

*Linda Cundy*

It is a Sunday morning. Within a mile radius of where I am writing, there are dozens of estate agents advertising Victorian properties with "original period features", many "retro" shops selling household items that are pre-owned but not yet antique, a wealth of "vintage" clothes shops and markets, and numerous "artisan" bakeries and craft stalls. There are even a couple of purveyors of knitting yarn and patterns. In the local playgrounds and parks, toddlers have the same names as my elderly aunties and grandparents.

Somewhere nearby, a young couple—"digital natives" (Prensky, 2001)—are sitting in front of their ornate tiled fireplace enjoying morning coffee from 1950s coffee cups with a slice of toast made from an artisan sourdough loaf, while little Maisie and Alfie are playing with their brightly painted wooden toys. Finishing his breakfast, the father reaches for his Kindle to read the next chapter of a sci-fi novel, and mother takes out her iPhone to take a snapshot of the children—they look so cute in their hand-knitted jumpers. She uploads the picture to her Facebook page, and then sends it via Flickr to her parents in Australia for good measure. When will Alfie and Maisie tire of their traditional playthings and reach for a handset or screen?

Of course, this is only one sector of my local, very mixed community. So, meanwhile, on the street outside this family's front door, a young woman is sauntering by chatting to her friends back home in Latvia, Poland, Brazil, or Russia. People are transferring money electronically to their families in India or Nigeria and finishing college projects at an Internet cafe. A couple of Turkish boys sit side by side on a wall playing computer games on their hand-held games consoles while listening to music on their iPods. And, it being a Sunday, the local Orthodox Jewish community are conducting business in Israel, America, or Belgium on their mobile phones.

There is nothing new about nostalgia. The world is always changing; we develop new tools and technologies so quickly that every now and again it seems we need to look backwards to appreciate what was good about life before, and make a place for the good things again in the present. The technologies addressed in this book developed in the late twentieth century but have permeated every aspect of our lives in just the past ten or fifteen years, radically transforming the ways we learn, conduct business, play, and communicate. It is timely to consider whether we are losing touch with anything vital and essential for our wellbeing so we can keep a place for it alongside our digital lives, ensuring that technology supports what matters to us—what makes us human—rather than undermining us. As Carter pertinently notes, "The trouble with evolution . . . is that it cannot keep pace with human ingenuity" (2000, p. 97).

* * *

John Bowlby was influenced by both Darwin and Freud, but the human beings they sought to understand are undergoing a dramatic shift. From the start, our species has been marked out by rapid creative development of tools, and new technology has always led to evolution of our bodies and brains as well as changes in our customs and cultures. The recent advances, leading to a host of digital technologies that enable communication across geographical and temporal space, are altering not only our lifestyles, but also the very nature of our self-experience. This has changed how and what we communicate with each other. Technology is now a third element in two-person relationships, mediating the exchange of information and the expression of our needs, desires, love, and hate. It brings us together, yet many also find these changes alienating, dehumanising.

We do not, as yet, have even one generation raised from birth to old age with personal digital technology as an "e-third" (Stadter, 2013) present throughout. Those of us whose first years were lived in a world of public telephone boxes, waiting for the postman to deliver hand-written letters, and *Two-Way Family Favourites* on BBC radio (where families back home sent messages and song requests for loved ones overseas) straddle pre- and post-"singularity" (Prensky, 2001), and we might look back with nostalgia or look to the future with alarm—we are facing inevitable global extinction. However, we will also be enjoying many of the benefits that new technology is delivering and adapting ourselves to this new environment. We have a special place in the evolutionary process, with one foot in the past and one in the future.

Counsellors, psychotherapists, and psychoanalysts are well placed to observe this cultural transition. Technology has crept almost unnoticed into our private lives and into our professional world. The stories our clients and patients recount about themselves are replete with references to digital media: from linking up via chat rooms and social networking, Internet dating and Friends or Families Reunited, addictions to online gaming, gambling, shopping, sex, or Google searches, cyberbullying, cyberstalking, and identity theft, virtual world experiences and digital devices as fetishes, working online and communicating with loved ones across the globe via Skype and Instagram, misunderstandings caused by text or email messaging—their lives and ours are intimately bound up with the Worldwide Web and communication (or miscommunication) through the ether.

Psychologists have their own tradition of researching the effects of these technologies on human behaviour: Sherry Turkle, a sociologist and psychoanalytically informed clinical psychologist, began publishing works on our relationship with computers and robots as early as 1984 (Turkle, 1984, 1995, 2007, 2011). Psychoanalytic interest in the psychic significance of cyberspace and digitally mediated communication is more recent (Akhtar, 2011; Balick, 2014; Carlino, 2011; Lemma & Caparrotta, 2014; Scharff, 2013). Attachment theory bridges the two realms of external and internal reality: Bowlby insisted we recognise the impact of actual events and the imprint of the social, historical, political, and relational matrix on the minds of our patients. His classical attachment theory drew on findings from other disciplines that threw light on human experience, including Darwin's evolutionary perspective, ethology (the study of species in their natural habitats), and laboratory studies such as those of Harlow on primate behaviours, and he incorporated these insights into psychoanalytic thinking. Influenced by cybernetics, Bowlby formulated an understanding of the conscious and unconscious mind informed by control theory and information processing, and attachment theory has since integrated aspects of linguistics, trauma studies, and neuroscience.

In his lifetime, Bowlby was accused of placing too much focus on the external world and observable behaviours at the expense of elaborating the rich complexity of individual internal reality. He acknowledged this in a talk given to the Tavistock Clinic Social Work Continuation Group when he was eighty: he was unrepentant, explaining that he had devoted his life to correcting what he viewed as a bias in favour of "fantasy" over reality in psychoanalytic theory. (A video recording of this talk was given to me by Regina Allen; she had trained in social work at the Tavistock while Bowlby was head of the Children's Department, and she had been present at the talk in 1987. She later became a patron of the Wimbledon Guild where I met her in 2001. By that time she was rather frail and unwell, and she passed the video to me for posterity. I was able to hand it on to Sir Richard Bowlby for his archive of material about his father. Nowadays, the videotape seems a rather clumsy receptacle for such precious memories.)

But there has also been a rapprochement between attachment theory and psychoanalysis, a growing together after the rift caused by Bowlby's challenge to Freudian and post-Freudian orthodoxy. For me, a synthesis of attachment and object relations theories is helpful in considering the effect of the external world of relationships and culture on the inner workings of an individual's mind and on his sense of self. Attachment theory has morphed into something more complex through absorbing new influences, while themes of danger and safety, connection and separation, deprivation and loss are still at the heart of it.

I imagine that Bowlby would have embraced today's digital technologies, with all that they can offer, while perhaps cautioning against the potential dangers that insecure children and adolescents, in particular, might be exposed to in online life. Would he have been open to the practice of psychotherapy via Skype? Why not? Concerning the clinical implications of attachment theory, Bowlby wrote,

> A therapist applying attachment theory sees his role as being one of *providing the conditions* in which his patient can explore his representational models of himself and his attachment figures with a view to reappraising and restructuring them in the light of the new understanding he acquires and the new experiences he has in the therapeutic relationship. (1993, p. 138, my italics)

He then outlined five "tasks" that form the basis of his approach to the work of psychotherapy, all of which may be equally well achieved "remotely". For Bowlby, the foundation of an effective therapy was this provision of conditions conducive to exploration, including the therapist's role as a secure base from which the patient can explore both his internal world and external relationships.

* * *

We humans evolve to adapt to the changing social and technological environment that we ourselves have created, yet we still retain the primitive instinct to attach. Fonagy (in Lemma & Caparrotta, 2014) argues that we have an equally strong and primitive instinct for communication, and it is probable that our species began to develop technologies to communicate information and ideas early in our evolutionary story. Certainly cave art, stone figurines, and even a mammoth ivory puppet dating back some 26,000 years hint at the desire of our Ice Age ancestors to relay something more profound than mere entertainment to each other and to the next generation (Taylor, 2010). Today's amazing digital tools had their origins in this impulse to share ideas, to teach, and to pass on culture. And, of course, communication technologies continue to evolve at a dramatic rate—no sooner have I learned to use a device than it is almost obsolete. The green-shelled iMac I was once so proud of, with its space age looks and sophisticated features, now speaks an extinct language. So, by looking back at our personal histories and right back to the origin of our species, perhaps we can remind ourselves of who and what we are, what matters to us, what really needs to be communicated. We can then adapt our tools to meet our needs more closely in the future, while handling them with care in the meantime.

* * *

Some years ago, while I was running a training course (Attachment From Cradle to Grave, for the Wimbledon Guild Counselling Service), a mobile ringtone rang out from a bag or a pocket somewhere in the room. I remember quipping that this was an example of attachment behaviour, and suggested that someone should research the relationship between attachment style and use of communication technology. Fast forward several years and I received an email from a person who had been in the room that day; Toni Rodgers, head of training at the Tunbridge Counselling Centre, was organising its annual conference and invited me to do the research myself and produce a paper for the event. She also wanted a second speaker to address issues of the Internet and addiction, and I knew just the man for the job. The conference was held in February 2012, and those two papers (John Beveridge's and the first chapter in this volume) have been reworked to form the basis of this book. Other colleagues were also beginning to think about the impact of computers, smartphones, and the like on our day to day and psychic lives, and their papers in this book explore the impact of digital communication technologies on various kinds of relationship: the bond between children and parents that lays the foundations of the child's sense of self, attachment between adult couples, the human need for community, and the special kind of "love" that exists between psychotherapist and patient.

Although each of the authors here is grounded in attachment theory, we are a diverse bunch where relationship with technology is concerned. While some chapters celebrate the potential of email, Skype calls, and social networking for improving communication, empowering people, and offering therapeutic options, others are more apprehensive about embracing change uncritically, and caution us to be reflective and discriminating in our relationships with digital media lest we allow ourselves to be controlled by it. After all, while digital technology and culture do not create psychopathology *per se*, they may stoke many latent pathological processes, such as addictions, acts of aggression and bullying, splitting between sex and relationship, primitive thinking, defensive behaviours, and erosion of psychic and interpersonal boundaries.

In writing our chapters, each of the authors has spent many, many hours in front of a computer screen rather than engaging in the "real world", relaxing with loved ones, or being available as an attachment figure to friends, partners, elderly parents, and children.

Whether you have borrowed this from a library (long may such fine institutions exist), bought it from your high street bookshop, or purchased it online, and whether you are reading it in conventional form or an electronic version, I hope it stimulates your thinking, sensitises you to the complex nature of our relationship with technology, and alerts you to some of the questions we should be asking ourselves as psychotherapists in a rapidly changing world. In addition, I hope it reminds you of what it is to be human, a member of a deeply social species whose astonishing ingenuity sits alongside powerful ancient instincts.

## *References*


Akhtar, S. (Ed.) (2011). *The Electrified Mind: Development, Psychopathology and Treatment in the Era of Cell Phones and the Internet.* Lanham, MD: Jason Aronson.

Balick, A. (2014). *The Psychodynamics of Social Networking: Connected-Up Instantaneous Culture and the Self.* London: Karnac.

Bowlby, J. (1993). *A Secure Base: Clinical Applications of Attachment Theory.* London: Routledge

Carlino, R. (2011). *Distance Psychoanalysis: the Theory and Practice of Using Communication Technology in the Clinic.* London: Karnac.

Carter, R. (2000). *Mapping the Mind.* London: Phoenix.

Fonagy, P. (2014). Foreword. In: A. Lemma & L. Caparrotta (Eds.), *Psychoanalysis in the Technoculture Era* (pp. xv–xxi). Hove: Routledge.

Lemma, A., & Caparrotta, L. (Eds.) (2014). *Psychoanalysis in the Technoculture Era.* Hove: Routledge.

Prensky, M. (2001). Digital natives, digital immigrants. *On the Horizon*: 9(5): 1–6.

Scharff, J. S. (Ed.) (2013). *Psychoanalysis Online: Mental Health, Teletherapy, and Training* London: Karnac.

Stadter, M. (2013). The influence of social media and communication technology on self and relationships. In: J. S. Scharff (Ed.), *Psychoanalysis Online: Mental Health, Teletherapy, and Training* (pp. 3-13). London: Karnac.

Taylor, T. (2010). *The Artificial Ape: How Technology Changed the Course of Human Evolution.* Basingstoke: Palgrave Macmillan.

Turkle, S. (1984). *The Second Self: Computers and the Human Spirit.* New York: Simon & Schuster (new edition Cambridge, MA: MIT Press, 2005).

Turkle, S. (1995). *Life on the Screen: Identity in the Age of the Internet.* New York: Simon & Schuster.

Turkle, S. (2007). *Evocative Objects: Things We Think With.* Cambridge, MA: MIT Press.

Turkle, S. (2011). *Alone Together: Why We Expect More From Technology and Less From Each Other*. New York: Basic Books.

CHAPTER ONE

# Attachment, self-experience, and communication technology: love in the age of the Internet*

*Linda Cundy*

## Introduction

The infant's sense of self, his patterns of defences, creativity, and social brain develop in intimate relationship with care-givers. Parental delight in, and attentiveness to, their child lay the foundations for pleasure in relating, while shared "moments of meeting" (Stern, Sander, Nahum, et al., 1998) boost vitality and the capacity for intimacy. These first relationships are internalised as a secure, or insecure, basis of the personality. Throughout life, in times of stress, we again turn to others for comfort, reassurance, and support. Is the communication technology of the twenty-first century an aid or a hindrance to secure attachment? According to Stadter, "we need to study not only what technology can do *for* us but also what it does *to* us" (2013, p. 3). This chapter explores the impact of mobile telephones and texting, communication by electronic mail, Skype, and through social network sites on the sense of self as it develops in relationship with our attachment figures, and throughout life.

* This paper was originally prepared for the Tunbridge Wells Counselling Centre Conference, February 2012.

Argentinean psychoanalyst Carlino writes, "Socio-cultural changes and technological innovations that settle into and circulate within society affect both reality and people's subjectivity" (2011, p. 1). How might the ubiquity of mobile phones, email, Internet chat rooms, social networking, and blogs influence our subjectivity and shape the development of a sense of self? How are traditional boundaries between self and other affected, and what might the consequences be?

## *Attachment*

Human beings are a social species. We have survived and flourished through social organisation, co-operation, and communication. According to Bowlby, our instincts evolved over millennia in the original environment our distant ancestors inhabited. Our primary instinct is survival, and we rely on others for protection against danger. Attachment enabled the survival of the species and maximised the chances of individuals in a potentially hostile and challenging habitat (Bowlby, 1969, 1979). We are born with innate behaviours designed to gain proximity to a protective adult; Bowlby listed grasping with the hands, suckling, moulding the body into parental arms, calling out, and babbling as earliest means of attracting the parent. Early in life we can follow, first with the eyes, later by crawling, and eventually on two feet. The infant's smile has a special place in our relational repertoire, seducing mother into falling in love with her baby and reassuring her that she is loved and needed (Bowlby, 1958).

Modern neuroscience points to the role of attachment in structuring brain architecture.

> Given our dependence on groups for our very survival, primates have evolved elaborate neural networks for interacting with others as well as reading their minds and predicting their intentions . . . These systems of attaching, predicting, and communicating are all functions of the social brain. (Cozolino, 2006, p. 21)

Evolutionary psychologist Andrew Whiten proposes that our species is characterised by its "deep social mind"—an extraordinary interpenetration of thoughts and feelings (2007). While Winnicott noted that there is no such thing as an infant without the involvement of another person, Cozolino suggests that "a single human brain does not exist in nature", and that the natural environment of our species is no longer a geographical but a relational landscape (Cozolino, 2006, p. 11).

The instinct to reach out to another person in times of potential danger, anxiety, or illness persists throughout life. We may think of the emergency services and the National Health Service as meeting attachment needs for survival. The armed forces organise personnel with this instinct in mind. Certainly, communication technology promotes survival by making others readily accessible; stories appear in the press frequently—a couple lost in the Amazon jungle were found as a result of a mobile phone call to coastguards in Britain (*Digital Journal*, 21 September 2011), and a sailor thrown overboard by rough seas in the English Channel was rescued as a result of a desperate call to a builder's merchant in Devon (*BBC News Online*, 24 May 2013). However, once survival can be more or less taken for granted, the *quality* of attachment has implications for psychological health, or psychopathology. Most parents manage to keep their offspring alive, but not all manage to raise stable, resilient, emotionally healthy children. "Those who are nurtured best, survive best" (Cozolino, 2006, p. 14).

Attachment is related to spatial and emotional distance. We need our protectors to be available in times of perceived danger, and we need them at a comfortable distance in order to feel a safe connection, a secure base. For some, attachment figures must always be close at hand and they are anxious when the gap is too great; they feel frighteningly alone and exposed. Others need more space, feeling suffocated by demands for intimacy. We develop psychological and behavioural defences to regulate the emotional distance between ourselves and other people, while still maintaining the connection. It is as if we are joined to our significant others with an elastic thread which is best kept slightly taught, neither slack nor overstretched. The length of the thread depends on our personal needs for intimacy and space. It is easy to observe in babies, who turn their heads away from overly intrusive attention, and toddlers who become alarmed if mum or dad is too far ahead in the park. As we grow, our tolerance of separation increases and young children parted from their families can be comforted by photographs and reassured by telephone and Skype calls. However, attachment-seeking behaviours also become more complex, more symbolic, and often distorted and disguised. This is likely to have implications for our use of communication technology.

Hungarian psychoanalyst Michael Balint, a contemporary of Bowlby, theorised that infants are stressed by contact with reality and long for moments of blissful safety and union that they experienced in the womb. They develop one of two patterns of defence as a result (Balint, 1959, 1968). Ocnophils are afraid of open expanses without human presence, and their defence is to cling to their objects or attachment figures. Conversely, philobats are alarmed by objects (people) and are drawn to the spaces between them in order to find homeostasis. The ocnophilic elastic thread is considerably shorter than that of the philobat. I postulate that the ocnophil uses mobile telephones, text messaging, Facebook, and Skype differently from the philobat. The former will rely on technology to feel closely connected at all times while the latter feels reassured by the remoteness that technology permits. He can maintain relationships at arm's length, and often on his own terms.

## *Attachment and communication technology*

Attachment theory is an evolutionary psychology. Our species, homo sapiens sapiens ("wise man"), is unique in developing a wide array of complex specialist tools. Our closest relative, homo neanderthalensis, also made implements, yet the design of these did not evolve into such a diverse toolkit. Technological creativity is in our DNA. Yet, while the geographical landscape of our species has changed, with fewer life-threatening features, our primitive instincts persist. Human beings have conquered the environment in many respects (though not all), and technology has greatly increased our ability to survive and to thrive.

Arguing in favour of "distance psychoanalysis", Carlino notes, "Today's human being is not the same as the one Freud studied more than one hundred years ago" (Carlino, 2011, p. 7). In some respects, the twenty-first century human being is not the same as that studied by Bowlby in the middle of the past century. Bowlby was influenced by the cybernetics of his day: how the brain processes information, prioritising some knowledge provided by our senses, defensively excluding other data that is too painful to confront and integrate.

Since then, sophisticated technology has instigated an evolutionary leap. It has changed the social landscape, providing new methods of communication, new forms of language, and new metaphors for thinking about ourselves. Recent research suggests that brains are changed by excessive computer use. While this is still being debated, I suggest that digital technology *is* shaping our relationship to reality and self-experience.

The computer has taken on some aspects of the ego. It is becoming an external hard drive, a satellite ego with many cognitive functions, including holding, retrieving, and sifting information, containing memories, and providing affect regulation—soothing and stimulating. Professor Susan Greenfield is alarmed by the rapid changes brought about by these technological developments, linking this with a reduction in communication skills, attention span, and ability for abstract thought. Human identity itself, she warns, is facing an unprecedented crisis (Greenfield, 2008, 2012).

Are we really facing the cataclysm Greenfield fears? Currently, it is believed that around fifty per cent of adults meet criteria for secure–autonomous attachment as defined using the adult attachment interview (George, Kaplan, & Main, 1985; Main, Hesse, & Goldwyn, 2008). Features of this optimal attachment style include valuing relationships, the ability to act independently but also to communicate needs openly and without shame, and the likelihood of providing a secure base for their own children. This leaves around fifty per cent of adults who lack the self-esteem, resilience, and relational reciprocity that typifies the secure–autonomous group. Dismissing and preoccupied adults have developed different defensive strategies for coping with stress (avoidance of intimacy with others or clinging to others), while those in the unresolved or cannot classify categories, lacking coherent strategies for seeking attachment or protecting themselves from harm, show features of severe psychopathology. The former have much in common with the diagnostic criteria for personality disorders, especially borderline personality disorder, while the latter exhibit a globally fragmented discourse style, internal world, and sense of self also seen in schizophrenia (Hesse, 1996, Main & Solomon, 1986).

When we feel secure, with a sense of belonging to a social group where we are known and valued, we are better able to act with self-agency. Mobile phones, email, text, Skype, and social network sites enable communication across geographical space and time zones, maintaining emotional connections with loved ones—a virtual community. Sometimes, the technology is literally life-saving. But does it increase *felt* security? Are there features of modern communication technology that may actually *increase* insecure attachment, alienation, and psychopathology?

I begin by considering how communication technology might aid or hinder attachment in the first crucial months of life, when base levels of neurohormones are set, neural pathways are being laid down, and patterns of attachment are being internalised, all influencing brain architecture and psychological defences. This is illustrated with vignettes from a recent infant observation.

## *Infancy*

The newborn is utterly dependent on adults for survival. His brain develops in the context of his earliest relationship with "mother"—the individual or group who provides maternal functions and relating (not necessarily the birth mother, not necessarily female). The responsibility of caring for a newborn requires the new mother to withdraw from her old life for a time. In order to attune to the baby's needs, she is helped by the presence of an internalised secure base founded on the sensitive and reliable care *she* received from her own care-givers in the past. She also needs to be assured that her current attachment figures are available to support her. Communication technology can certainly provide access to the reassurance of partner, friends, and family to mitigate feelings of isolation, and emergency health services are also easily reached in case of crisis. With this safety net, a securely attached care-giver can abandon herself to enjoying contact with her baby.

The sense of self is founded on a core that is fundamentally bodily. According to Winnicott, the experience of being safely held and handled with delight leads to the baby *having* a body, coming to inhabit his own skin (Winnicott, 1965a). The maternal functions of holding and handling are essential for the integration of the infant's mind and body, psyche and soma. Winnicott suggested that the mother's pleasure in her infant's body provides the context for "indwelling", for his mind to take root in his body, and for the self to be experienced as an embodied entity. An infant who is not securely held, or held in mind, who is not handled with pleasure, who is overwhelmed by too much contact with the outside world, or deprived of exciting engagement with the shared world, grows with the sense of himself as lifeless, fragmented, disembodied, or depersonalised. He is not safely contained within a psychic skin.

### *Infant observation*

> Feeding was functional with no communication of warmth and affection. Baby Harry was usually fed by bottle at arm's length, either propped against a cushion at the end of the sofa or on the floor in a baby chair. The mother made use of this time to read messages on her laptop or mobile phone, to check social networking, or make telephone calls. There was no skin contact, little eye contact, and seldom any words. The mother did not notice Harry gazing at her face as she was engaged in another activity on her screen. She would look at photographs of the baby on her computer, while the real baby in front of her was trying in vain to attract her attention.

Here is an infant deprived of bodily, emotional, or social contact, whose attachment-eliciting behaviours go unnoticed. I believe that his experience is not uncommon—we will all have seen similar scenarios enacted between carers and babies in public spaces. Communication technology is used to meet the care-giver's attachment and affiliation needs, but it interferes with the infant's developmental needs. This will have implications for the kind of attachment figure he internalises, the self-soothing strategies and defences that become habitual, the unconscious schema he develops of relationships, and the fate of his social brain.

In the first few months of life, base levels of neurohormones are established through relational experiences. Pleasurable skin-to-skin contact stimulates production of oxytocin, the bonding hormone, in both partners. High base levels of oxytocin boost the immune system, protect against anxiety and depression, and enhance social bonds (Cozolino, 2006). Developmentally, the physical organ of the skin also takes on a psychological function and meaning. The question of what is inside oneself and what is outside is key to healthy psychological development—the ability to experience oneself as a whole individual encompassed by a skin ego (Anzieu, 1990). The psychic skin is the semi-permeable interface between self and others. The infant experiences psychological containment through skin-to-skin contact, and "until the containing functions have been introjected, the concept of a space within the self cannot arise" (Bick, 1968, p. 484). We need a sense of what is generated and held inside us and what is external, other, in order to feel whole and real.

Winnicott also referred to the maternal function of object presenting: introducing the outside world to the infant in manageable chunks, stimulating him to an optimal level (Winnicott, 1965b, 1971). Too much too fast is impinging, traumatic; too little too rarely starves the infant of much-needed excitement which feeds his vitality. Khan (1963) describes "breaches in the mother's role as protective shield" (her failure to recognise when the infant is overwhelmed by too much reality) as cumulative trauma. Cortisol is produced by the aroused state and is initially pleasurable; optimal arousal actually contributes to structural growth of the left hemisphere of the brain during the second year. However, high levels of stress hormones flood the infant's vulnerable nervous system, leading to a toxic stress reaction (Cozolino, 2006; Gerhardt, 2004; Schore, 1994).

## *Infant observation*

> Harry was encouraged to hold and to watch the smartphone from around twelve months of age. It was used as a source of entertainment, as a distraction while mother busied herself or left the room, and was sometimes placed in the baby's hands as a self-soothing object when he was distressed. The device was symbolically important for the mother, who acknowledged feeling dependent and disliking being "on her own". Her smartphone connected her to important others in her life—her partner, parents, and social network. I was also struck by the cold hardness of that object, especially when offered as a soothing substitute. Mother discouraged play with soft or cuddly toys from Harry's first birthday because "they don't *do* anything".

The tactile feel of the phone—cold and hard—reminds me of Tustin's concept of the autistic sensation object (Tustin, 1990, 1992). She suggests that an autistic child will hold a rigid object in his hand and experience it as both an extension of his body and as protective armour wrapped around him. She writes, "hardness helps the soft and vulnerable child to feel safe in a world which seems fraught with unspeakable dangers" (Tustin, 1992 p. 115), and autistic sensation objects "give rise to the illusion of being encapsulated by a shell" (Tustin, 1990, p. 41).

It is not only autistic children who feel held together by contact with something solid and hard-edged. In the Strange Situation Test, toddlers of twelve to fifteen months and their mothers settle in a room with toys on the floor. A "stranger" enters and attempts to engage with the child. After a few minutes, the mother is asked to leave and the little one's reaction to this temporary separation is observed. On the basis of this separation and subsequent reunion, the relationship between mother and toddler is either considered to be secure or assigned to one of several insecure categories. A securely attached child will leave off playing to follow mother to the door and protest at her leaving, but where the relationship is avoidant the child will continue to play. However, on closer inspection, it is clear that the quality of play has changed. The toddler is struggling to contain his anxieties and typically picks up a hard object, such as a toy car or building brick, that he holds on to in a distracted way. Again, it is as if the rigidity of the object and its hard contours are experienced as helpful in holding the self together under great duress.

In the infant observation cited above, the mother uses her smartphone as an umbilical cord, the elastic thread keeping her connected to other people much of the time. However, initially, Harry could not have understood the purpose of the object, only the *feel* of it in his hands. He might have found this useful in containing himself when the adults around him failed to recognise his attachment needs or soothe his distress.

In contrast is the self-soothing behaviour of John, aged seventeen months when he entered a residential nursery for several days while his mother gave birth to her second child. James and Joyce Robertson, colleagues of Bowlby, filmed John's experiences as part of an attachment research project in 1969. John and his mother had enjoyed a secure relationship prior to this separation, and the toddler was overwhelmed by confusion and grief at being parted. However, rather than resorting to an autistic sensation object to create the illusion of a hard shell around him, John sought out human contact initially, and later clung to two large teddy bears that probably represented his parents and their usual capacity to comfort him. He was able to imbue them with living qualities, while Harry was denied soft toys because they appeared passive, inanimate, and perhaps infantile to his mother.

Turkle has written extensively about our relationship with computers and robots (1984, 2011). It seems that we have a great capacity for anthropomorphism, for attributing humanity to electronic circuitry if it is programmed to react to us or appears to initiate contact. "Sociable robot pets" have been developed to provide an illusion of companionship to the young and the elderly (Turkle, 2011). We project parts of ourselves on to them, such as our need for love and affection. I wonder whether there is a qualitative difference between the personalities we ascribe to complex technological creations that simulate some human capacities, and soft toys that are entirely passive. I wonder whether the mobile telephone in Harry's hand generates different fantasies from the soft toys of his first year. I also wonder whether he misses having a teddy bear to cuddle up to.

A baby has very limited means of managing hyperarousal. Gaze aversion is the most primitive defence against being overwhelmed by impingements. As he grows, other methods of self-soothing become available for those occasions when the attachment figure fails to provide the necessary affect regulation. Not all of his self-soothing techniques will be healthy. Schore (1994, 2003) postulates that *all* psychopathology originates in difficulty regulating affective states.

* * *

Several months later, Harry can discover what the mobile telephone *does*—it is now a toy.

### *Infant observation*

> At seventeen months, Harry was able to pick up the phone from the coffee table and had learnt the sequence required to switch the handset on. He would then pick out and double click on an icon that brought up a cartoon game related to a popular children's television programme. Although he could not yet take part in the game, he enjoyed mastering the physical procedure and accessing the resulting pictures. Despite his ability to manipulate devices, at eighteen months Harry had not yet started to speak.

I contrast this with a vignette from my own infant observation, conducted in the 1990s, before digital technology was widespread. It presents a very different attachment style.

> Claire, the mother, received frequent telephone calls from family and friends. In the first months, she would ignore the ringing telephone when she was breast-feeding, and later she might answer briefly, saying that she would call back shortly. Baby Ella showed curiosity about these exchanges. Sometimes, she would ask for the telephone to be given to her, and often Claire would hold the handset out for her to take. Increasingly, Ella became annoyed when her mother was distracted talking on the telephone. She did not show the same frustration when Claire was talking to me (as observer) or to another adult in the house. However, she did become irritated if her mother paid attention to Ollie, Ella's brother, then aged four. When Ella was ten months old, I observed her mother taking a long call from a colleague (she was planning to return to work part-time) and the infant complained vigorously. Claire picked her up but she tried to grab the telephone from her mother and was put down again. Ella returned to her toys then reached for her new upright walker. She looked at me, directing my attention to her new toy as if to say, "If mummy won't play with me, at least I know you will pay me attention". I waved to her and she waved back, grinning. She pulled herself up to her feet with the aid of the walker. Whatever she was engaged in, she looked back to make sure I was watching her. Claire later bought Ella her own brightly coloured toy telephone and it became a favourite. I often observed her babbling seriously into the receiver, then banging it back down on the cradle with aggressive pleasure.

* * *

Another demand on the good-enough mother is to put aside her own interests for a time and instead to identify with, and delight in, her infant's creative efforts (Winnicott, 1965a). The experience of having his efforts celebrated stokes healthy narcissism and builds a secure and resilient sense of self-agency. Claire exemplified this ability, but the mother who imposes her own ideas and needs on her baby instils an adaptive false self, where the infant has no faith in his fundamental existence as a separate individual, and insecure attachment results. Harry again:

> There was a period in the early months where there seemed sometimes a disconcerting tendency for mother to objectify Harry and regard him as

an entertainment or a toy. The infant was photographed in various adornments and fancy dress outfits. The photos were then uploaded to social networking sites. Comments as a result of these postings amused the mother. At these times, it felt as if he was a figure of fun for mother and others.

I recently heard of the practice of uploading footage captured on smartphones of babies and small children crying, along with witty explanations of why the child is upset. These clips attract a great deal of amused attention on sites such as YouTube. From an adult's perspective, the reason for a child's distress might seem comical, but I find it disconcerting that a parent is more concerned with entertaining friends than comforting his or her infant.

## *Rapprochement*

The infant of a narcissistic mother must distort his needs and behaviours to maintain proximity to her as his attachment figure. He may learn to disguise his anxiety, to precociously contain himself, if mother cannot tolerate his demands for reassurance and contact: avoidant attachment (Ainsworth, Blehar, Waters, & Wall, 1978). Or he may develop behavioural defences, literally clinging and demanding attention of a tantalising but inconsistent attachment figure: ambivalent attachment.

Shortly before Christmas at a local shop, I witnessed a toddler of about two with her mother. Mother pushed a supermarket trolley and was speaking to a friend on her mobile phone. The conversation appeared to be superficial and not urgent, about television programmes and so on. The toddler stood by the vegetables and pointed, trying to gain mother's attention, saying "garrots". Mother ignored her, so she persisted, "Look, mummy, garrots. Garrots mummy, mummy ..." Her mother continued talking on the telephone and walked away from her daughter. The little girl followed, still trying to converse. She clung on to her mother's clothes. The woman asked her friend to wait a moment while she issued a sharp rebuke followed by a slap. The child was stunned and began to cry. Her mother moved off, having resumed her conversation as if nothing had happened. The child was distressed and had not noticed her mother leaving. When she did, a wave of panic came over her and she ran, crying, in search of her mother. When she found her she began to wail. The woman, holding the telephone at arm's length, then screeched at her daughter, "You're a BAD girl. Now Father Christmas won't be coming."

Mahler refers to this stage of development—from about eighteen to twenty-four months—as the rapprochement period, or crisis (Mahler, Pine, & Bergman, 1975). The toddler is beginning to realise that he and mother are not one unit, but separate people. This means that he can be abandoned or lost, and can find himself utterly alone in the world—the elastic thread could be broken. Existential dread causes him to pursue mother and cling to her. However, he also fears losing his growing independence, being re-engulfed in a regressed, enmeshed, and suffocating relationship. This anxiety causes him to pull away and protest at any curtailing of his autonomy. We have the "terrible twos", a phase characterised by ambivalence. This developmental stage can be safely navigated when aided by sensitive but consistent responses from care-givers. The toddler then begins to experience himself as a separate person in relationship to reliable others. He has introjected his primary attachment figure as a secure base and can move away from her to explore his world and return to her for emotional refuelling. He can increasingly use symbols to represent her, such as transitional objects. In the supermarket vignette, the mother did not help the toddler manage her anxiety but withdrew from her, activating the child's attachment system, and the child was then punished for needing comfort. The message appears to be "For goodness sake grow up and stop needing me! You're a nuisance".

A further consideration here is rivalry and envy. Envy is stoked when the child perceives that there are not enough resources to go around—there is not enough of mother available to attend to everybody. In the above example, the toddler must share mother not with father or even a sibling, but with an invisible competitor. It might seem to her that mother is having a relationship with an ethereal other from which she—the child—is excluded. The child is effectively invisible to her mother and must either protest loudly, risking admonishment, or quietly accept her fate and manage the narcissistic blow in hope of gaining some scraps of parental approval. These are the ocnophilic and philobatic options: to cling to people or to contain oneself and take refuge in the spaces between them.

## *Adolescence*

Separation and individuation are revisited during adolescence as the teenager renegotiates relationships with parents, redefines himself, begins to find a place for himself in the world, and to make new attachments. This reworking of old conflicts results in "firmer boundaries and greater stability of both self and object representations, with a resistance to shifts in cathexis" (Keiffer, 2011, p. 47).

Communication technology can make this process more manageable for everybody: a discrete text message from teenager to parents letting them know what time he will be home, and Skype calls when the young person has flown the nest, can maintain contact and reduce anxieties. Some parents, however, cannot tolerate their children having independence or any privacy of mind. They fear being abandoned, as if attachment roles have reversed. They might try to curtail the young person's developmentally healthy desire for autonomy by instilling their own anxiety about the outside world. They might closely monitor his use of the Internet and chat rooms in the guise of protecting him from harm. These are "helicopter parents", hovering nearby and monitoring the young person's world for signs of danger. They might insist upon being a Facebook "friend", having access to the social life of their child, or maintain frequent intrusive contact via mobile phone while they are apart.

There are certainly legitimate concerns about the safety of our children. Bullying via text messages, exposure to pornography and other explicit material online, peer pressure to behave inappropriately (such as uploading photographs of themselves naked or in compromising situations), cyberstalking or grooming by paedophiles, websites promoting anorexia, self-harm, and suicide are all parental nightmares. The instinct to protect our children is activated, yet it seems impossible to ensure their safety from something so insidious.

Conversely, the inevitable conflict between teenager and parents may become focused on use of the Internet, social network sites, and computer games. Conflict is developmentally normal as the young person revisits oedipal struggles, challenges boundaries, and provokes reactions to his experimentations. However, there is a greater gulf between the current generation of adolescents and their parents than in previous times. Prensky described today's young people as "digital natives" (Prensky, 2001); they have been born into a world where digital technologies inform most aspects of their lives, from education and leisure to social relationships. Young people are indigenous to the Internet world with its language, customs, and culture. In comparison, their parents are "digital immigrants"; they have had to learn an alien culture and few of them are as fluent in the language or can find their way around cyberspace as efficiently as their teenage children. Prensky highlighted this generation gap in a paper on education:

> Today's students have not just changed incrementally from those of the past, nor simply changed their slang, clothes, body adornments, or styles, as has happened between generations previously. A really big discontinuity has taken place. One might even call it a "singularity" – an event which changes things so fundamentally that there is absolutely no going back. This so-called "singularity" is the arrival and rapid dissemination of digital technology in the last decades of the 20th century. (Prensky, 2001, p. 1)

Teenagers have always felt misunderstood by their parents' generation; indeed, Winnicott believed it is developmentally important that young people *do* mystify adults as they struggle to establish a meaningful, congruent sense of personal identity (Winnicott, 1965a). The dramatic technological advances of even the past decade can make the world inhabited by our teenage children puzzling to many parents, and the young people themselves might seem alien.

A major developmental task of adolescence is to move towards greater independence, renegotiating relationships with parental figures. Graham (2013) points out that "The many ordinary rites of passage of adolescence migrate into the digital domain, and young people are learning and testing themselves in this space" (p. 273). They may experiment with identity on second life-type websites, explore their sexuality through online pornography, and vent aggression in combat games. And in the teenage years the peer group takes on a key role, offering a transitional space through which to separate from the intimacy of the family unit. Teenage friendship groups provide a "skin" to contain their members, with implicit relational rules, roles, and hierarchies. Groups can provide a sense of safety and belonging in a changing landscape, as well as opportunities to practise care-giving, the complement to attachment seeking. Adolescent loyalty is strong, and group affiliation is maintained through social network sites, apps, and messaging. These recent technologies foster group cohesion, as all members of the cohort can access messages and photographs posted online simultaneously. Yet, these same media can widen the gap between generations.

A patient, a young man born a few years before the widespread use of mobile phones, pointed out that until recently teenagers' social contact was, to some extent, mediated by parents. He spoke of developing social skills through holding polite conversation with his friends' mothers and fathers on the household telephone before the receiver was passed to the intended person. In particular, he commented that parents once acted as "gate-keepers", protecting their daughters when they began dating. This opportunity to know and be known by the families of friends, and the protective parental function, are diminishing now as adolescents and younger children communicate directly on mobile phones and social network sites.

Adolescence is also a time of dramatic restructuring of the brain, putting under great strain the capacity to manage levels of arousal and to control impulses.

> The changes in the brain's reward circuitry required for new attachments during adolescence can also lead to confusion, disorientation, and depression. These biological and behavioral shifts are no doubt connected to the many impending life transitions that lay[*sic*] ahead. Unfortunately, these shifts are fraught with dangers related to risky behaviors and addiction coupled with poor judgment and lack of adequate impulse control. (Cozolino, 2006, p. 45)

Primitive defences evoked by adolescent anxieties can lead to splitting, scapegoating, envious attacks, acts of cruelty, and poor judgement. Aggression can easily become sexualised, and, in the digital era, acting out often takes place on the very public stage of social network sites.

In some situations, it is the adolescents rather than parents who are unable to tolerate separation and individuation. They lack an internal secure object relationship to support them in the world beyond the family, and they have no trust that help will be forthcoming. Indeed, they may feel ashamed of ever needing help. For them, the Internet brings the outside world into their bedrooms and virtual reality is as much reality as they can tolerate. Often addicted to online fantasy games, they lose all relationship to real others and to time, cut off from contact with the rational world. I think it is relevant that teen fiction is obsessed with vampires, werewolves, ghosts, and other creatures of the night, as so many adolescents themselves become nocturnal, inhabiting a liminal "as if" world at their computer keyboards and games consoles.

According to Turkle, "We're lonely, but we're afraid of intimacy. And so from social networks to sociable robots, we're designing technologies that will give us the illusion of companionship without the demands of friendship" (Turkle, 2012). The virtual life, a life lived in cyberspace, is a psychic retreat. It is a withdrawal from demands on the integrated psyche (Steiner, 1993). Denying the needs of the body for exercise, daylight, healthy food, and human touch, increasing numbers of young people spend their lives in front of computer screens, replacing real friendships with virtual relationships. Some create avatars and project their aggressive and sexual feelings on to these and out into the ether. Anna Freud described the defence mechanism of asceticism typical of adolescence—self-denial as avoidance of overwhelming primitive sexual and aggressive impulses. Informed by drive theory, she understands this attitude of self-deprivation as an attempt to master the instincts that disturb both body and mind at a critical time when the attachment relationship with parents is changing (Freud, A., 1936). A crucial developmental task of adolescence is to renegotiate the relationship with attachment figures in preparation for establishing new relationships outside the family. The anxiety evoked by this next stage of separation and individuation may also be dissociated during the hours spent living a virtual life.

In Japan, hikikomori is a recognised and alarming social phenomenon. Adolescents become hermits in their own bedrooms, often for years, relying on parents to deliver food to their doors. Parents of a hikikomori are tied to him like serfs, unable to take a holiday or separate from him, yet also unable to communicate with him. During their self-imposed retreat from the world, these young people play computer games ordered from the Internet, and communicate with others like themselves in dedicated online chat rooms. There is even animated online counselling aimed at reaching these recluses, complete with avatar therapists. I predict that, like sushi, hikikomori will become familiar in the west. Increasing numbers of people who cannot tolerate the give-and-take of ordinary human contact will conduct relationships online while holding their families hostage.

## *Later life*

Most people born before the 1990s spent their formative years without the benefits (and drawbacks) of digital technology. The devices we take for granted today were the stuff of science fiction and *Tomorrow's World*. Computers were mainframe and occupied whole rooms. Communicating with loved ones overseas entailed writing letters on thin, blue airmail paper and waiting weeks for a reply, or gathering around the radiogram on a Sunday to listen out for a message from home on *Two-Way Family Favourites*. Staying in touch required commitment, and separation felt more like loss.

These older generations straddle pre- and post-"singularity". Recent technological advances have been likened to the advent of the printing press, but it is unlikely that newspapers and books found their way into homes across all social strata, or had such a major influence on lives all around the world in such a short space of time. Even the telephone took longer to relocate from the red boxes on street corners to the hall tables of every home (and thence into our pockets). The nearest analogy might be the arrival of the radio and then television, which were quickly adopted as essential household assets, allowing access to information and culture as never before. Most of us were passive recipients at best, but families often sat together to listen or watch, and people chatted to one another about the latest news item or soap plot.

What we have now are new means of communicating, working, playing, living, and loving. Many of us have adapted to the emerging culture, either with alacrity or resistance. Wondering whether attachment style played a part in our eagerness to embrace technology, I undertook a brief, and purely impressionistic, piece of research among colleagues about the place of digital technology in their private lives. All participants are experienced psychotherapists and counsellors, and all are "digital immigrants" who described their relationships with different aspects of communication media. I then asked them to hazard a guess at their own attachment styles (all had studied attachment with me previously).

Here is a quote from Nina (who feels she has "earned security"), about her mobile phone use:

> I use it to make and receive calls and texts to friends and family. I use it in a spontaneous way on the spur of the moment if for instance I

hear a joke that I know a particular person will get, I'll send it on. It gives me a sense of security, knowing that I can be in touch if I need to. I also use it in a practical sense when meeting up; "I'm here," "What time?" "Where are you?" I have a photo gallery so I'm carrying friends and family on that. Impact on my life: very positive. It is good to know I can contact someone if the unexpected occurs.

Penny (describing herself as originally preoccupied but now secure–autonomous) wrote,

I have an iPhone, and I love it, I am very attached to it indeed. Not quite so far as going to the loo with it, but I do take it around with me, and use it a lot. I take a lot of photos and videos on it, and use What's App, which is a free messaging service, to send them to others, especially my son, who is away at Uni. I also use texts a lot to keep in touch in a reasonably low key way with friends and family, as well as phone calls. I check it for emails/texts about every hour or so. I have about ninety contacts. I also like the look and feel of my phone, and appreciate how easy and user-friendly the design is. I have a rather smart red leather cover for it. As I write this, I am aware I am feeling anxious about the prospect of ever losing it . . .

Meanwhile, Steve and Karen speak for many:

My idea of hell is to be available 24/7. I want to be in control of when and how I engage with people. Technology, particularly the mobile phone, can sometimes feel like an invasive tormentor. But I really value and enjoy the Internet, spend far too much time on Amazon and Google. The Internet is great and I think my life is enriched by it, but it's a bit like alcohol, should only be consumed in moderation.

People get annoyed with me when I say I don't have a mobile. They can reach me by landline, Royal Mail, email, knock on my door or by carrier pigeon – how many more ways do they need?

Both view themselves as having achieved security, but one feels the original attachment style was dismissing, while for the other it was preoccupied.

While some respondents "filled dead time" making phone calls to family and friends, others prefer to stay in touch via email:

For quick interchanges on a 'need to know', I have befriended email. I now find it invaluable for group emails of various sorts. I like the feel

> of being able to communicate with a group all at once. It has a 'all inclusive' feel to it.
>
> Email is a very useful tool early morning and late evenings when I do not want to interrupt a person.

Some reactions to Skype had an almost phobic quality:

> As for Skype – I have no clue what that is. Bluetooth is another mystery. I just know these words but don't know anything about them. I have a bit of a fear of technology, which is strange considering that in my former life [prior to becoming a psychotherapist] I was a PhD scientist.

However other people "took" to Skype naturally:

> Wonderful for contacting our children when they've been abroad . . . in fact amazing! Our daughter lives in Montana with her husband and we love to Skype. My other daughter, when in Vancouver for a year, used to move the laptop round the room so we could feel we were there with her. Of course the difference is real communication, being heard and seen!! I feel at home with this and it is technology overcoming the physical distance between people and creating connection.

Only one of my eleven respondents regularly used social network sites. June wrote, "Since my grandson was born it has been a lovely way of keeping up with his life, his parents take lots of photographs and videos and send them to me or paste them on to Facebook or Flickr."

Barbara, who had studied computer science and assembler language in pre-PC times, and had even taught Word and Excel, felt nostalgic: "I would be happy to go back to the world without computers and back to the fountain pen". But there has been an evolutionary leap: there is no going back.

In later years, we are faced with physical decline and an accumulation of losses in life. Attachment needs increase as we become less able to care for ourselves, and often the world begins to feel more like an unfamiliar, even hostile, environment. This is a time when easy access to family and other support should increase felt security. In general, however, elderly people find technological advances alienating and frustrating rather than reassuring. The cost of devices, their small screens and keyboard pads, the foreign navigation systems and language, and the rapid speed of change tend to exclude the elderly. In fact, the ubiquity of computerised systems for a range of necessities, such as paying bills, arranging services, making appointments, and so on, contributes to the experience of the modern world as dehumanised and threatening for many elderly people. Various projects have encouraged this section of the population to become "silver surfers" by offering free training, but we might need to wait until the digital natives themselves get older before innovators develop technology that is better suited to use by the elderly. There is a newly established telephone helpline for the "silver generation", offering confidential one-off support and regular scheduled befriending calls to isolated, lonely, elderly people. Perhaps, in a few years' time, that service will meet the attachment needs of its user group via Skype or FaceTime—or whatever they evolve into. Let us hope that in the future, avatars or sociable robot pets programmed to simulate empathy will not replace these counsellors and befrienders of the elderly.

## *Boundaries*

I want to return to the subject of boundaries, of psychic skin, of a contained internal space and privacy of mind that protects against psychosis. Psychosis, here, refers to a failure to differentiate, a confusion between "me" and "not-me", and between the personal internal world and external reality. It seems that skin was the earliest organ to evolve and is found even in primitive sponges (*New Scientist*, 2010). The ability to separate a creature's insides from the environment was vital in the evolution of complex bodily structures; being able to rely on a protective psychic membrane to keep internal reality from being overwhelmed by external impingements facilitates individual development and an appropriate sense of interpersonal boundaries.

According to Frank (2011), "The world of cyberspace has altered many traditional boundaries—work and play, serious discourse and entertainment, adulthood and childhood, and public and private" (p. 36).

The separation of work and child-care can be blurred, as, with access to the Internet and conference calling, parents may feel that they can work from home and attend to children at the same time.

This is not always in the best interests of the child, whose needs might be perceived as less urgent, and whose envy and rivalry are stoked excessively. Parents might struggle to impose appropriate boundaries on their child's use of the Internet and computer games, either intruding too much into the child's private world or leaving him unprotected in a potentially dangerous environment.

On the other hand, we increasingly inhabit a global village. Couples meet on dating sites online and might go on to develop strong and happy relationships (one UK online dating service currently claims that "one in four relationships now start online", while an article appeared in the *New York Daily News* (2013) claiming that "one third of married couples in U.S. meet online"). New forms of media allow people in areas of civil unrest to draw the world's attention to their plight, and social media can be used to campaign for a fairer world. Information and disapprobation can have a regulatory effect on the greatest excesses. Ordinary citizens can contribute their journalistic skills via blogs, challenging the supremacy of government-sanctioned news, and are using social media to engage disaffected voters in a new kind of democracy.

Skype enables people to communicate and be together regardless of geographical distance. It can maintain family cohesion and friendships across continents, promoting secure attachment, but it also has the potential for more malign uses regarding exhibitionism and voyeurism.

Cyberspace has not just altered, but eroded, many boundaries. This is evident in any public venue. Loud music and mobile phone calls intrude into other people's personal space on public transport, the addictive beep of "you've got mail" shatters the "as if" transitional space in cinemas, theatres, art galleries, and consulting rooms. Other people's lives are thrust into our faces and ears without regard for privacy. Personal information is disseminated to all on social network sites. The Internet offers a worldwide stage where narcissistic exhibitionism is encouraged. Details of our daily lives, personal habits, sexual fantasies, and romantic relationships are casually proclaimed to "friends" on Facebook or Twittered to the world.

The other side of exhibitionism is voyeurism. A great deal of private information about each of us is now easily accessible to anyone who cares to search online. This makes life easy for stalkers and extremely difficult for people who wish to remain invisible, such as victims of domestic violence, witnesses to crimes, psychiatric and prison staff, and possibly counsellors and psychotherapists. Broadcasting personal information about other people without express permission strikes me as an outrageous infringement of civil liberties, yet one that hardly seems to ruffle any feathers. I suspect that more than civil liberties are being eroded, such as the sense of appropriate private boundaried space.

* * *

We have a curious relationship with hackers, people who infiltrate and illegally gain access to confidential information. There is a new archetypal hero or heroine who breaks into secure and seemingly impenetrable strongholds to access secrets. The likes of Julian Assange, founder of WikiLeaks, or Edward Snowden and Bradley/Chelsea Manning, who both leaked American official secrets, are applauded by many for their activities, seen as championing democracy and challenging censorship, while others, including their governments, condemn them for irresponsibility and playing into the hands of terrorists. Fictionally, we have Lisbeth Salander (Larsson, 2008) and Penelope Garcia from television's *Criminal Minds* among many who bring the bad guys to justice by computer wizardry, exposing evil and corruption. However, there is public abhorrence at the hacking of emails and mobile telephone messages by journalists, especially where the subject is an ordinary member of public who is already traumatically exposed and victimised, such as schoolgirl murder victim Millie Dowler and the parents of Madeleine McCann.

Guilt—moral anxiety—is a feature of the psychic skin that helps us to contain ourselves, and our more destructive impulses. The seeming anonymity of cyberspace permits unboundaried, guilt-free behaviour. Combat and virtual reality games can be used to play out fantasies of cybersex and violence. While acting out these impulses in a virtual world may detoxify them, such activities can have a compulsive life of their own. The real world of real people begins to feel unreal, while the virtually real world of ethereal people begins to feel more significant, elaborated, and compelling. In one tragic incident, a South Korean couple starved their baby to death while preoccupied with raising a virtual baby in a virtual world (*Telegraph*, 2010, also cited by Akhtar, M. C., in S. Akhtar, 2011). The potential for television programmes and online fantasy games to dehumanise the other and increase aggressive acting out on the streets has long been debated.

## *Psychopathology*

Stalking, bullying, grooming, addictions, self-neglect, avoidance of intimacy with real others, avoidance of separation, and becoming a "real" whole person—these are familiar ills reconstituted for the digital age. Technology has also changed the pace of life. We are always in a hurry, bombarded by emails and texts, spam, and messages requiring a quick response. It is difficult to turn off the computer or mobile phone, to ignore the insistent beep of "you've got mail". There is little space for quiet reflection, a temporary withdrawal into the restorative inner world, or intimate human connection.

We have become used to accessing information instantly. Delay causes frustration. We are over-stimulated, primed for instant gratification. Winnicott wrote that it is vitally important for healthy development that the good enough mother gradually *fails* to respond immediately to her infant's demands; it is through learning to wait, to trust that needs will be met, that self-containment, intellect, memory, and hope flourish. "What releases the mother from her need to be near-perfect is the infant's understanding" (Winnicott, 1958, 1971)

Finally, back to the body, which, in the digital age, is increasingly neglected and dissociated from the mind. Psychoanalysis developed from Freud's work with hysterics. Hysteria was a scream of protest against the philosophical backdrop of the body–mind split (Herman, 1992), physical symptoms created by troubled minds. Perhaps, as we enter a new era of dissociation between psyche and soma, a new form of hysteria will present itself and new desperate measures will be concocted to feel real in an alienated body.

## *Conclusion*

In *Far From the Tree*, Andrew Solomon writes about the phenomenon of children who are dramatically different from their parents. He interviewed families whose children were born with disabilities and dwarfism, where a child was diagnosed with autism or schizophrenia, and where the child grew up to be a murderer (Solomon, 2013). Yet, as I write, all but the youngest of parents have offspring who are radically different from themselves, children born into an advanced technological era and seemingly almost primed to grasp for a digital device as much as our species is primed to reach out for a human hand. What will these digital natives be like as parents to the next generation? What kind of father might baby Harry be when his turn comes?

Will we become more, or less, secure as a result of societal changes brought about by the Internet and various forms of communication? Given the relatively recent evolution of digital technology and its central place in our personal and professional lives, it is not yet clear how attachment and the sense of self have been and will be affected. Perhaps it will take another one or two generations for the full impact to become evident in the Strange Situation Tests of the future.

According to Balick (2012, p. 122), "the virtual world both enables and obstructs a variety of ways of relating". Mass culture is global and we are all exposed to it when plugged into our computers. Our social brains, without personal boundaries, may be shaped by constant communication, often of a fairly superficial content. We might become the Borg! (An alien Collective from the television series *Star Trek*, the Borg assimilates beings into the Collective using cybernetic implants to link individuals to the "hive mind".) While this might increasingly be the fate of one group of insecurely attached people (preoccupied/ocnophilic), I believe that another group (dismissing/philobatic) will become increasingly isolated and alienated, turning to technology rather than fellow human beings for comfort and company.

Where there have been failures in creating secure attachment, psychopathology flourishes. However, where early relationships have provided security, confidence, containment, and boundaries in the critical early years, communication technology makes ongoing intimate and supportive contact between individuals possible. Knowing that loved ones are available if needed, the secure person has a sturdy and resilient sense of self, and the capacity to provide sensitive, reliable care-giving to the next generation. However, parents, grandparents, child-minders, and other care-givers might need to put away their digital devices sometimes in order to provide the conditions for a generation of securely attached children.

## Acknowledgement

My thanks to Jan for kind permission to use disguised extracts from her infant observation paper, and also to all from the Wimbledon Guild training who took part in my informal research into attachment and the use of technology.

## References

Ainsworth, M. D. S., Blehar, M. C., Waters, E., & Wall, S. (1978). *Patterns of Attachment: A Psychological Study of the Strange Situation.* Hillsdale, NJ: Lawrence Erlbaum.

Akhtar, S. (Ed.) (2011). *The Electrified Mind: Development, Psychopathology and Treatment in the Era of Cell Phones and the Internet.* Lanham, MD: Jason Aronson.

Anzieu, D. (Ed.) (1990). *Psychic Envelopes.* London: Karnac.

Balick, A. (2012). TMI in the transference LOL: psychoanalytic reflections on Google, social networking, and 'virtual impingement'. *Psychoanalysis, Culture & Society, 17*(2): 120–136.

Balint, M. (1959). *Thrills and Regressions.* London: Maresfield Library [reprinted 1987].

Balint, M. (1968). *The Basic Fault: Therapeutic Aspects of Regression.* London: Tavistock.

Bick, E. (1968). The experience of the skin in early object-relations. *International Journal of Psychoanalysis, 49*: 484–486 [reprinted in J. Raphael-Leff, (Ed.), *Parent–Infant Psychodynamics: Wild Things, Mirrors and Ghosts.* London: Whurr, 2003].

Bowlby, J. (1958). The nature of the child's tie to his mother. *International Journal of Psychoanalysis, 39*: 350–373.

Bowlby, J. (1969). *Attachment and Loss: Volume 1: Attachment.* London: Hogarth Press and Institute of Psychoanalysis.

Bowlby, J. (1979). *The Making and Breaking of Affectional Bonds.* London: Tavistock.

Carlino, R. (2011). *Distance Psychoanalysis: The Theory and Practice of Using Communication Technology in the Clinic.* London: Karnac.

Cozolino, L. (2006). *The Neuroscience of Human Relationships: Attachment and the Developing Social Brain.* New York: W. W. Norton.

Frank, J. L. (2011). The epidemic of information: pros and cons. In: S. Akhtar (Ed.), *The Electrified Mind: Development, Psychopathology and*

*Treatment in the Era of Cell Phones and the Internet* (pp. 35–42). Lanham, MD: Jason Aronson.

Freud, A. (1936). *The Ego and the Mechanisms of Defence*. Reprinted 1993, London: Karnac.

George, C., Kaplan, N., & Main, M. (1985). The adult attachment interview. Unpublished manuscript, University of California, Berkeley.

Gerhardt, S. (2004). *Why Love Matters: How Affection Shapes a Baby's Brain*. Hove: Brunner-Routledge.

Graham, R. (2013). The perception of digital objects and their impact on development. *Psychoanalytic Psychotherapy, 27*(4): 269–279.

Greenfield, S. (2008). *ID: The Quest for Meaning in the 21st Century*. London: Sceptre.

Greenfield, S. (2012). Modern technology is changing the way our brains work. *Daily Mail*. Available at: www.dailymail.co.uk. Accessed 2 February 2012.

Herman, J. L. (1992). *Trauma and Recovery: From Domestic Abuse to Political Terror*. London: Pandora.

Hesse, E. (1996). Discourse, memory, and the adult attachment interview: a note with emphasis on the emerging cannot classify category. *Infant Mental Health Journal, 17*(1): 4–11.

Keiffer, C. C. (2011). Cyberspace, transitional space, and adolescent development. In: S. Akhtar (Ed.), *The Electrified Mind: Development, Psychopathology and Treatment in the Era of Cell Phones and the Internet* (pp. 43–62). Lanham, MD: Jason Aronson.

Khan, M. M. R. (1963). The concept of cumulative trauma. *Psychoanalytic Study of the Child, 18*: 286–306.

Larsson, S. (2008). *The Girl With the Dragon Tattoo*. London: Maclehose Press.

Mahler, M., Pine, F., & Bergman, A. (1975). *The Psychological Birth of the Human Infant*. London: Hutchinson [reprinted London: Karnac 1991].

Main, M., & Solomon, J. (1986). Discovery of an insecure–disorganized/disoriented attachment pattern. In: T. B. Brazelton & M. W. Yogman (Eds.), *Affective Development in Infancy* (pp. 95–124). Norwood, NJ: Ablex.

Main, M., Hesse, E., & Goldwyn, R. (2008). Studying differences in language usage in recounting attachment history: an introduction to the AAI. In: H. Steele & M. Steele (Eds.), *Clinical Applications of the Adult Attachment Interview* (pp. 31–68). New York: Guilford Press.

*New Scientist* (2010). Skin was the first organ to evolve. 16 December. Available at: www.newscientist.com. Accessed 11 January 2011.

*New York Daily News* (2013). One third of marriages start online. 4 June. Available at: www.nydailynews.com. Accessed 11 September 2013.

Prensky, M. (2001). Digital natives, digital immigrants. *On the Horizon*: *9*(5): 1–6.

Robertson, J., & Robertson, J. (1969). *Young Children in Brief Separation: John*. Film, Tavistock Child Development Research Unit.

Schore, A. (1994). *Affect Regulation and the Origins of the Self*. Hillsdale, NJ: Lawrence Erlbaum.

Schore, A. (2003). *Affect Dysregulation and Disorders of the Self*. New York: Norton.

Solomon, A. (2013). *Far From the Tree: A Dozen Kinds of Love*. London: Chatto & Windus.

Stadter, M. (2013). The influence of social media and communication technology on self and relationships. In: J. S. Scharff, (Ed.). *Psychoanalysis Online: Mental Health, Teletherapy, and Training* (pp. 3–13). London: Karnac.

Steiner, J. (1993). *Psychic Retreats: Pathological Organizations in Psychotic, Neurotic and Borderline Patients*. London: Routledge.

Stern, D., Sander, L. W., Nahum, J. P., Harrison, A. M., Lyons-Ruth, K., Morgan, A. C., Bruschweilerstern, N., & Tronick, E. Z. (1998). Non-interpretive mechanisms in psychoanalytic therapy: the 'something more' than interpretation. *International Journal of Psychoanalysis*, *79*: 903–921.

*Telegraph* (2010). Korean couple let baby starve to death while caring for virtual child. 5 March. Available at: www.telegraph.co.uk. Accessed 4 December 2013.

Turkle, S. (1984). *The Second Self: Computers and the Human Spirit*. New York: Simon & Schuster (new edition Cambridge, MA: The MIT Press 2005).

Turkle, S. (2011). *Alone Together: Why We Expect More From Technology and Less From Each Other*. New York: Basic Books.

Turkle, S. (2012). Connected but alone? *TED Talk*. Available at: www.ted.com. Viewed 14 April 2013.

Tustin, F. (1990). *The Protective Shell in Children and Adults*. London: Karnac.

Tustin, F. (1992). *Autistic States in Children*. London: Routledge and Kegan Paul.

Whiten, A. (2007). The place of "deep social mind" in the evolution of human nature. In: C. Pasternak (Ed.), *What Makes Us Human?* (pp. 146–163). Oxford: Oneworld.

Winnicott, D. W. (1958). Mind and its relation to the psyche-soma. In: *Through Paediatrics to Psychoanalysis: Collected Papers* (pp. 243–254). London: Tavistock [reprinted London: Karnac 1992].

Winnicott, D. W. (1965a). Ego distortion in terms of true and false self. In: *The Maturational Processes and the Facilitating Environment* (pp. 140–152). London: Karnac.

Winnicott, D. W. (1965b). *The Family and Individual Development*. London: Tavistock.

Winnicott, D. W. (1971). *Playing and Reality*. London: Tavistock.

CHAPTER TWO

# A tangled web: Internet pornography, sexual addiction, and the erosion of attachment

*John Beveridge*

> "Children today have everything but they are lost, like tiny boats at sea"
>
> (Mongolian farmer, *BBC World Service*, 2014)

## *Introduction*

We have become used to living in a "sexed up" climate of fear and paranoia in an increasingly frightening world, and there is plenty to be paranoid about. While there is talk of economic recovery for some, we have been surviving for years on the edge of global financial meltdown, and the squeezed and demoralised middle classes are beginning to understand how the poor citizens of New Orleans felt after Hurricane Katrina, when they were abandoned to their fate by the people they had elected to power. Manufacturing jobs and its pollution have been exported to the Third World, followed by the service industries which replaced them, and nobody seems to be accountable for corporate tax-evasion, the banking crises, the treachery of pension companies, and the gradual erosion of safe, universal, healthcare provision. Whole countries, cities, regions, and sections of the economy are being written off as failing, while others make grotesque profits.

In the first half of 2012 in Britain, 953 chain-store shops closed down in the continuing recession (Smithers, 2012), and they are not coming back. Unless you want to pawn something or place a bet, our high streets are dwindling in importance as places to meet. But does that really matter when we can order everything we need online, and Tesco or Asda will deliver it to our doors? Bookshops might be closing, but some people can get all their reading material by post from Amazon, or download it directly to their Kindles. And libraries? Who needs them now that Google is hoovering up every book in print in the world and we can retrieve them, online, from the "Cloud"? You do not even have to leave the house.

"Online" is increasingly the preferred method of communication for the majority of businesses and government services that are almost impossible to access either in person or on the telephone. I wonder if the credo, attributed to Margaret Thatcher, that "There is no such thing as society", came back to haunt us in the consumerist riots of 2011.

It might be just me getting old, but people seem to have little sense of spatial awareness, mutual respect, or even manners, as we move through public places, texting and wired for sound, in our own private worlds. It can only be a matter of time before interactive chips will be implanted in our heads so that content can be downloaded directly into our brains. When I have an appointment to see my doctor, she swivels between her computer and me, feeding it with data, relating to her screen, while I just seem incidental to the process.

These few examples of the weakening of the ties that bind us are a small price to pay for the advantages brought to us by the mind-boggling pace of technological change and are, perhaps, nothing more sinister than bad habits, but modern life seems to be working against a sense of attachment and intimacy. The government endorses the intention to supply broadband to every home in Britain, which a recovering sex addict client said "is like putting free cocaine into every bathroom cabinet in the land". It seems that all this apparent connectivity is loosening the social threads that hold us together, replacing them with pseudo "social networks" which are turning into sexual networks, so we can all fiddle with ourselves while Rome burns.

It concerns me that I might be perceived as an ageing Luddite, beached on the shores of progress because I grew up in the 1960s, in a house with one heated room where we gathered to watch a television with a choice of two channels and no means of recording the content. For a long time, we had to go to Mrs Hanlon's next door if we needed to use a telephone. Today, unless tuning in to "event" programming such as *The X Factor*, where voting and eviction create excitement around watching TV live, the idea of whole families in front of one screen is outdated. Even in the poorest households there are infinite ways and different devices from iPods to Xboxes, from Wiis to mobile phones, from Kindles to computers, on which different members of a family can consume their games, films, entertainment, or even filth, simultaneously, each on their personal screens.

I remember, in our early teenage years, my brother and I would leave our annoying parents and siblings in the living room to sit in the kitchen in the dark, in the glow of the wireless, listening to pop music on Radio Luxembourg. I recall feeling full of those indefinable longings, which were probably sexual, for something or someone beyond my immediate horizons. That simpler life in the 1960s was not perfect, but at least we were not watching pornography.

## *Pornography*

Today and every day, there are apparently sixty-eight million search engine requests for pornography and over four million websites, which are all part of a huge industry whose profits have outstripped those of Hollywood and the music industry. In these troubled times, the three escapist industries that seem to be recession-proof are communications technology, computer games, and pornography. The publishers of porn have never needed sales strategies or planning meetings, and neither do they have to advertise or market pornography; it just sells. There were sexually explicit paintings on the walls of houses of Pompeii because people, mainly men, have always used graphic images of bodies and people having sex as a stimulus to masturbation. The sale of erotic and pornographic images has spread and prospered as delivery systems and technology have become more sophisticated. After the invention of the printing press, followed by photography, film, then video and DVD, there came computers.

In the past, men, to satisfy their needs, were compelled to go searching for material from sex shops, seeking in magazines and films the kind of girls and boys you could never take home to mother, doing things that you could not or would not ask of a partner. With digitalisation, file-sharing, and social networking, moving images can now be downloaded to one's mobile telephone, and, I am told by Robert Weiss (2012), there are even sexual aids into which one can insert oneself, or put into oneself, which, when connected to a viewing device, will throb in time to the images on the screen. Aside from sexual appetite, "accessibility, anonymity, and affordability" are the main drivers of the use of Internet pornography. Online and feeling invisible, people do not have to verbalise their requirements to others who might judge their choice or preferences.

With high-speed access to onscreen menus of multiple, thumbnail "tabs" offering film clips of people having sex, devoid of plot or preamble, just the cum-shots, people can become acquainted with, and turned on by, infinite variations of sexual experience and practices of which they might not have been aware previously. Because they can then fast forward to more exciting material, the Internet hastens and perpetuates arousal and is responsible for a rapid growth in the numbers of potential sex addicts who are losing the ability to control their usage of porn, sex, or masturbation. Men, who are visual creatures sexually, are biologically set up to be susceptible to pornography, being concerned with the external appearance of things rather than the content. In successful television comedies, such as *Friends* and *Peep Show*, likeable and funny young men make jokes about their use of pornography, and it might seem acceptable to have a porn habit because the subject is never seriously discussed.

Men might not have to address their usage of pornography, or recognise that it is problematic, until they try to stop and find they cannot. Riemersma and Sytsma define sex addiction as "a disorder characterised by compulsive sexual behaviour that results in tolerance, escalation, withdrawal, and a loss of volitional control, despite negative consequences" (2013, p. 308). Addiction to pornography thrives in the consumer's compulsive need for novelty, and, because it is more exciting than satisfying, images quickly become threadbare in their power to arouse and stimulate. In order to constantly increase excitement, the content has to become more extreme. A teacher told me that some teenage girls had asked her if it was normal during sex that a boy might ejaculate on the girl's face: a practice known in the porn industry as the "money shot".

The effects of pornography are insidious because young boys are learning how to have sex from porn and they are now seeing sexual practices which thirty years ago would have been considered perverse. The portrayal of "hard core" scenarios such as anal sex, double penetration, threesomes, water sports, "ass to mouth", and BDSM (bondage, discipline, sadism, and masochism) is now so regarded as the norm that they are described as "vanilla". With the Internet, for the first time in history, people can access, at the touch of a finger, pictures that the Marquis de Sade could only imagine. Stoller (1975), who described perversion as a form of hatred, writes,

> That these forms are common does not mean that they do not arise as solutions to conflict, distress, frustration and anger ... pornography spares one the anxieties of having to make it with another person; the people in porn know their place and do as directed. (p. 87)

The average guy, when asked in therapy, what kind of porn he might watch, will often minimise the content by saying, "Oh, normal stuff, men and women", but the effects of hard porn are sinister because it has always been about the control and degradation of women. Today, slapping, hair-pulling, and choking are common practices in depictions of sex and it is mostly women who are on the receiving end. I have observed that my patients, nice, middle-class men, try not to think of the coercion or trafficking which might lie behind the manufacture of these films, or the anger that they might be acting out against women when they are excited to orgasm by seeing them traduced. There is an old joke that "a standing dick has neither taste nor conscience". Writing about pornography, Moye says. "It provides a vicarious means of escape and solace for men. It displays the old assumption of women's subordination and their complicity in it, in the teeth of all the changes to the contrary" (1985, p. 52).

Let me state that I am not privileging one kind of sexual behaviour over another in a hierarchy led by heterosexual, vaginal, penetrative sex, within a committed relationship. There is nothing wrong with recreational sex, gay or straight, or engaging in masturbation, especially for teenagers. Problems begin when people feel compelled to engage in sexual acts and do not feel as if they have the power to make choices, whatever kind of sex they are having. We can only really say we are making a choice when we have the ability to say no. Sexually addictive behaviour has been around for a long time and has been given many descriptions: "nymphomania" in women, and "satyriasis" in men, "hyper-sexuality, erotomania, and sexual compulsion", are terms that therapists have long used although, paradoxically, some are uncomfortable with labelling people "addicts".

The acceleration of sexual compulsivity in today's culture might be part of a serious malaise. I have seen young men in my practice who are increasingly unable to become excited by ordinary sexual experiences. Some say that they prefer the look of "fake tits", and that they have to masturbate to porn to finish themselves off when having sex with a real woman, who has, unlike her pornographic counterparts, pubic hair and body smells and desires and wishes of her own.

A pornographic sensibility has permeated films, billboards, fashion, television, magazine adverts, and music videos, affecting how people have sex with themselves, how men and women see each other, and how we relate—and it is affecting young people growing up. People who argue that sexual addiction does not exist are like the people who tell us that global warming has not yet been proved, while we can see the evidence of it everywhere. The majority of people still think it is funny to say, in a "nudge, nudge" kind of way, that "sex addiction, might be an addiction worth having". I have seen journalists ask, "Whatever happened to old-fashioned promiscuity anyway?" Many people seemed to react angrily to the suggestion that the sexual behaviour of Tiger Woods was compulsive, saying that "The term 'sex addiction' is just an excuse for bad behaviour"—as if to say, "He had his cake, he ate it, and now he wants our sympathy, too?"

Many young people, either with a degree and saddled with debt or without, have been unable to find entry level jobs as a whole generation has been consigned to the scrapheap by a society that does not appear to care. It might not seem to matter if they lose interest in the ordinary pleasures of life; the pursuit of work, study, and the joys of sport might all just seem dull, boring, and unrewarding if they have been prematurely turned on to sex. What effect does the habitual use of pornography have on young people whose characters coalesce and form around the experiences they encounter growing up? And what happens to the appetites of teenagers who can now enjoy unlimited fantasy scenarios that might have made a Roman Emperor blush? Do they not need something upon which to cut their emotional teeth, a necessary degree of frustration against which they might grow?

I am seeing some young men experience loss of libido which might be normally expected thirty years later, and, since they can still get it up for porn, the problem is in the mind, not the penis. This is caused by a continuous over-stimulation of their sexual response, which has changed their brain chemistry.

## *Neuroscience*

Having worked for years trying to help people to recover from chemical dependence and addiction to sexual behaviours, I would often become frustrated by people who relapsed after having expressed a strong desire to change. Despite my experience and understanding of addiction, I still confused their behaviour with morality and judged them accordingly. My understanding was changed dramatically, and I was able to evoke a more empathic response, when I heard a recorded talk by Dr Kevin McCauley, who defined addiction as

> . . . a dysregulation of the mid-brain dopamine (pleasure) system, due to unmanaged stress, resulting in symptoms of decreased functioning, which results in loss of control, craving, and persistent drug or behaviour use, despite negative consequences. (McCauley, 2004)

I was to learn that people's behaviour is affected by their brain chemistry, which accounts for the disparity between how people intend to act and what they might actually do in a crisis. It is helpful to understand addiction as a disease of the dopamine system, so that we can learn to stop punishing addicts because of their behaviour. Sex addiction, like addiction to gambling, is a process addiction, arising out of self-generated chemicals and hormones that behave like powerful drugs. We produce these drug-like chemicals in response to our environment, and we carry them with us everywhere we go. If a knife-wielding maniac burst into the room, our brains would respond by flooding our bodies with adrenalin to facilitate our flight or fight response. When the danger had passed, we might start to shake, which is our body's way of getting rid of the accumulation of adrenalin. Perhaps we like to think we might behave in a heroic manner, but as the captain of a sinking cruise liner recently found, we do not know how we might act until we are at mortal risk.

We produce a simple organic chemical called dopamine which functions as a neurotransmitter in the brain and rewards us by making us feel good when we engage in activities that help us survive. If we monitor newborn babies, we can see that dopamine is produced when the infant turns its head towards the breast, and the rewards for this first act of searching brings immediate mood alteration in anticipation of food or attention. The repetition of these experiences forms neural pathways, which change the brain, and we call this process learning. When we sit next to someone in a meeting or at the cinema and we notice them casually reach for a phone to check for messages or go online, then their boredom threshold has dropped and they are refreshing their dopamine levels. So, when we go searching online, either for an academic paper or houses for sale in France, it changes the way we feel and, so, too, does looking online for sexual material.

McCauley (2004) describes experiments in which drugs are administered and the subject's brain is then scanned; the mid-brain, or limbic system, is seen to respond dramatically. This part of the brain is linked directly to the basic functions that have maintained our survival as a species: the three "Fs" of "feeding, fighting, and fucking". This has been described as the "mammalian brain", which responds and reacts first to all incoming information from the environment. "Emotions are generated in the limbic system, along with most of the many appetites and urges that direct us to behave in a way that (usually) helps us to survive" (Carter, 2000, p. 42). Our ancestors once had to learn where to get food and sex and, if anyone obstructed their intention, they would fight them because their lives depended upon these things for survival. In addiction, our appetites have this life-or-death quality to them.

When a person watches pornography, he or she builds sexual excitement, raising and maintaining tension by producing dopamine, and when orgasm is reached, endorphins are released bringing relaxation and relief, so that a self-contained method of mood alteration has been learnt. In effect, this is an addiction to our body's self-generated opioids. When levels decrease post orgasm, endorphins are replaced by anxiety inducing stress hormones that "activate the urge-making areas of the brain" (Carter, 2000, p. 105), thus perpetuating the addictive cycle.

According to Lewis:

> "[W]anting" and "liking" are distinct psychological states underpinned by distinct neural processes. It's the opioids that cause liking—the sensation of pleasure or wellbeing. And it's the dopamine that produces wanting—the feeling of desire or attraction. (2011, p. 134)

James Olds conducted experiments in the 1950s where rats were trained to press levers to obtain a rewarding hit of drugs. They became habituated to repeating these actions to feel the effects of the drug despite harmful consequences, such as foregoing food or having to run across heated plates to reach the lever. Someone who masturbates habitually might know cognitively that they are not having "real sex", but their bodies are fooled into releasing those same exciting chemicals. There is YouTube footage of a tortoise with a faraway look in its eyes, rhythmically humping a training shoe, oblivious to the fact that it is not another member of its species.

Dopamine raises the pleasure threshold, the "hedonic level" of the brain, which operates like a thermostat, and then the ordinary pleasures in life do not mean as much as they once did.

When people take drugs or get high from sexual excitement, or both together, the mutation from habit to compulsion and addiction requires a helping hand, such as opportunity and availability, and what is better suited than the Internet? A patient told me that there is always the feeling that there is something elusive and more stimulating just around the corner. Some men I have worked with have found themselves, when looking at porn, falling into a trance-like state, searching for hours on end and sometimes escalating to extreme, perverse, or illegal genres, amplifying porn's hyper-stimulating effects by forcing the release of a never-ending stream of dopamine spikes.

There is something inherently different about looking at images on the printed page, compared to spending hours looking at seemingly infinite exciting images on an illuminated screen in a state of adrenalised sexual arousal. Describing the plasticity of the brain, Doidge (2007) writes,

> The men at their computers looking at porn . . . had been seduced into training sessions that meet all the conditions required for plastic change of brain maps. Since neurons that fire together wire together, these men got massive amounts of practice wiring these images into

> the pleasure centres of the brain, with the rapt attention necessary for plastic change. (p. 108)

Internet porn is free, easy to access, available within seconds, twenty-four hours a day and seven days a week. For the susceptible person, the effects of compulsively using Internet pornography has been compared to those that crack cocaine has on the nervous system of cocaine users, causing an acceleration of addiction (Mary Ann Leyden, US Senate Testimony, October 18, 2004). Some people have always been prone to addiction, because they have responded to early experiences of stress by becoming able to dissociate, which is a process of unconsciously splitting off parts of the mind. As well as protecting them from pain, this can lead people to defensively detach from the natural need for attachments that organise and stabilise our emotional experience across the human lifespan.

### *Addiction: craving, self-soothing, splitting, and shame*

Our sense of self and our personality, our belief systems and the values that inform our behavioural intentions, are all located in the frontal cortex. This is the most advanced structure in the brain and it is shaped by early experiences with our attachment figures; it embodies the superego and fosters the ability to contain, rather than act on, our primitive impulses. However, when someone feels threatened, or during addictive and drug-like experiences, this part of the brain can go "offline". People with no understanding of the addictive process might say, "Well, we all get stressed but we don't become addicts, they are just weak and have no willpower!" Yet, some people in extremis will take drugs or engage in compulsive behaviours because, when they feel threatened, there are certain genes that affect our impulse to seek novelty and risk. People are then prone to becoming addicted because their habitual physical and emotional reaction to stress has now become craving. According to Carnes, Carnes, and Bailey,

> During a craving, the area of the brain that creates drives is activated, while the areas that restrain these urges are deactivated. The result is a person who can't defend against the craving. It is essentially a high-jacking [*sic*] of the rational part of the brain. This all happens at a subconscious level. (2011, p. 79)

I have seen addicts face extreme symptoms of distress when they cannot act out with their old, self-soothing behaviour. With the erosion of willpower, their ability to resist diminishes, because craving feels like grief and grief is separation anxiety. Anyone who has experienced bereavement might recognise the spiky, volatile, angry, agitated, and restless longing that platitudes cannot put right. To say to an addicted person "Just say no" is missing the point. McCauley (2004) points out that their survival imperative, operating out of the mid-brain, kicks in, urging, "Get me something NOW to get me through the next ten minutes—We'll worry about all that 'life' stuff, like work, family, and children, tomorrow!" When faced with any threat, addicts will feel at mortal risk because "The pleasure producing cycle is now unconsciously and inextricably linked with the mid-brain, the survival mechanism part of the brain, so that survival has become the drug" (McCauley, 2004).

I have worked with many sex-addicted clients committed to religious beliefs, who see themselves as weak and sinful when they succumb, once again, to acting-out behaviour after making firm pledge to stop. This sense of being split that people have experienced as a result of historical religious attitudes to sexuality reflects the struggle between intentions and actions operating out of different parts of the brain. Ulman and Paul say that the addict, unconsciously:

> . . . induces a self hypnotic trance (i.e., the hypnoid defense) within him or herself that flips unconscious subjective experience from one characterized by an excruciatingly painful mood of narcissistic mortification (reflective of being out of and having lost control) to one characterized by a mood of narcissistic bliss (indicative of a temporary and fleeting feeling of rapture). (2006, p. 118)

With minds obsessed and preoccupied by continuous fantasies of body parts and part-objects, there is a growing sense of separation, increasing fear and paranoia, activated by those primitive anxieties that the acting out was supposed to keep at bay. Dissociated from their attachments, values, beliefs, morals, and spirituality, a sense of disintegration is common among sex addicts. Self-punishing thoughts lead to shame and the need to alleviate that shame creates more cycles of acting out, causing damage in the relational field by eroding people's ability to respect themselves, to love and make love, to be intimate, vulnerable, attached, and to be good partners and parents. The first half of the title of this chapter, "A tangled web", is from an oft-remembered family trope: "O what a tangled web we weave, when first we practise to deceive".

## *Deception of self and other*

Rather like an addiction to drugs, which has a built-in dishonesty factor because of their illegality, the shame of sex addiction and its consequences thrives in secrecy and denial. I have often remarked that a surprising number of men who might identify as sex addicts do not have sex with their partners. If a spouse enters a room where their husband or wife is online and the screen is abruptly disappeared or changed to the weather forecast, he or she senses that something is going on, and they feel (rightly) that they are being deceived because their intuitions are being denied. Because many men have maintained a secret sexual life, away from the marital couple, they fail to comprehend that women often regard the watching of porn by a partner as a form of betrayal, equal in seriousness to a physical encounter or an affair (see Chapter Three in this volume). In order to protect their behaviour, the sexually compulsive person is often difficult to pin down to exact timings; they create extra time spaces around commitments so they can be unaccountable and be left alone to masturbate, or worse. The addict, in a state of constant self-deception, might maintain a defensive disavowal that "It doesn't mean anything", but, remembering the three Fs mentioned earlier, if a partner is perceived as blocking their attempts to get to sex (survival), then he or she has become the enemy. Frustration and anger arising from perceived restrictions might be acted out by engaging in more deceptive behaviour and the enjoyment of more degrading, abusive, and violent sexual fantasies.

For the partners of sex addicts, this covert hostility can be crazy-making, causing them to worry that the lack of emotional availability in the other means that there is something wrong with themselves; this can lead to obsession about the addict's behaviour, driving them to play detective by trying to catch him or her out. Binges of sexual acting out where drugs like methamphetamine, poppers, cocaine, and crack are used can extend masturbating and sexual sprees for hours.

Disinhibition can lead to interactive online activity with other people and real life encounters with strangers, leaving the user in volatile emotional states for days afterwards. If children find a parent watching porn, they can be emotionally blackmailed into becoming collusive in covering up this secret behaviour, out of fear that its revelation might cause the break-up of the family.

While I have used gendered terms for the description of the addict and partner, the term sex addict can apply to people of both sexes as well as people in same-sex couples. There might be a tendency to think that it is mainly men who use pornography and the Internet to get sex, but it must be remembered that when heterosexual men are sex-texting, looking at images, masturbating, having cam-to-cam sex, searching online for massage with prostitutes, visiting strip clubs, or having affairs, it is usually women with whom they are engaging. Women might like to place themselves at the love and romantic end of the addiction continuum, perhaps believing that they are looking for love and security through online dating, but their searching is just as mood altering and can become compulsive. In trying to find the love they seek, women have also become addicted to having sex with partners found on the Internet. There are also numerous "second life" sites where they can spend hours online as exotic "avatars", that is, cartoon fantasy versions of themselves, conducting real-time conversations involving romance, weddings, and online sex, while their husbands and children are ignored in other rooms.

## *Therapy*

Many men in their twenties present for therapy after they have entered a real relationship and, wanting to commit sexually to a partner, they realise that their online behaviour cannot be as easily relinquished as they had hoped. Sometimes, in order to be apprehended, the addict might create a crisis by forgetting to erase their online history, thereby unconsciously setting themselves up for the discovery of shocking or illegal images on computers or mobile phones by partners or employers, so that they have to stop. I worked with a woman who found a prostitute's telephone number on her partner's phone, which he had let her borrow, two weeks before their wedding. This can lead to a recovery that is often described as "spouse led". We need to understand that, despite the revulsion that their behaviour might cause us to feel, addiction to the sex chemicals in the body and the behaviours that stimulate and protect them, are as serious and as difficult to treat as heroin addiction, even among clients who are highly motivated to change. Also, unlike heroin, accessing online pornography is less risky and generally free of charge.

Shaming or punishing people who are addicted has never affected a cure, as the prison population, who are, more often than not, alcoholic or chemically dependent, would testify. I once found myself feeling angry and taking it personally when a man informed me that he had relapsed after I thought the therapy was going well. I heard myself saying, "Well, maybe you are just one of those people who never get recovery." I later felt the need to apologise and tell the client about the angry feelings I had experienced at his lapse, and I pointed out the countertransferential dynamic where, like his father and numerous previous employers in his past, I had been set up to be just another authority figure who had rejected him. That was a turning point in this man's recovery, helping him recognise the unconscious payoff he had in his core belief of feeling himself to be unacceptable.

Therapists who have not yet taken the time to become informed about the drivers of sexual compulsivity and its treatment can sometimes be dismissive of sexual addiction; an ex-therapist of one of my present clients told her "not to worry, all artistic people have high sex drives" when she was full of shame about her sexual behaviour.

Whenever I work with people who identify as being addicted to sex or pornography who are seeing themselves through the lens of self hatred, I explain that their compulsive behaviour is an attempt at self-soothing to help them cope with the stress of their lives' struggles. I also add that when they appear to be most out of control in their addictive behaviour, they are, emotionally, at their most defended. They immediately ask, "So what do I do to stop doing this?" This response is understandable among people who have always been able to *do* something, or reach for something that they thought could help, often unaware of what they might be avoiding or defending against. Of course, what they have traditionally done in order to cope eventually becomes the presenting problem, the compulsive behaviour, which can sometimes lead a therapist to collude in a moralistic drama of preoccupation with the addict's behaviour rather than with their hidden emotions or distress.

When we ask about the sex lives of our clients, we also need to ask if they regularly use pornography, and what effect that use might have had on their desire, their relationships, and their attitudes to sexual partners. Despite our fear of appearing prurient, it might also help to know what sexual fantasies actually arouse them; what many people think about when they are having sex might not be what they are actually doing. Having explored the sexual fantasies of over 19,000 adults, Brett Kahr recapitulated Stoller's theory; if we examine our clients' most secret thoughts and the fantasies they use to trigger orgasm, it will often reveal the story of their lives: "Thus, our sexual fantasies protect us and shield us from something potentially dreadful. Yet in doing so, these fantasies reinforce our wish to masturbate, and hence avoid exploration of what lurks beneath" (2007, p. 291).

Our clients' scenarios of acting out sexually—which they might never have told anyone—can often reveal hidden trauma, which they bring under their omnipotent control at the point of orgasm, turning trauma into triumph. According to Stoller,

> Since his infantile traumatic experiences live forever inside him however, his triumphs last only a short while and must be endlessly repeated. Where a sense of despair and inferiority rides too close to the surface, it must be repeated rapidly and endlessly. (1975, p. 126)

As psychodynamic therapists, it is important to recognise the connections between sexual addiction and fantasy, masturbation, perversion, and dissociation, which many practitioners, including myself, encountering sexually compulsive clients had half intuited, but not thought through in terms of brain chemistry and neuroplasticity.

Mark, a gay patient, found that he had become addicted to watching abusive, heterosexual porn, finding himself most excited by images of men taking aggressive sexual pleasure, without thought or consideration for their female partners. He felt shame that his behaviour went against the conscious, liberal values he held about women, but this guilt only seemed to add to his erotic charge, making this secret material difficult to discuss. "Political correctness", of which the unconscious has no conception, is perhaps the last arena in which we can feel truly sinful. In therapy, we were able to associate his intense arousal to his early memories when, as an infant, he was placed in his parents' bed. He now believed this was to forestall marital rape, which he imagined to have happened on the nights when his father has been out drinking. He had been caught in the intense sexual force field between his father's desire to penetrate and the mother's determination to resist. He became conscious of the angry feelings about the use that had been made of him by his mother, and his own need of the secondary gains that he had enjoyed in his relationship with her, where he felt special and chosen over his father. In time, his enjoyment of seeing the besting of the women in pornography became less intense and no longer necessary.

## *Treatment*

As with any addictive or compulsive behaviour, if we want to support someone who wishes to stop using, we need to ask the question, "What happens when they try to give up their problematic behaviour?" I usually find that when an addicted person aims for a period of abstinence from all sexual activity, so that we can begin to understand the emotional needs that might have been sexualised, they very quickly go into a physical withdrawal, just like a drug user. They can sometimes experience intense bodily reactions, such as headaches and flu-like symptoms. Often, they are also exposed to deep and debilitating feelings, indicating the strength of the emotions they have might have been trying to evade, perhaps for a lifetime. Even renunciation brings grief, and, since grief is connected to loss, the questions here are, "What has been lost, and when?" As it was for Mark, so it is for others: the sense of bringing unconscious primal scene anxieties under one's own omnipotent control through watching porn is illusory.

When, in therapy, we relinquish the illusions that have given us a sense of power, we are losing something dear to us. The feeling states of bereavement, including denial, bargaining, anger, despair, and depression, which might have been unconsciously entrenched but unexpressed for years, can now be recognised. When "solutions" such as addiction and avoidant or disorganised attachment behaviour no longer keep out awareness of early abandonment, sexual abuse, or emotional neglect, these tragedies might then have to be mourned.

New information gained from neuroscience can help us understand the strength and tenacity of the dependence upon sexual acting out, but it does not give people an excuse or a "green card" to behave as they wish by saying, "I can't help it—it's the dopamine!" For addicted clients, I strongly recommend attendance at, and support from, one of Britain's fastest growing, twelve-step sex addiction recovery groups, Sex and Love Addicts Anonymous (SLAA, www.slaa.uk.org), whose membership, surprisingly, comprises almost equal numbers of women and men. They offer a structured treatment programme which helps addicts learn, with peer support, how to go through difficulties without acting out, and helps them take responsibility in their relationships by making reparation for the pain that their actions, or avoidance of action, has caused. This can be helpful for people coming out of hiding and shame. The mind can be altered for the better with the acquisition of alternative coping mechanisms, so that the building of self-respect can become a new and powerful motivational reward system. They can then move on to find or rebuild healthy relationships, where sexuality is brought into balance and where they can operate as reliable attachment figures to their partners and children.

Once sexual sobriety is established, deeper psychodynamic work can be done in psychotherapy to reveal and release the trauma that has remained locked within sexual fantasies, allowing people to grieve and mourn the losses that addiction has left in its wake. Support from groups involving "mindfulness" practice can break the tyranny of isolation and fantasy. All addictions are really addictions to what the fantasy of acting out always promises, but seldom delivers. "In the midst of such an illusory spell, which cannot be so easily broken, an addict exists as a figment of his or her own imagination" (Ulman & Paul, 2006, p. 315).

Mindfulness practice can help people learn how to observe their own thought processes and to determine whether the thought or the feeling comes first. They can begin, in times of stress, to operate from their observing ego, engaging the frontal cortex. People can practise thinking, "I am not someone who is going to die if I don't do something immediately to take away my pain". They can begin to see that "I am just someone having a feeling or thought that I am going to die if I don't do something immediately!" In treating sexual compulsion, I look for, and expect to find, early experiences of overt or covert sexual or emotional abuse and disorganised or avoidant attachment histories. Because of previous dysfunctional relationships where rage has been eroticised, it can take time to lower the hedonic threshold and live an ordinary life, bringing emotions within the window of tolerance. Developing a non-compulsive sexuality may lack the drama and intensity of hyper-stimulation and continuous over-arousal.

In the past twenty years, there has been a recognition that many recovering chemical addicts, successful in living sober lives, had found that their compulsion had moved from alcohol or drugs to other self-defeating behaviours, such as overeating and anorexia, or, very often, sex addiction. There has been a growing awareness of, and more research into, this condition, coming out of the "recovery movement", with certified training for therapists becoming available in the past ten years from organisations such as the International Institute for Trauma and Addiction Professionals (IITAP) in Europe and the USA, and the Association for the Treatment of Sex Addiction and Compulsivity (ATSAC) in the UK.

There is clearly much more work to be done. With many pre-teen children regularly accessing sexual material on the Internet, it has been said that there is a tidal wave of addiction heading towards the therapeutic world. Riemersma and Sytsma (2013) make an important distinction between the "classic" addict, most often met in the past in adult males, and what we might be recognising today as a new manifestation that they describe as a "contemporary" form of sex addiction, "rapid in its onset", which is "disrupting normal neurochemical, sexual and social development in youth" (p. 307). They alert us to the delayed therapeutic response of the professional community and the paucity of research in this area, saying that

> ... effectual therapy with this population will likely require child and adolescent developmental expertise due to the increasing numbers of young people who are predicted to be impacted by "contemporary" sexual addiction. Alternatives to adult- oriented talk therapy and 12 step groups for example, will be needed. Informed consent and parental release will be important legal issues in this population. (Riemersma & Sytsma, 2013, p. 316)

The vulnerability to predation that the condition of sexual compulsion already creates in teenagers might also make attendance at adult groups or adult treatment centres problematical. We will have to develop new forms of treatment and therapeutic responses to this condition.

### *Young people and online addictions: cumulative trauma*

Young people presenting in therapy for sexual compulsion today might not have suffered early relational trauma or come from sexually abusive homes like the "classic" sex addict; their addiction to pornography may have had an opportunistic element. They seem to have become addicted simply because it was there. The effects of being continuously excited by extreme and shocking material, repeatedly opiated after orgasm, together with the isolation that pornography encourages, may, over time, have become traumatic experiences in themselves to brains that are still developing.

It might also be worth considering that some symptoms, such as attention deficit hyperactivity disorder, depression, obsessive–compulsive and mood disorders, lack of sexual desire, and social anxiety in young people, might be the effects of habitual pornography use. Riemersma and Sytsma write,

> It is suggested that these are typically the result of modern sexual addiction (rather than the driving force as may be the case with the "classic" addict), given that compulsive, virtual sexuality drives impairment in the very human, interpersonal and sexual connections that are protective against mood disorders and addictions. (2013, p. 315)

Then there are the physical effects of online compulsivity and screen addiction: the brains and the minds of children and adolescents are more plastic and, therefore, more vulnerable to being overwhelmed by over-stimulation and stress. Laurance described a study on the brain-altering effects of Internet addiction on seventeen game-addicted adolescents in China who had been diagnosed with "Internet addiction disorder". Their brains were scanned and compared with those of their peers, and "the results showed impairments of the white matter fibres in the brain connecting regions involved in emotional processing, attention, decision-making and cognitive control". (Laurance, 2012)

Screen compulsivity may also be the result of a particular kind of neglect. Today and everyday, we can see evidence everywhere of people around thirty, "digital natives", bringing up children to whom screens are given as toys to keep them quiet. One wonders if parents are fully aware of their children's online behaviour and whether, as attachment figures, they have tried hard enough to protect them from the dangers to be found in cyberspace. It is hard to quantify the effect of care and attention that is missing.

## *Conclusion*

Whenever anyone writes a book about sex addiction, it is usually the first third, the exciting part revealing the shenanigans and the crazy things that addicts do, that is often read avidly. The last third, which talks about healthy sexuality and the building of relationships, the difficult bit, often goes unread. Healthy relationships—with other people and with ourselves—are not marked by intense highs and lows, but by a sustained and sustaining reliable commitment to making them work, which is neither glamorous nor exciting.

Psychoanalysis in Freud's time of infant mortality and short life expectancy, when most people were acquainted with sorrow and grief, was focused on working towards the removal of sexual repression that was being converted into hysteria and other symptoms. Since then, all that freedom of sexual expression does not appear to have made us happier. Today, due to the commodification of everything from sex to debt, and the unwillingness or inability to cope with grief or stress, the diseases of our time that we meet in our psychotherapy rooms and treatment centres seem to be narcissism and addiction. It is not just addicts; we increasingly live in a world that has forgotten how to suffer. As a culture, we do not know how to wait, how to work through pain, and few people seem to understand the concept of loss any more, evidenced by the ubiquity of advertisements for "no win-no fee" injury compensation lawyers. We want compensation, and we want it now! The term "retail therapy" is established in the culture where shopping, buying online, and consuming are regarded as recreational activities, recognised as ways to reduce any unwanted feelings of stress, boredom, or discomfort.

According to James (2012), the portrayal of the male sex addict in the film *Shame* can tell us a lot about the way we are living now:

> [T] he rest of us Westerners consumed as if there is no tomorrow – and now, there is no tomorrow. Name your poison – the one that caught you up in the consumer boom. Gadgets? Heels? Guitars? Cocaine? A huge DVD collection? (p. 34)

Even in the most recent recession, although we had maxed out the credit cards, we were still being encouraged to consume our way out of trouble. Indulgence is condoned and endorsed in a "live now and don't pay later" culture, where we take what we want, without struggle or challenge, "because we're worth it!" This ethos goes right to the top of governments who will financially enslave, exploit, or invade other countries so that they can supply us with what we perceive to be our due.

In just a few years, a virtual, push button, so-called interactive way of communicating has become the norm. It has made enormous inroads into our collective behaviours and it is not going away. Young people can spend the equivalent of a working week in front of screens, affecting how they relate to themselves and others because they are often having contact, but not relationship with real people.

This might all seem rather bleak but there is hope for addicts, both "classic" and "contemporary", who feel trapped in secrecy and shame around their sex addiction. The information available to us from the field of neuroscience shows that brains can be rewired when people learn to care for themselves and others. We are born seeking proximity with other human beings and we need to engage in working through the friction and challenges of building real, productive, relationships by learning how to manage and transcend conflict, and this can reinforce our sense of self-worth. In SLAA, they say that "love is a committed, thoughtful decision, not a feeling by which we are overwhelmed". People can recover from addiction and can practise, over time, how to be present with their own discomfort and the wounded parts of themselves by learning how to wait, how to grieve, and how to mourn. But they need relationship with real others to help them with recovery.

Inviting people to suffer is never going to be an easy sell. Is there an App for that?

## *Web resources*

Association for the Treatment of Sex Addiction and Compulsivity (ATSAC) at www.atsac.co.uk

International Institute for Trauma and Addiction Professionals (IITAP) at www.iitap.com

## References

*BBC World Service* (2014). *From Our Own Correspondent*. www.bbc.co.uk. Broadcast 7 February 2014.

Carnes, P., Carnes, S., & Bailey, J. (2011). *Facing Addiction: Starting Recovery from Alcohol and Drugs*. Carefree AZ: Gentle Path Press.

Carter, R. (2000). *Mapping the Mind*. London: Phoenix.

Doidge, N. (2007). *The Brain that Changes Itself: Stories of Personal Triumph from the Frontiers of Brain Science*. London: Penguin.

James, N. (2012). Sex and the City. *Sight and Sound Magazine, 22*(2): 34–38.

Kahr, B. (2007). *Sex and the Psyche: the Truth About Our Most Secret Fantasies*. London: Penguin.

Laurance, J. (2012). Addicted! Scientists show how Internet dependency alters the human brain. *The Independent*, 12 January 2012. www.independent.co.uk/news. Accessed 4 February 2012.

Lewis, M. (2011). *Memoirs of an Addicted Brain: A Neuroscientist Examines His Former Life on Drugs*. New York: Public Affairs.

McCauley, K. T. (2004). *The Disease Model of Addiction: Families, Friends & Employers*. Part I. CD available from: www.instituteforaddictionstudy.com. Accessed 12 December 2013.

Moye, A. (1985). Pornography. In: A. Metcalf & M. Humphries (Eds.), *The Sexuality of Men* (pp. 44–69) London: Pluto Press.

Riemersma, J., & Sytsma, M. (2013). A new generation of sexual addiction. *Sexual Addiction and Compulsivity: The Journal of Treatment and Prevention, 20*(4): 306–322.

*Shame* (2011). Film4/See-Saw Films, UK.

Smithers, R. (2012). Chain stores close business. *Guardian*, 17 October 2012. www.theguardian.com. Accessed 10 December 2012.

Stoller, R. J. (1975). *Perversion: the Erotic Form of Hatred*. London: Karnac.

Ulman, R. B., & Paul, H. (2006). *The Self-Psychology of Addiction and its Treatment: Narcissus in Wonderland*. New York: Routledge.

Weiss, R. (2012). Personal communication.

*CHAPTER THREE*

# Net gains and losses: digital technology and the couple

*Anne Power and Linda Cundy*

## *Introduction*

Influenced by the discipline of ethology (the study of animals in their natural environments), John Bowlby described observable repertoires of behaviours in terms of motivational systems. Although the specific behaviours may vary, attachment and sexual systems are universal among mammals; attachment is a strategy to maximise individual survival while sex ensures survival of the species. In a few species, including our own homo sapiens, sex may have functions other than procreation, such as pair bonding, release of tension or aggression, and pleasure. Ethologists also study the courtship rituals that bind two adults together. Among humans, courtship rituals are complex and varied, and the advent of the Internet has opened up new arenas for flirting, display, the dance of attraction, and mate selection.

We are social animals, but different cultures organise along different lines. Polygyny is openly practised in a few, with one man supporting a number of wives who each bear him children. Polyandry, the practice of one woman taking two or more husbands, is a rarity. However, covert polygamy in the form of affairs is common the world over.

In much (but not all) of the developed and developing worlds, monogamy is the approved model for adult bonding. It is unclear where or when we began to organise relationships differently from our closest relatives: neither gorillas nor orang-utans, chimpanzees nor bonobos are monogamous. It seems likely that the preference for family units based on stable relationships between two adults would have been encouraged by the development of agriculture around ten or twelve thousand years ago, with populations foregoing nomadic or semi-nomadic lifestyles for permanent settlement. Kinship bonds would have been maintained through attending clan gatherings where young people could meet and pair up. The extended family unit was probably important then, as it still is now in many cultures, with relations between families forged and maintained through the practice of arranged marriages between them.

Ten millennia or so after our ancestors began to farm the land of the Fertile Crescent and the world has changed radically. Many societies now favour the nuclear family as the basic unit—the extended family structure is increasingly unwieldy in an economic system that requires geographical mobility—and the range and complexity of our technological toolkit is bewildering. Parents, grandparents, aunts and uncles, cousins and siblings may live on different continents rather than sharing a family compound or living in adjoining homes, but communication technology and social networking enables distal relationships to be maintained as never before. Despite this ongoing contact, relatives might not be on hand to help with child-care or to give practical assistance to the nuclear family. The couple as a unit might come under greater pressure as the primary source of attachment for both partners—and, of course, for their children.

* * *

Although attachment behaviours are most obvious in children who elicit a care-giving protective response from parents, Bowlby (1969) insisted that the need to reach out to another person in times of stress, illness, and worry is normal, and the capacity to do this is healthy throughout the whole of life. Parents may continue to function as attachment figures well into our adult lives, with sibling relationships and friendships also serving our needs for comfort and reassurance when we are distressed. What marks out attachment between adults from that between child and parent is mutuality: an individual may, at times, seek out the presence of another person, yet can reciprocate when the tables are turned. In our society, there is an expectation (felt by many as a pressure) that adults will form a relatively enduring relationship with one other person, and that this bond will encompass the needs of both partners for intimacy, companionship, sex, and attachment—and possibly provide children, too. In many cases, this might be a hopelessly unrealistic goal. However, communication technology plays an increasingly significant part in all these areas of relating—companionship, attachment, and sex.

This chapter explores how the Internet is having an impact on couples with regard to attachment, on the process by which couples find each other and form relationships, on the longer-term development and maintenance of an exclusive relationship, and on the ways that adult relationships might end.

Long-term monogamous relationships have two distinct phases in addition to an ending stage (whether that be a separation, divorce, or death). Initially, there is the projective process we call falling in love and, subsequently, there is a gradual evolution of an attachment bond over the years, which may be more or less secure, or even abusive. The transition between these two states is a significant developmental task for a couple and hinges on their tolerance for disillusionment and for the loss of idealisation in favour of reality. The evolution of passion to attachment is not automatic and many couples part before the eighteen month–two-year watershed when the erotic charge generally calms. If the transition is made, then the long-term couple face the question of whether they can retain enough of their early passion to sustain a companionable connection, whether they can integrate sex and attachment. But first they must meet.

## *Casting the net*

It seems that finding a potential life partner has become more difficult, not because there are fewer eligible mates, but perhaps because of the pace and pressure of life and work, with reduced opportunities to socialise with groups of people. Dating websites offer access to large numbers of potential matches and can effect an initial introduction. This may be particularly valued by people with hectic work schedules, who are socially isolated, or for whom the biological clock is ticking and time to start a family is passing quickly. It is possible to "meet" specific groups of people more easily than at a club or bar: whether your preference is for redheads, vegetarians, people who work in uniforms, or horse-lovers, there is a dating website for you. Or there may be other reasons why people are turning more comfortably to the Internet in the initial stages of searching for a partner. In a seemingly dangerous world, it might feel better to get to know a stranger in the safety of an online environment before meeting up, the easy attention of a number of interested parties who "like" one's profile might stoke narcissistic pleasure, or the fun of voyeurism found in sizing up the available options gives a buzz. And for all of us—those brought up with digital technology and those who have adapted to it—so much of life is already lived online.

As more couples are formed through Internet dating sites, we might wonder whether matches that begin online make for more, or less, satisfying long-term relationships. Dating websites are big business, and, in order to compete with each other and with the more traditional methods of courtship, many research and publish their success rates in generating long-term relationships, weddings, and happy marriages. The outcome of this research and the statistics produced are likely to be somewhat skewed; we will probably need to wait for another generation to grow old together before a true picture emerges, and it is possible that this shift in couple formation will make no difference to relationship outcome.

Let us eavesdrop on two people who join an online dating website. They have both chosen a particular site, drawn by its reputation and targeted marketing that seems to hold out the promise of meeting their specific desires. They complete questionnaires and create profiles presenting an edited version of reality, perhaps exaggerating some qualities and minimising or omitting others they prefer to keep hidden. Each selects a photographic self-portrait with the hope of catching the eye of a certain kind of viewer. "Do I look young enough, slim enough, friendly or intelligent, successful, fun, fit, and sexy?" Consciously or otherwise, each has a notion of the ideal mate and the kind of relationship they might have together, and they construct their profiles with this in mind. They hope there will be "chemistry"—or alchemy.

Bollas has described the first relationship between infant and mother in terms of transformational experiences: the mother transforms her baby's unpleasant sensations and emotions into pleasure through her sensitive attentions (Bollas, 1987). Sadly, some disturbed mothers transform the relatively calm states of the infant into anxiety and fear, projecting their own distress into the little one. These early relational patterns form an internal template for the child, who then pursues experiences throughout life that replicate those of his first relationship with his transformational object: someone or something to lift him out of depression, to soothe him when he feels overwhelmed, to raise his spirits beyond the mundane, to make him feel special—the biggest fish in the pond. Or, possibly, he looks for someone to make him feel real by creating havoc with his equilibrium . . .

In attachment terms, our representational models, constructed from everyday encounters with our care-givers in the first months and years of life, create internal maps that we use to navigate around relationships, predicting the ways other people will behave and how we will feel in our dealings with them (Bowlby, 1979, 1988). If we are fortunate enough to have internalised secure relationships, then we face the world with optimism, expecting to be liked and respected, anticipating pleasure in social contact. However, insecure attachment sets up something more complicated: the unconscious expectation, influenced by established internal working models, is that other people will behave in unhelpful ways (tantalising but withholding, for example), but alongside that there may be a fantasy of a relationship that is very different, totally and reliably satisfying and secure, a relationship to heal old wounds.

So, she and he (or he and he, she and she) arrange the website payments with their online banks and then press "send". Like SOS messages in bottles thrown out to sea, our couple-to-be has sent out beacons into cyberspace.

This is the twenty-first century equivalent of travelling to a gathering of the clan in order to find a mate. However,

> Rather than relying on the intuition of village elders, family members, or friends to select which pairs of unacquainted singles will be especially compatible, certain forms of online dating involve placing one's romantic fate in the hands of a mathematical matching algorithm. (Finkel, Eastwick, Karney, et al., 2012, p. 3)

Our imaginary protagonists have cast their nets, but they may have different motivations from each other, and their conscious motives might be at odds with an unconscious undertow. The choice of dating website and the psychological profile should highlight whether the relationship being sought is for temporary hooking up and uncommitted sex, or long-term romance and attachment, but both parties might feel some ambivalence or lack of clarity about what they want. And they might decide to lie. Perhaps one believes that the best hope of getting sex is to dangle the carrot of a committed relationship. The other, meanwhile, might be afraid of frightening off a potential life-partner by seeming too needy or broody. Some websites are set up explicitly to enable individuals to link up for casual sex, and this can work well for those who keep attachment and sex separate, who are effective at denying a need for attachment, or are just not ready to settle down. But what might our two characters be looking for?

## *Falling in love as a method of partner selection*

Contemporary western culture is unusual in relying largely on romance to settle the critical question of finding a life partner; in previous centuries and in other cultures, the family held more power and the individual, particularly the woman, rather less. Marriage was viewed as more of a financial contract than it is now. Perhaps match-making by Internet site has proved so popular because the romantic solution has not been particularly successful in producing satisfactory long-term partnerships.

In popular stories, two people may fall in love when their gaze meets with unexpected intensity, and in real life it can, indeed, happen across a crowded room. At that moment, each person is seeing something of great meaning in the other; from one perspective they are recognising a quality in the other that is fascinating or lovely. With our powerful unconscious antennae, we can sometimes accurately identify traits that are carried unobtrusively by another, but, from a different perspective, those desirable characteristics are projections; the individual who is falling in love is attributing to his beloved qualities that have been lacking in his own self and life.

However, the idealisation which overwhelms us when we fall in love has major flaws as a mechanism for partner selection if what is sought is a companion, sexual partner, and attachment figure all rolled into one: first, it can lead to a dubious choice in terms of suitability, and second, there will be a challenging transitional stage to negotiate when the initial phase of idealisation fades. Lyons (1993) describes this task: "It involves the attempt to convert what was originally a largely unconscious, instinctive choice into a conscious commitment" (p. 45). There is a great deal of difference between falling in love and feeling a mature love for the other—love as a "commitment device" (Kirkpatrick, 1998).

When human beings fall in love, they experience a flood of feel-good neurotransmitters such as phenylethylamine—a kind of endogenous amphetamine (Ratey, 2001). But what is it that makes one person so powerfully attracted to another? An explanation in terms of sexual attraction is suggested in the notion of erotic templates (Morin, 1995), while object relations theorists offer an understanding of psychic attraction. From the perspective of attachment theory, our attachment patterns and accompanying representational models alert us when we identify someone whose own internal world supplies a promising mix of similarity and difference.

It is intriguing to consider how this unconscious process of recognition and projection begins to happen online when the individuals are connecting only through the ether—when their eyes meet across cyberspace. They might believe that a mutual interest in hill-walking brought them together and that they love the sense of humour demonstrated in their online exchanges, but the biggest pull may be unconscious. Perhaps the understated, sensitive personality of the one embodies a disavowed part of the other; meanwhile, the other partner might have sensed in the online profile the warm, capable parent they had always longed for. This kind of fit could apply in both heterosexual or same sex couples; attachment theory does not distinguish between heterosexual and homosexual relationships, but between secure and insecure ones. Usher (2008) describes what the unconscious is looking for in functional terms when we seek a mate: "An individual has to find a partner who will contain their projections and whose projections they are able to contain" (p. 19).

Bramley's analogy of a job advert seems particularly apt when we are considering online searches:

> In jobs and in love we tend to go for a set-up where we can carry on doing what we are talented at, while getting something fresh and extra out of the new situation, or at least the promise of further in-service training. (Bramley, 2008, p. 23)

She makes the point that applicants for a job know to read between the lines in order to tune into the hidden agenda, and her metaphor is even more apt when courtship happens online. Our attachment histories create patterns of defence that help us to get some of our needs met. Clinging and demanding attention, for instance, can ensure some scraps of affection from others who have the capacity to love but are unreliable. Another useful strategy is to present oneself as being without needs, appearing strong, competent, and capable. This pattern might appeal to another who cannot tolerate the demands of intimacy, or someone who is better at asking for comfort than providing it. Bramley suggests that we unconsciously seek out a partner who "fits" with our particular defensive strategies—our representational models—but who also brings something new to the equation. With online dating, we pick up clues from the other's textual conversation, including speed of response to messages, what is responded to and what is dismissed, emotional vocabulary, length of communication, and so on: human beings are acutely sensitive to the form, as well as the content, of communication.

* * *

Back to our couple-to-be: scanning the profiles of eligible "dates", they dismiss many as unsuitable but are drawn to each other's. According to Finkel, Eastwick, Karney, and colleagues, "encountering potential partners via online dating profiles reduces three-dimensional people to two-dimensional displays of information" (2012, p. 3). Perhaps this missing dimension creates the very space in which imagination can flourish. Carefully selected words and photos settle in the mind like grit in an oyster shell, and fantasies begin to cluster together, layer upon layer. Sparse phrases are fleshed out by projections and transference. First contact is made—a statement of interest is posted. As yet, the "other" has no body and possibly no voice, just a photographic portrait and text typed into a keyboard. During initial online conversations, with little to ground our two protagonists in reality, embryonic fantasies gestate.

### *Internet dating and the client in therapy*

When a therapy client is using a dating site, thinking together in detail about what happens on Internet-mediated dates can be very creative and enlightening: who decides where to meet, who keeps the other waiting, who signals to whom that the evening is not working, how the pair ends the date. Circular questions from systemic therapy explore projections and highlight gaps in communication: "How would he have known that you felt x?" "If someone had noticed you in the bar together, what would they have observed?"

Dating experiences might shed light on attachment patterns a patient has struggled with for years. For instance, if he is getting plenty of willing attention and interest, but never feels he is finding the right person, he might feel bewildered and disheartened, but it does challenge any belief that the difficulty lies outside of himself. This can give the therapeutic pair a chance to think about what is really going on—perfectionism is a great defence against intimacy or commitment.

It is often helpful in therapy to enquire about the specific dating website selected and reasons for this; there are so many to choose from, each with its own target audience and reputation. Some purport to help subscribers find love, others are aimed at companionship or people to have fun with, and others still are implicitly or overtly about sex. The financial cost varies enormously, too, and where individuals cannot afford the most expensive they might feel that any "match" they find will invariably be second-rate. This could repeat a relational pattern of feeling disappointed and deprived of good-enough love. A further relational dynamic is at play when any potential date selected by algorithm is immediately rejected as undesirable. It may be helpful to enquire about the patient's relationship with authority in general, and parental figures in particular: what kind of partner might the parents feel is appropriate?

It is also noteworthy that many clients now also search for a therapist online, sifting through profiles on websites, perhaps reacting to photographs and looking for clues that this might be a satisfying relationship, a good match. It is an intriguing parallel for patients who are also registered with online dating services.

## *Matchmaking*

Online sites funded by advertising revenue allow customers to post their own profile, to browse through those of available others and to decide if they want to send a message of interest. A profile, as Paumgarten observes, "is a vehicle for projecting a curated and stylized version of oneself into the world" (2011, p. 41). Sites charging a fee usually ask members to complete a questionnaire and then perform a deliberate sifting and matchmaking function on their behalf. While the simpler sites operate in a similar way to old-fashioned flirting, spotting someone who appeals and making a play for their attention, those using more sophisticated selection processes are closer to traditional matchmaking practices in many middle-class Asian and Jewish families. In fact, Asian and Jewish populations embraced online searches for suitable partners early on, with websites such as JDate and Asiand8. Perhaps this approach to matching couples is particularly helpful not only when populations are geographically dispersed, but also where there is already a recognised cultural tradition of matchmaking.

Sites which use questionnaires and algorithms to match their members now have an enormous pool of data about what makes for a satisfied customer/couple outcome, and their computer programmes can constantly learn from the millions of members whose dating experience is stored in their software: for instance, the eHarmony survey includes 250 questions to aid accurate matching (Online dating statistics, www.statisticbrain.com). Fisher (2007), an anthropologist whose ideas of partner selection are behind Chemistry.com, has analysed feedback from members after a first meeting. Her finding—that there was an initial attraction to people with different cognitive and behavioural profiles—is unsurprising, but perhaps significant given the volume of data examined. At eHarmony there is less enthusiasm for difference; Gonzaga and colleagues, who conduct research for this company, endorse studies that demonstrate similarity as a predictor of relationship satisfaction. They write, "Similarity may benefit a relationship by coordinating partners' responses to the environment, increasing understanding of each other's internal states, and promoting higher levels of validation" (Gonzaga, Carter, & Buckwalter, 2010, p. 635). But how do we make sense of these findings alongside the theory of couple fit developed through psychodynamic practice? Are the kinds of projective fit we consistently find in couples too elusive, too unconscious to be picked up in questionnaires?

Each commercial company adopts an implicit or explicit theory of couple fit that informs selection and matching procedures. Perhaps, in many cases, the computers are programmed along the lines used by matchmakers for generations: similarity is desirable in practical matters such as levels of education and income, while complementarity is desirable for various personality traits. The new process seems remarkably similar to the traditional one. Previously, and in some cultures still, a parent might say, "your auntie knows someone who works in the media—he sounds like he might be right for you, would you like to meet him?" Nowadays, a computer generates invitations to link up with possible matches. One difference in the traditional scenario is that not only the couple, but also both families are involved, and this may help to deter later infidelities (or, at least, make the straying partner extra vigilant about being discovered).

If online flirting needs a slightly different set of skills from meeting in flesh and blood, then it may favour a slightly different group of people, but the essential impetus to convey "Do you fancy me?" and "I fancy you" is perhaps not very different. It could be less humiliating to be rejected online than in person in a public place. Those who cope with flirting in the actual world seem also to enjoy it electronically. Some people thrive on dating sites, feeling affirmed by the attention, but how does the online experience work for those who want to take the next step, to be part of an ongoing couple?

It would seem that for those with either an unusually low or high estimate of themselves as sexual beings, online attention or rejection might entrench their self-image. Advertising oneself on a dating website is necessarily exhibitionistic—we put our profiles out into the ether for others to react. The experience is inherently one of being judged, and people might be wounded by this or cope by hardening their defences. When two people become an item, those around them often comment openly about whether their son/daughter/friend could have "done better", and perhaps that question is present in the partners themselves at some level of consciousness. There does seem some risk that Internet dating might heighten the sense of trading; it certainly makes more explicit the sense that any one individual has a market value, and this may fuel insecurities about believing in the choice one has made, as well as about one's own worth. It might also speed up a process, encouraging one party to "snap up" the other before somebody else muscles in. After all, according to one of the major online dating sites, there are Plenty More Fish in the Sea, and some of them might be predatory.

### *The next step*

The next developmental phase for our couple-to-be might involve a shift to other modes of communication. Some dating websites offer this facility, or there might be an invitation to become a Facebook friend, or the exchange of mobile telephone numbers. By this time, a cathexis could already be made, each having invested the other with significance and hope. Perhaps they check for messages more frequently now, are more disappointed if there is nothing waiting in the inbox, elated when there is. In time, giddy with a cocktail of excitement and anxiety (and maybe just an undercurrent of doubt or pessimism), they arrange to meet.

Up to this point, the other has been a disembodied virtual character, an avatar of him or her self. Both parties have their own histories of relationship, their own perceptions of who and what they feel themselves to be, their own ideas about who and what will complement them to make a viable match. "When adults come together to form an intimate relationship, each person releases into it unresolved issues from their transgenerational pool of unconscious fantasies" (Raphael-Leff, 2001, p. 10), and "they enter it dragging their psychological histories behind them" (Raphael-Leff, 2005, p. 195).

Before the advent of the Internet, the getting-to-know process happened during social meetings and dates. This was the gestational period, when fantasies were formed and modified. Now, much of this happens prior to the first meeting. I am reminded of a pregnancy where so much preparation for relationship goes on before the parents and newborn meet face to face. Initially, the baby is not a whole person in the mind of his parents, but a jumble of hopes, expectations, and fears. When they finally "meet", the parents need to renounce the imagined baby in order to welcome the real one (Brazelton & Cramer, 1991; Raphael-Leff, 1993). So, for our couple, about to meet for the first time in the flesh, the encounter will reveal many of the projections and fantasies to be products of imagination. The relative anonymity of cyberspace has enabled both of our players to stoke fantasy by stage-managing the flow of information and withholding certain facts they fear are unpalatable. Can each give up the idealised imaginary lover in order to make a relationship with the real other?

Attachment history plays a part in the ability to accept the other for who he or she is. An adult with predominantly dismissing attachment may be easily deterred by a mismatch between fantasy and reality, returning to further online browsing in search of the ideal. Someone with a more preoccupied pattern, who tends to feel insecure and anxious when alone, might be more inclined to persist despite disappointment rather than be abandoned. Perhaps those best prepared to adapt to reality are people who have internalised secure relationships, whose higher levels of self-esteem and social ease enable them to be genuinely curious about the other person without needing to merge with him or her.

Western popular culture promotes the notion of romance and the dream lover. The specific dream lover is tailor-made by each individual, a unique blend of attachment figure and sexual partner designed to meet the needs for each. The archetype, however, is usually distinguished by being utterly devoted, totally attuned and considerate, always available for intimacy, play, and even perversion if that is what is required. I have worked with several insecure patients who found that relationships with real people were difficult and disappointing, but who each constructed a perfect imaginary lover to turn to. In more than one case, the patient actually felt guilty when dating, feeling that they were being unfaithful to the one (fantasy) person who would never let them down. Online profiles can provide a template for an ideal lover, but nobody can ever fill their perfect shoes.

Dating sites can make it possible for two people to meet, but the test of whether they both feel "that spark" happens when they come together face to face, and for some couples this flesh and blood meeting will follow a long online courtship and even a commitment to each other. While Internet sites, with their intelligent algorithms, may in many cases produce more sensible matches than chance romance, perhaps random and romantic meetings have a special meaning to a couple, as Paumgarten writes: "Serendipity and coincidence are the photosynthesis of romance, hinting at some kind of supernatural preordination, the sense that two people are made for each other" (Paumgarten, 2011, p. 44).

The first meeting is loaded with complicated feelings. There may, indeed, be "chemistry"—pheromones now play a role as two bodies come into physical contact. Sexual attraction may be strong, and it seems that many first dates where the couple met online end in sex (Aboujaoude, 2011). Perhaps the reality of a physical presence, a body that has been absent previously proves irresistible. Conversely, awkwardness, disappointment, or even revulsion may dominate, along with anger at being misled. Sometimes, the embarrassment of having deceived the other, and fear of "being found out" also create tension and self-consciousness that spoil the moment.

For our couple, the first date goes well and one or other texts to say, "Had a gr8 time. Wld love 2 meet again". He or she then waits for a response, and if it does not arrive immediately, insecurity sets in. The website is checked to see if the "date" is still actively soliciting new interest. Meanwhile, the other actor in our scenario is holding back an impulse to reply straight away, afraid of appearing too eager or desperate. Perhaps his or her attachment style is more dismissing, wanting relationship but afraid of revealing too much, wishing to seem relaxed and confidant while actually feeling awkwardly shy. The responding text finally arrives a day or two later. What does the delay mean? The more eager of the two now feels embarrassed and confused. Perhaps he misread the signs of attraction? Or maybe she made a fool of herself; how could she believe her date was really interested in her? Human beings, with our complicated brains, need to make sense of experience, and, in the absence of information, we fill the gaps with imaginings. There is no culturally agreed behaviour, "netiquette", for when and how to reply to telephone messages, emails, or texts, and this creates misunderstanding, even paranoia.

Tronick and his team devised a powerful experiment to observe relationships between mothers and small infants, usually eight to twelve weeks of age (Tronick, Als, Adamson, et al., 1978). The mother is asked to engage with her baby for a time, and they are filmed relating to each other in ways that are more or less typical of this dyad (though the presence of researchers and cameras is bound to influence behaviour). After a few minutes, mother is signalled to freeze her expression and not respond to any of the infant's cues. During this still-face phase, most infants initially seem to view mother's behaviour as part of the game and they intensify attempts to engage her. When this fails, the babies appear confused, their behaviour becomes disorganised and—in a few cases—the infant's posture collapses. Their averted gaze hints at the painful experience of shame. Once mother resumes relating, the baby usually re-engages quickly, with no harm done, but in those dyads where mother has been diagnosed with depression or borderline personality disorder, the infant might remain disengaged or disorganised for long periods. Fast forward to adulthood and two people flirting online, by phone or text. Communication flows playfully between them until there is a sudden, inexplicable silence. The more resilient secure–autonomous person will tolerate waiting for a response, containing herself until she can check the reality of the situation rather than jumping to conclusions. She does not necessarily take it personally, accepting that the other person has a life of his or her own as well. But those with insecure attachment histories might fill in the gaps created by silence with fretting, jealous brooding, and fearing that the other is disappointed with them. Feeling rejected may trigger feelings of anger, shame, and panic, even leading to acting out. In retaliation for imagined infidelity, or in order to self-soothe and boost self-esteem (at least temporarily), another search might be started for a partner or a one-night stand.

### *From passion to attachment*

According to Holmes (2007) "As the pair-bonding dance progresses each member of the potential couple may be mutually exploring whether sexual attraction and secure attachment can be mapped on to one and the same individual" (p. 20).

The longer-term satisfaction of a relationship and its ability to weather the loss of early idealisation will depend on how well it functions as a container (Colman, 1993). Attachment theory frames this containing function in terms of a secure base, with the relationship itself helping to regulate feelings; Hazan and Zeifman (1999) identify the transition from a state of being in love to an attachment bond at the point where the presence of the partner becomes less arousing and more soothing. We can think of this shift in neurochemical terms, with higher levels of the amphetamine-like substance phenylethylamine present during the sexually charged early phase of high arousal, and increased levels of endorphins, vasopressin, and oxytocin—the "bonding hormone"—as the attachment bond strengthens (Eagle, 2007). Liebowitz (1983) writes of "two distinct chemical systems for romance; one basically serves to bring people together and the other to keep them together" (p. 90).

A romantic couple relationship is built on the three elements of attachment, care-giving, and sexuality (Hazan & Shaver, 1987); the balance of these three varies considerably between couples and over the years of a long relationship. Methods devised to assess attachment in a couple determine how well the relationship functions as a secure base and also gauge the capacity of each partner for both care-seeking and care-giving (Fisher & Crandell, 2001). From this perspective, the relationship itself can be seen as having an attachment style, even though the two partners may differ in their separate patterns. The hallmarks of a secure attachment relationship are accessibility, reliability, and responsiveness, and partners provide mutual comfort as well as a secure base from which to go out and explore the world. Digital technology can provide a channel for communication between them, keeping them accessible and "logged on" to the relationship while apart.

There are many positive ways in which digital technology supports established couple relationships. After playing a part in bringing them together, the increased capacity to stay in touch that is afforded by the plethora of communication channels promotes pair bonding. Thus, a partner who needs to travel can still access her safe base for emotional refuelling (Mahler, Pine, & Bergman, 1975). At times, this could be critical for the wellbeing of the relationship: separation during the early stages of a union, when the home alone partner might feel abandoned, or, later, when the partner at home is single-handedly caring for children, or when one partner is unwell or has reduced mobility. Emails, mobile telephone calls, Instagram messages, and Skype conversations provide reassurance and continuity, building the foundations of secure attachment. Even the small everyday communications between partners sharing thoughts, information, plans, and feelings help to bind them together as a unit, supporting the transition from the first to the second phase of couple relationship.

## *The couple online*

The opportunity to access information on the Internet and to make other supportive connections will have a benefit to couples that is hard to assess. Where there are fertility difficulties, online contact with others in similar situations can dispel some of the feelings of isolation, anxiety, shame, and grief that otherwise put undue pressure on the pair. Some couples find crucial help with parenting, and this makes a substantial difference to their relationship. Others find information about sex that reduces anxiety and normalises their experience, thus freeing their erotic life. Communicating with friends and family through social network sites can diffuse the intensity of a two-person relationship, easing the pressure to "be everything" for the other. Information and support found on the Internet and on social network sites could also be crucial to individuals and couples from minority groups; this can be the case for gay and lesbian people and those who feel their sexuality is constrained within their own families and communities: being welcomed into an online community can reduce loneliness and it might serve as an extended family or clan where a pool of potential partners may be found.

Two partners—gender is immaterial—live and work in different countries. They maintain their bond through supportive text messages, emails, telephone, and Skype conversations. They are committed to each other and visit each other for weekends every month. It is a long-term, stable relationship, with each person feeling secure in the knowledge that the other is committed to it continuing, and trusting the other—more or less—to be faithful. There is an implicit understanding that any indiscretion will be minor and will never be revealed. Both not only manage to live with this arrangement, but they seem to need the geographical and emotional space it allows, perhaps to focus on careers. We might describe this as a stable relationship between two people who are insecure, both having dismissing relational styles. The brief periods of real intimacy during visits might feel very special and enough to maintain them as a couple, but too much of this intense contact would feel suffocating. Communication technology has made these kinds of relationship increasingly sustainable, and perhaps the structure of society in the twenty-first century requires more couples to live this way. Contemporary social and economic pressures might even be creating the conditions for more of this avoidant attachment style, where self-sufficiency and commitment to career is prized above intimacy. It is not an ideal arrangement for family life, and perhaps difficulties must be faced in old age, when there is no work or travel to distract from the struggles over intimacy, and when the need to depend on others necessarily increases. Although potentially stable, such a long-distance relationship might lack the features of a truly *secure* adult attachment, but, in the meantime, it is an increasing feature of adaptation to the economic environment.

This contrasts with a truly secure relationship that serves as a safe haven for each partner, a source of comfort and reassurance where each feels known and accepted. Needs are communicated clearly and without manipulation or shame, with the expectation of a helpful response. Insecure couples, however, have difficulty achieving a good enough balance between their needs for autonomy and for intimacy. If one partner has a preoccupied pattern and the other a more avoidant or dismissing attachment style, then an approach by the former is likely to provoke a retreat by the latter. This pursuer–pursued pattern can endure throughout a long relationship. In such cases, the avoidant partner might even seek work abroad and leave the ambivalent partner to cope alone with their profound anxiety. If the two are living in different time zones, the frustration for the abandoned anxious partner will be great, and the avoidant one is likely to wake up to a queue of angry messages on his or her telephone.

Established couples might need to negotiate the amount of contact they maintain during a day, especially the quantity of communication sent and received during work hours. In many situations, it is not appropriate to manage personal life during office hours, but an insecure partner could experience these limits as a rejection. Feeling excluded can lead to increased anxiety about being abandoned, or jealous fantasies of infidelity.

Many couples run into trouble about how much of their life to post online, and this happens when one partner objects to the level of exposure on social network sites that the other one imposes. Having an online presence as a couple has the hazard that if there is a break-up, the process may become rather public. If messages about a break-up are posted too swiftly, it might make it hard to come back and repair, and if rows are conducted by means of exposure and denunciation, then the Internet can become a weapon in a personal vendetta.

The problem of the Internet gobbling up time is aptly depicted by cartoonists who have drawn couples in bed with their digital devices, oblivious to the warm flesh and blood beside them. Like children or pets, these gadgets can become a third in the bedroom, cutting into the scraps of time when busy, tired partners might have cuddled up and unexpectedly found the energy and desire to take things further.

As previously stated, sex and attachment are different behavioural systems that are not easily integrated into one complete bundle. We are familiar with situations where companionable attachment goes on at home while the frisson of sex is kept separate. Various societies have practised this duality overtly, or, at least, with a degree of acceptance (usually with women as either wife or mistress/geisha and men moving between them). It is less frequently acknowledged that some people stay in committed relationships while their longings for meaningful platonic intimacy are met elsewhere. This could happen if the person in question is a carer for his or her partner, an attachment figure whose own needs for love and support must be split off and sought outside the primary relationship. Social contacts can be established online, for instance through support groups, to which carers turn at the end of a difficult day, and some of these flourish into loving relationships that help each person endure the hardships of fulfilling commitments to their long-term partners. There might, of course, be hopes that in time the online couple can come together openly—but that is another story.

## *Sexual media and the couple*

Couples will vary in the degree to which they see sexual media as problematic. Pornography is easier to access now than ever before and the range of imagery from mild to hard core is probably much wider than pre-digital times. For some individuals, all pornography is distasteful or felt to be a threat. For others, the specific details of the content are the issue, or the amount of time a partner spends in viewing it. Where one partner uses cybersex compulsively, he or she may "engage in the perverse behaviours with a virtual object as a way to avoid actually being in a relationship with an actual object" (Cebulko, 2013, p. 45).

Writing in a pre-Internet age, Stoller offered an interesting definition of pornography: "No depiction is pornographic until an observer's fantasies are added: nothing is pornographic per se" (Stoller, 1975, p. 63). Stoller's statement indicates how much of our sexuality goes on in our minds, and this presents our generation with the challenge of understanding or identifying what we mean by Internet infidelity. Gonyea (2004) suggests that it involves directing sexual energy (thoughts, feelings, and behaviours) out of a couple and, thus, draining the real relationship of life. She stresses that cybersex includes much more than arousing images to accompany masturbation. The equivalent of telephone sex in the twenty-first century is sex talk and mutual masturbation on Skype, or cybersex in virtual reality worlds, and this can be between people in a committed relationship, with a stranger, or within an affair.

Studies show that, for erotic stimulation, women tend to prefer chat rooms and real-time conversations to voyeuristic use of cybersex. Naïve users who are less familiar with connecting to strangers online can become more involved than they expected; Barker (2013) comments, "Intimacy can build quickly, as the anonymity in online forums enables us to reveal more about ourselves, and more quickly" (p. 33). Reading and writing slash literature (defined as a genre focusing on sexual relationships between fictional same-sex characters) is another online sexual behaviour which appeals to women more than the simple use of pornographic imagery, as is conducting an affair through an avatar in a virtual reality world.

Studies on heterosexual couples have suggested that where only one partner uses sexually explicit material, the impact on the couple tends to be negative, with men experiencing more difficulty in arousal if a partner uses pornography, while women's self-perception is negatively affected if their partner accesses porn (Daneback, Traeen, & Mansson, 2009). Reviewing several studies, Bridges and Morokoff (2011) found that the impact was more negative for women than for men; contrastingly, they report that when a couple use sexual media together, this tends to have a positive impact on relational satisfaction.

In couple therapy, just as in other areas of the client's narrative, a key task is to generate exploration of the nature, meaning, and function of the behaviour within the life of the couple. When use of pornography has become problematic, either for the partner or the user, the therapeutic task will often be to identify to what degree the porn is the cause of difficulties or a response to other problems. In some cases, it might simply be a vehicle for expressing anger or hurt which arise in the relationship, while in others, the porn might actually be the cause of the trouble (see Chapter Four in this volume). In each case, the types of erotic narratives favoured and their meaning to the viewer will be significant. Almost always there is quite a narrow range of erotic behaviours that are engaged in repeatedly, with the person using porn seeking a particular kind of hit which is felt to be missing or difficult to access in the "real relationship".

The therapist's role is to engage the client's curiosity in their choice of material and in how this is working for them. It is essential to demonstrate open-minded interest and be aware of points where our own values and codes of behaviour might influence what we take note of and what we comment on. If the two partners disagree on the meaning of cyber porn in their relationship, as therapists, we need to recognise the risks of personal inclinations aligning us with one partner against the other.

## *Online infidelities*

Easy access to the Internet, social network sites, personal emails, and text messages on mobile phones can have a malignant influence, one that can sometimes spell the end of a relationship. It can impinge traumatically on the life of a couple by making opportunities for infidelity more readily available. The betrayal might be a reconnection with a former lover, accessing a site that arranges no-strings-attached sexual liaisons, or conducting a clandestine online affair via webcam, email, or online forum. Some partners might furtively pursue a secret object of obsession, as occurs in erotomania, while others join virtual reality worlds and live out romantic or sexual fantasies among avatars, meanwhile rejecting their real-life partner. There is nothing new about infidelity, but cyberspace makes it so much simpler and offers such a menu of options to choose from; where once a wayward partner had to be proactive to have an affair, now there is a chance to make it happen at the very moment the thought strikes. The window of opportunity to reflect before betraying the trust of one's life partner has narrowed to the length of time it takes to press "send".

The myriad ways that people can connect erotically online, and the anonymity that cyberspace can afford, takes the concept of infidelity way beyond the traditional affair and brings the presence of a third person into the home more than ever before—covert polygamy.

Contemporary couples might need to talk about where they want to draw the line. In a couple where the attachment style is dismissing, each person might appear to accept the other's erotic online interests; such a partnership seems to function smoothly with pseudo-independence, but can then be unexpectedly disturbed when one partner reaches the limit of his or her tolerance. At that point, their limited capacity to either give or receive care makes it difficult to repair the relational rupture. In contrast, preoccupied couples tend to have a high level of both vigilance and disappointment (Schachner, Shaver, & Mikulincer, 2003), perhaps making them more susceptible to feeling threatened and injured by online behaviours that some other couples would tolerate, such as continuing to be a Facebook "friend" with an ex.

When one partner is getting his or her needs met through an Internet liaison, the impact on the long-term couple will have much in common with regular affairs, but, in this case, the real relationship is competing on a particularly unfair playing field: the virtual world is even more idealised than an old-fashioned affair and there is very little need to be authentic or to stay with discomfort. Perhaps a significant long-term result of Internet relating is that we become accustomed to instant access and immediate responses; through this speeding up of relational processes we could undermine our tolerance for holding experiences. The ease of accessing an online affair partner might increase the amount of time and energy given to the clandestine relationship, and an illicit text message can be sent or received while sitting at the dinner table with one's spouse.

If there is a propensity to keep love and sensuality apart, habits that encourage this split may drain erotic charge from the couple, and the Internet, by its nature, deepens that rift (see Chapter Two, this volume). Freud summed up the challenge of combining our erotic and attachment needs in one relationship, especially when there has been poor oedipal resolution: "where they love they do not desire and where they desire they cannot love" (Freud, 1912d, p. 183). We cannot measure how much the Internet is really contributing to infidelity, but what does seem likely is that for more couples now there will be a significant secret, which, if disclosed or discovered, could rock the relationship. While these remain hidden, we might only hear of them in individual therapy rather than in couple work.

## *The Internet and obsession*

Some people are addicted to online gaming, gambling, shopping, or pornography. Others feel compelled to conduct Internet searches, check emails and social network sites. Like other addictions, these impact on the life of a couple when one partner loses control over the impulse to log on.

A male client was periodically obsessive about a former colleague whom he had always fancied but never dated. He tracked her career through professional network sites, noting what training she attended and planning his own conference bookings to allow him to see her. Without the Internet, my client would probably still have obsessed to some degree, but I think the information he could so easily acquire online fed and sustained his rumination. We might argue that the externalisation of the behaviour prompts an individual to recognise the obsession and to confront it, where the silent internal fantasy might have aroused less self-scrutiny. Perhaps this is an example of technology helpfully bringing some of our internal workings into the open.

In this case, the online behaviour was a symptom of general anxiety and it was not clear how much the searching was the client's attempt at regulating anxiety or whether it was a punishing, self-destructive act. As in addiction, the hit (in this case finding a new piece of information) was always followed by guilt and shame. Attempts at managing these uncomfortable feelings led to relapsing into further searches in the need for another high. This client was in a long-term relationship and planning a family. His partner, who seemed to have some preoccupied traits, would have liked much more of his attention, and possibly the online behaviour was an additional strategy for maintaining distance, which suited his more avoidant style. However, the guilt he felt towards his partner was a burden rather than a useful trigger to help him contain his impulses.

## *The beginning of the end*

As well as oiling the wheels for those who are open to an affair, the Internet intrudes markedly into the process of trying to repair damage caused by infidelity. We now have the means to turn private detective ourselves rather than employing one to "dig the dirt".

Several years into their lives together, and our imaginary couple barely communicate. Technology—laptops, mobile telephones, and computer games—are a constant presence in their relationship. One person finds it impossible to put a boundary around career and private life, so the laptop is always open. Working from home means writing reports and responding to emails into the night, and the partner is asleep when he or she gets to bed. Resentments build, but perhaps this affair with technology is itself an act of anger or revenge. Or, possibly, the intimacy of a two-person relationship is too demanding for someone with dismissing defences . . .

One day, a laptop or mobile phone is inadvertently left unsupervised. Suspicions have been quietly gathering in one person's mind and this temptation cannot be resisted. Detective work is furtively carried out—emails, text and phone messages, history of Internet usage are all checked for signs of infidelity, pornography, online gambling, or a secret life. Our investigator is full of self-loathing for harbouring doubts and for succumbing to voyeurism, but what is discovered proves those hunches were correct. Photographs on social network sites attest to the double life of the partner, caught on camera *in flagrante* at the Parisian hotel where the long-term couple had spent their honeymoon, or dressed to the nines with a stranger at a familiar restaurant. We may wonder about the parapraxis, why the evidence was left tantalisingly available for discovery, why the need to be caught in the act. Can the relationship survive? From my experience in the consulting room, often it cannot. Trust is frequently destroyed irrevocably by such duplicity. Both parties feel betrayed and aggrieved. Intolerable shame is avoided by demonising the other.

The Stony Brook Attachment Relationship Project (Crowell & Treboux, 2001) recruited couples who were "going steady" or about to marry for longitudinal research into adult attachment. After five years, the rate of relationship break-up was about twenty per cent, regardless of whether partners were secure, insecure, or a mixture of both. However, the reasons why couples separate and the manner in which they go about untangling their lives together may differ according to attachment style. Secure–autonomous adults value relationship, have the capacity to empathise with others, and to work cooperatively with them. They are typically resilient and willing to work at problems to try to find solutions. When facing the loss of someone close, they are able to grieve. It is probable that secure couples will try to identify difficulties in their relationship and address them, try to repair damage done. When this fails to bring them closer, they are likely to feel sadness at ending and continue to have warm feelings for each other. They often find it possible to maintain friendly contact, especially when there are children involved.

Dismissing adults are poor at communicating feelings and have private inner worlds. They cannot allow themselves to become dependent and feel trapped by a partner who needs intimacy and support. Over time, they might become more remote, seemingly disengaged, and less willing to seek help for the relationship for fear of having to expose their emotions, perceived inadequacies, or secrets. They are more likely to give up and walk away. Feeling uncomfortable in the world of feelings, they might adopt manic defences, immersing themselves in work, suppressing the grief and anger of separating with alcohol or other addictions. They might hunt for a new partner straight away—subscribing to dating websites and pairing up again before the ink on divorce papers has dried.

Preoccupied individuals tend to make enmeshed relationships, doubting their ability to manage alone. They are afraid of being abandoned or betrayed by partners and are suspicious about the other person's online activity. They are jealous of the partner's contact with other men or women, and even the digital device (laptop, mobile phone, games terminal) may be experienced as a rival. Endings are messy and often protracted. Partners, perhaps feeling suffocated, may suggest "time out" to cool the situation down, but this will feel risky for the preoccupied person. A day—or even a few hours—without contact can feel unbearable. I have worked with individuals in this situation who believed it was acceptable to send text messages every day when they had been asked not to make telephone calls. Feelings run high, with a great deal of brooding, blaming, and pleading. It is difficult for preoccupied individuals to accept loss, so they protest and cling, and sometimes can only leave a relationship by destroying it completely. Or, when a partner has left, they might engage in stalking him or her and obsession is fuelled by the plethora of information available online, on social network sites, and messaging apps. This refusal to let go is an inability to work through mourning, a failure to "relocate the lost object" (Bowlby, 1980) and move on in life.

## *Conclusion*

Our primitive instincts, evolved millennia ago on the plains of Africa, survive in this new world of cyberspace. Communication technology mediates all areas of couple relationships, from finding a mate, falling in love, pair bonding, developing a mature mutual attachment, sex, and family life. It can promote secure attachment, but also has the potential to threaten, destabilise, and destroy intimacy. It can become a third element in a two-person relationship, creating a rift, and the negative impact of online behaviour is now showing up in divorce courts. American lawyers report the types of Internet use most frequently cited: the largest category was meeting a new love interest online, followed by compulsive use of pornography, excessive time using the computer, and unreasonable involvement in Internet chat rooms (Kalman, 2008). Whether you work with couples or individuals, these relational difficulties will be coming to a consulting room near you in the therapy of the future.

## *Web Resources*

Online dating statistics. Available at: www.statisticbrain.com. Accessed 6 December 2013.

## *References*

Aboujaoude, E. (2011). *Virtually You: The Dangerous Powers of the e-Personality*. New York: W. W. Norton.

Barker, M. (2013). *Rewriting the Rules: An Integrated Guide to Love, Sex and Relationships*. Hove: Routledge.

Bollas, C. (1987). *The Shadow of the Object: Psychoanalysis of the Unthought Known*. London: Free Association Books [reprinted 1994].

Bowlby, J. (1969). *Attachment and Loss Volume I: Attachment*. London: Hogarth Press.

Bowlby, J. (1979). *The Making and Breaking of Affectional Bonds*. London: Tavistock.

Bowlby, J. (1980). *Attachment and Loss Volume 3: Loss, Sadness and Depression*. London: Hogarth Press.

Bowlby, J. (1988). *A Secure Base: Clinical Applications of Attachment Theory*. London: Routledge.

Bramley, W. (2008). *Bewitched, Bothered and Bewildered: How Couples Really Work*. London: Karnac.

Brazelton, T. B., & Cramer, B. G. (1991). *The Earliest Relationship: Parents, Infants and the Drama of Early Attachment*. London: Karnac.

Bridges, A. J., & Morokoff, P. J. (2011). Sexual media use and relational satisfaction in heterosexual couples. *Personal Relationships, 18*: 562–585.

Cebulko, S. (2013). Internet pornography as a source of marital distress. In: J. S. Scharff (Ed.), *Psychoanalysis Online: Mental Health, Teletherapy, and Training* (pp. 37–47). London: Karnac.

Colman, W. (1993). Marriage as a psychological container. In: S. Ruszczynski (Ed.), *Psychotherapy with Couples: Theory and Practice at the Tavistock Institute of Marital Studies* (pp. 70–96). London: Karnac.

Crowell, J., & Treboux, D. (2001). Attachment security in adult partnerships. In: C. Clulow (Ed.), *Adult Attachment and Couple Psychotherapy* (pp. 28–42). Hove: Brunner-Routledge.

Daneback, K., Traeen, B., & Mansson, S. (2009). Use of pornography in a random sample of Norwegian heterosexual couples. *Archives of Sexual Behaviour, 38*: 746–753.

Eagle, M. (2007). Attachment and sexuality. In: D. Diamond, S. Blatt, & J. Lichtenberg (Eds.), *Attachment and Sexuality* (pp. 27–50). New York: Analytic Press.

Finkel, E. J., Eastwick, P. W., Karney, B. R., Reis, H. T., & Sprecher, S. (2012). Online dating: a critical analysis from the perspective of psychological science. *Psychological Science in the Public Interest, 13*(1): 3–66.

Fisher, H. (2007). The laws of chemistry. *Psychology Today, 40*(3): 76–81.

Fisher, J., & Crandell, L. (2001). Patterns of relating in the couple. In: C. Clulow (Ed.), *Adult Attachment and Couple Psychotherapy* (pp. 15–27). Hove: Brunner-Routledge.

Freud, S. (1912d). On the universal tendency to debasement in the sphere of love. *S.E., 11*: 179–190. London: Hogarth.

Gonyea, J. L. (2004). Internet sexuality: clinical implications for couples. *American Journal of Family Therapy, 32*: 375–390.

Gonzaga, G. C., Carter, S., & Buckwalter, J. G. (2010). Assortive mating, convergence, and satisfaction in married couples. *Personal Relationships, 17*: 634–644.

Hazan, C., & Shaver, P. R. (1987). Romantic love conceptualised as an attachment process. *Journal of Personality and Social Psychology, 52*: 511–524.

Hazan, C., & Zeifman, D. (1999). Pair-bonds as attachments: evaluating the evidence. In: J. Cassidy & P. R. Shaver (Eds.), *Handbook of Attachment: Theory, Research, and Clinical Applications* (pp. 336–354). New York: Guilford Press.

Holmes, J. (2007). Sex, couples and attachment: the role of hedonic intersubjectivity. *Attachment: New Directions in Psychotherapy and Relational Psychoanalysis, 1*(1): 18–29.

Kalman, T. P. (2008). Frontline: clinical encounters with Internet pornography. *Journal of Academy of American Psychoanalysis, 36*: 593–618.

Kirkpatrick, L. (1998). Evolution, pair-bonding, and reproductive strategies: a reconceptualization of adult attachment. In: J. A. Simpson & W. S. Rholes (Eds.), *Attachment Theory and Close Relationships* (pp. 353–393). New York: Guilford Press.

Liebowitz, M. R. (1983). *The Chemistry of Love.* Boston: Little, Brown.

Lyons, A. (1993). Husbands and wives: the mysterious choice. In: S. Ruszczynski (Ed.), *Psychotherapy with Couples: Theory and Practice at the Tavistock Institute of Marital Studies* (pp. 44–54). London: Karnac.

Mahler, M., Pine, F., & Bergman, A. (1975). *The Psychological Birth of the Human Infant: Symbiosis and Individuation.* London: Karnac.

Morin, J. (1995). *The Erotic Mind.* London: Headline.

Paumgarten, N. (2011). Looking for someone: sex, love and loneliness on the Internet. *New Yorker,* 4 July. Available at: www.newyorker.com. Accessed 12 October 2013.

Raphael-Leff, J. (1991). *Psychological Processes of Childbearing.* London: Chapman & Hall [reprinted London: Anna Freud Centre, 2005].

Raphael-Leff, J. (1993). *Pregnancy: The Inside Story.* London: Sheldon Press [reprinted London: Karnac, 2001].

Ratey, J. (2001). *A User's Guide to the Brain.* London: Little, Brown.

Schachner, D. A., Shaver, P. R., & Mikulincer, M. (2003). Adult attachment theory, psychodynamics, and couple relationships: an overview. In: S. M. Johnson & V. E. Whiffen (Eds.), *Attachment Processes in Couple and Family Therapy* (pp. 18–42). New York: Guilford Press.

Stoller, R. (1975). *Perversion: The Erotic Form of Hatred.* New York: Pantheon Books.

Tronick, E., Als, H., Adamson, L., Wise, S., & Brazelton, B. (1978). The infant's response to entrapment between contradictory messages in face-to-face interaction. *Journal of the American Academy of Child Psychiatry, 11*: 1–13.

Usher, A. F. (2008). *What Is This Thing Called Love? A Guide to Psychoanalytic Psychotherapy with Couples.* London: Routledge.

CHAPTER FOUR

# Desire and memory: the impact of Internet pornography on the couple relationship, and processing of early trauma in therapy

*Jenny Riddell*

## Introduction

The use of Internet pornography in an increasingly casual manner is common. This is known about and yet, while access gets easier as smartphones and tablets get smaller and the problem of instant gratification gets bigger, we know too little of the long term effects of this usage. In couple therapy we also know how Internet pornography can sometimes have a deeply disturbing and destructive role in a couple's relationship. The kind of pornography chosen, the meaning ascribed to it by one or other of the couple, the way it is accessed, engaged with, and related to, are all significant and require exploration. The possible function being served by pornographic material for the mind of the participant when the activity becomes habitual, compulsive, and even obsessive also has an impact on those around the consumer. I use the word consumer deliberately, as it reflects the combination of spending, devouring, and cost. The expensive use of time, energy, money, and life are evident. These concerns come into the consulting room as a presenting problem, or can emerge as the therapy progresses. Couples might use pornography together or separately, or one partner accesses it while the other does not. This might not cause any difficulty and could even enhance the relationship: this chapter will not address this scenario, but explores when the use of Internet pornography creates a rupture affecting not only the sexual dimension of a couple relationship, but also the nature of attachment between them.

How couples come together, fit together, grow together, and grow apart is linked to the interweaving of their individual attachment histories. Our attachment patterns clearly have influence on our sexual expression as well as on how we manage intimacy. Sex and attachment are complex bed-mates. The use of Internet pornography by one or both of the couple may add to this complex dynamic. Power and Cundy (this volume, Chapter Three) have addressed the theoretical model of couple fit from an attachment perspective, and I refer the reader to their clear and well-researched work for the theoretical basis to this case study.

However, there is also another side to the use of Internet pornography that is significant; the way it might function for an individual as a form of communication between the unconscious and the conscious mind, rather like a waking dream. This, then, proves rich material for the psychoanalytic therapy. If the couple have presented together in therapy, then the question is how to engage with this material, and how much individual and couple therapy can be achieved alongside one another.

## *Elaine and Graham*

This is the story of a brief therapy, which lasted fifteen months and concluded by mutual agreement between couple and therapist. I have sought and received permission to present this case study; however, I have also disguised the material to protect confidentiality.

For the purpose of this chapter, discussion will be focused predominantly on the impact on the couple of the man's preoccupation with Internet pornography, but in the context of wider family dynamics.

## *Referral*

Elaine and Graham were referred to me by a colleague I had supervised for a number of years, and who was now retired. Elaine rang me initially and was in considerable distress; she said that her partner, Graham, had announced that he "had to end the relationship". She felt bewildered and frightened at this threatened loss. She knew there were considerable difficulties of which both were aware, but this announcement of a firm decision, not an invitation to talk about things, had come "like a bolt from the blue". She was phoning on behalf of them both, as Graham wished to help her with his painful decision and was keen to attend therapy, too. He was fifty-two, Elaine was forty-nine: she worked as an illustrator and he as a sculptor.

How a referral arrives is particularly interesting when working with couples. The approach comes from an individual, even if overtly on behalf of the couple. Although the Internet means email contact is increasingly the mode of contact, usually there is also a telephone conversation prior to meeting. A contact has been made, a voice is heard, and a connection experienced by one partner but not by the other. An attachment, or at least a potential attachment, is beginning, as may be an early transference.

## *Presentation and assessment*

When this couple arrived, they demonstrated a demeanour of wary apprehensiveness, which I was better able to understand later in the session. They had travelled a long distance—attending therapy entailed a two-hour journey each way—and I came to see their willingness to undertake this journey as an indication of their depth of commitment to the process. However, it could also be seen as reflecting ambivalence towards their home, or as a desire to be seen far away from home. These possibilities ran through my mind.

I began by acknowledging that I had spoken to Elaine, but not Graham. Graham chose to begin. His initial comments, though swiftly moved on from, proved to be highly significant. He said that their present crisis was largely due to his unhappiness. He had been in a deep panic about his identity and where his life was going, and this had been growing since his mother's death the previous year. He said, "I had always felt shut out, excluded from her, since my sister was born when I was ten years old." He was eager to tell me that the six-month gap between the diagnosis of his mother's brain tumour and her death had offered the opportunity to resolve deep resentments from the previous years. He had visited his mother often and they had become close, though his sister, who lived close to the mother, had nursed her through her final illness. Elaine countered this with a story of her own; she paired her partner's tale with the story of her own mother's death five years previously, which was also very traumatic but "led to a resolution". The relating of these two specific factual events evolved into a more general narrative history and offered further information. However, I noted the theme of bereavement present at the outset and recognised that loss activates the attachment system. I wondered what form attachment seeking might take between these two, and how they might each respond to the expressions of attachment needs by the other.

They shared the presentation of the relationship problems as they saw them, passing the baton of description and association between them. They were cautious and respectful of each other, prompting each other's hesitation or supporting with facts rather than interrupting or contradicting. Having said they felt there was no specific incident in the relationship that led to the present crisis, they chose to give a history of the relationship as a way of beginning. They saw their lives as complex, and both felt that a series of impinging events had gradually eroded their energy and sense of ability to cope. The smooth quality of this co-presentation contrasted sharply with the discord and oppositional needs they described. They said there had been bitter rows, told of cruel and vicious things being said. However, in the room they were the opposite. Thus, I was presented with a couple who appeared generally securely attached to each other, but with aspects of an anxious attachment, especially when provoked by a perceived threat: a couple who were responding to a bereavement of one of Graham's parents, which had evoked an earlier bereavement of one of Elaine's. This had dysregulated their attachment bond and feelings of security, leaving them both confused and fearful.

Their relationship had begun as a love affair seventeen years previously, shortly after Graham's first marriage, always fragile, had finally broken down. He and his former wife, Sally, had had four children in rapid succession—a daughter, twin sons, and then another daughter. The second and third pregnancies were unplanned, resulting from failed contraception. Both Graham and his wife felt overwhelmed and panicked by the responsibility and demands and, as he described it, it was a case of who left first; both felt the urge to run away. His wife fled, initially making no contact, but then establishing herself nearby and seeing the children regularly but sparsely. She remained an intermittent and unreliable influence on all their lives. Graham was the children's secure base and remained closely attuned with them.

Elaine had moved in shortly after Graham and Sally separated, and took up the role of stepmother. In describing this, she was self-critical, appeared resentful of the burden, and felt she had "failed the children, Graham, and herself". What was to emerge was a co-parenting relationship where she held the discipline, boundary keeping, and control, and he held the freedom, play, and indulgence—a not uncommon "soft cop–hard cop" split in parenting which becomes unhelpful only when the roles become fixed in the parental couple, rather than flexible and interchangeable. However, they did not recognise this system as complementary, only as conflictual. For the past three years, only the youngest daughter, Lucy, was living with them, and the triangular relationship was stressful to all. She was now nineteen and, having started university away from home, was struggling with separating and came back most weekends. Elaine felt guilty about her relief at Lucy going, resentful of her frequent returns, and apprehensive about how they would be as a couple, now alone together for the first time. Graham felt caught between his partner and his daughter, wanting to keep both happy and trying to keep the peace.

As the initial session drew towards a close, I spoke of my experience of them as cautious and apprehensive with each other, while acknowledging this to be understandable in a first session. After all, they did not know me, and were telling me their worries. Privately, I thought this wariness was the anxiety behind their balanced, calm, and cohesive presentation. Both could readily relate to the caution I named, Graham saying he wondered how much he could say and indicating a concern for Elaine's emotional fragility. She appeared willing to go along with this explanation, though I wondered if *he* was feeling more fragile than he realised. After all, he had quite recently lost his mother, his youngest child was on the cusp of leaving home, and rather than turning to Elaine—his attachment figure—for comfort, his response appeared to be a decision to end his relationship with her.

They then linked the caution with a recent experience of couple therapy elsewhere. Both had been involved in alternative self-help groups and healing movements, intensively and exclusively at times in the past. One member of such a group had been therapist to each of them individually, and had continued this role occasionally in spite of also becoming a friend. They had returned to see her individually and together recently, seeking help with the present crisis. It was at this point that Graham's preoccupation with Internet pornography was mentioned for the first time.

Elaine explained that, in individual sessions, the therapist told her that Graham had an incurable "addiction", and it was inevitable that the relationship would fail. It seems that Graham, meanwhile, was told he needed to "follow his path and discover himself without the constraints of a relationship". The couple had been bewildered and distressed by this advice, but also believed it, and discussed it with a friend (my ex-supervisee) who suggested they come to see me.

Hearing this, I felt a range of possible reactions might be expected of me. I thought there was an invitation to criticise and question the therapist's behaviour, that I was also being invited to offer hope in exchange for despair, that I was a second opinion who needed to present a diagnosis, and that I was being tested. As these ideas came to my mind, I recognised my own sense of needing to be cautious about what I would say, and how this might mirror their caution. I also reminded myself to avoid becoming attached to one of these ideas, but to try holding all possibilities in my mind.

### *Early case material*

As the therapy developed, I learnt more about the pornography and its meaning to them as individuals and as a couple, but this was to take some time. Graham's use of Internet pornography was both subtly and substantially different from other erotic material that they were familiar with using, either individually or together for sexual stimulation.

The second session brought a flight into health; they had been away for the weekend, had great sex (which had been infrequent and boring in recent months), and had fallen in love again. They described this experience as "healing". They did not want to discuss the pornography "problem" at this time, but the triangular relationship between the two of them and Lucy, and how to change it. Retrospectively, I believe this area of work was a way into the pornography issue, and the more disturbing triangular relationship they were caught up in between them as individuals and pornography as a "third" in their relationship. This could not be addressed directly early on: I was aware of the need to continue developing a secure base in the therapy, and that trust and safety do not necessarily evolve quickly.

However, the work they did on parenting was creative and reassuring as evidence of their capacity to work effectively together. The secure attachment between them was strengthened as they explored how the "soft cop–hard cop" split in their parental roles had evolved, and how they could shift this through small behavioural changes. The oedipal triangle and oedipal triumph that had led to rigid demarcation of parental roles was also explored. For instance, they negotiated a different approach, so that Elaine invited Lucy back for the weekend, taking her out shopping and for lunch, while Graham tackled his daughter about her mismanagement of money, reversing usual tasks. Lucy's bedroom was moved from next to theirs to another part of the house, coinciding with them allowing her boyfriend to sleep over. My role as therapist in this work appeared to be to stand back and observe. I was a witness and affirming mirror to this creative and thoughtful couple. In both attachment and psychoanalytic terms, I was being experienced as a benign mother, and in return I developed a strong countertransference of affection for, and interest in, them.

As I listened to stories and incidents reported, I became aware of how much mothering Elaine had done over the years (Lucy was only two when she moved in). Paradoxically, the picture of her competent mothering developed through material presented by Elaine to evidence her failure, inadequacy, and resentment in bringing up the children. For instance, she lamented the fact that Lucy had not come to her when she started her periods; she (Elaine) reasoned that she must be unapproachable, cold, and hostile as a stepmother. When I explored how she knew Lucy's periods had started, she said she noticed the sanitary towels she had given her some months earlier had been opened. She had then spoken to Lucy, who openly affirmed that she had had her first period.

Elaine viewed parenting as solely action, doing, and did not appreciate her own value as a container or observer, or recognise her ability to reach out before being summoned. As I offered back evidence of her mothering skills that I gathered in through the stories I heard, she began to claim the status and authority she had so well earned. As she did, so could Lucy and Graham through her example; it was as if her self-doubt had infected them all. Graham was thoughtful about how he had failed to see this earlier, and wondered at how blinkered he had been. He thought it was unlike him not to notice such things; this lack of insight disturbed him, and he returned to this theme often.

Lucy clearly yearned for Elaine's mothering to be named. In the midst of a domestic row about tidiness, Elaine yelled at her, "Because I say so and I'm the one who's been here for you all these years." Lucy responded with a sense of relief, stating, "Now I finally feel I belong here!" Subsequently, she addressed a birthday card to Elaine as "Mum".

It is hard to convey the impact this had on Elaine. We reflected on how her low self-esteem and the negation of her importance as a mother had affected Lucy's sense of belonging and self-worth. This had probably added to Lucy's need for compensatory comfort in the oedipal intimacy with her father. Gaining a mother, as well as a boyfriend, made losing that oedipal triumph so much easier.

### *Internet pornography*

Alongside their effective and creative parenting, I began to hear more about the Internet pornography. Graham would spend long sessions on the computer scrolling through images. He often masturbated, but also continued to look at the images after sexual relief. This indicated to me that the pornography was providing an additional psychological function, as yet unclear. Elaine was torn between a politically correct attitude of his "right" to use pornography if he wished, and an increasing anger at his withdrawal from her, his preoccupation and unavailability. The more he withdrew from her, the more anxious and alone Elaine felt and the more she protested—we can see here how anger is representative of attachment behaviour. Graham played down his preoccupation with pornography, saying it was irrelevant to the relationship, but that he could understand her feeling that it was a waste of time. However, when we explored how much time was involved, it became clear that Graham was losing time, in a fugue state, dissociating. He also struggled to hold on to the content of the pornography. It was hard to engage either of them with this dissociation.

The couple shared a philosophy concerning converting bad to good. As with their parenting and what they had described about resolving their bereavements and "unfinished business" with their dead parents, other examples of reparation and resolution were offered. Financial and work worries (both were struggling in their careers) and managing the extended family all fell into this area. They did not expect life to be easy, but saw difficulties as a challenge that they could learn from, and through learning they would know what to do to resolve the issue. These are hallmarks of secure attachment, and they tried to apply this philosophy to the pornography.

Elaine would trace Graham's activity on the net and also found DVDs and magazines he had stowed. This evidence was not exactly hidden, but neither was it openly available—she looked and found what he left to be found. On one occasion, she watched one of these DVDs and found it arousing, also masturbating to it. When Graham came home, she told him and this led to "great sex" between them. This continued for a while, but what they described as "great" sounded manic and driven to me. I became concerned about behaviour that seemed to be escalating, increasingly detached from truly relating to each other. Frantic action appeared to replace thinking and reflecting and even feeling, beyond sexual stimulation.

They began to tell me in detail about what they did sexually, and in the countertransference I started to feel like an unwilling voyeur. They were incorporating images from the Internet pornography into their sexual practice, several involving specific penetrative sexual acts. They had rejected the previous therapist's implication that Graham was "really homosexual"; what they were doing was represented as exciting, experimental, and life enhancing. Thus, I saw them as gradually slipping into a shared manic defence whereby sexual stimulation replaced thinking or relating. What was happening now was different from any of the various phases of sexual activity over the years of their relationship. Sex was exaggerated, elaborate, and had a dramatic "staged" effect, and this, I felt, led to my sense of voyeurism. My countertransference had become a lot more complicated.

On one occasion, the couple arrived emotionally raw and distressed. Elaine began; she was frightened and revolted. She recognised that she had been fooling herself and Graham by participating as she had in their recent sexual experimentation, and had realised this was "not ok" after all. She had been "going along with something" which was not really acceptable for her. The previous day she had followed Graham's trail on the net and found the images he had most recently been viewing. One in particular horrified her. It was a close-up of a vagina, stretched and distorted by an unlikely household object inserted into it. As she looked at these and other images Elaine felt defiled and disturbed. She struggled to identify specifically how and why these images had disturbed her (as they as a couple would struggle to understand when presented with a difficulty). She believed that if she could understand it, she could sort it.

Graham was enormously upset at her distress, but could not relate to it at any level; they were just images to him. I noticed that whenever he spoke of pornography he became dissociative, in contrast to his usual manner, which was much more relational. He was detached, unemotional, and distant on this subject. All the images he was drawn to were close-ups, and he saw only parts of bodies. However, *she* saw the whole body and person behind the part. She wondered about the circumstances that led a woman to model for such photographs. She felt abused by looking at something that appeared abusive, and was fearful that her partner did not. He saw images of sex, which were like part objects, unconnected with reality. The pornography problem was terrifying because they just could not work out what it meant or what to do about it. Also, neither could understand how the other saw it, they who generally could empathise with each other and see things through each other's eyes so readily.

As we three struggled with this upset, Elaine was able to identify some of her disturbance. "It is as if things which should be on the inside are pulled out and are on the outside," she said, while graphically demonstrating a kind of dissection with her hands. Graham listened to her, but could not engage or respond. This had not happened before and I was concerned at his detachment.

Elaine appeared to be re-establishing a psychic skin boundary around herself; in attempting to fuse with Graham and enter his world, she had lost her sense of self, perhaps to hold on to their relationship, and now she was finding her way back. While this offered a great sense of relief to her, it also left her feeling distant and detached from her partner, which increased other anxieties. Their previous, more familiar and recognisable, way of relating to each other, a rather anxious sensitivity to the other which could look and feel symbiotic, was breaking down. As Graham became episodically dissociative, appearing cut off, unfeeling, and disconnected from his partner, Elaine's anxiety and insecurity increased. She was differentiating herself from him, feeling revolted and confused, and was simply unable to understand the man she had known and loved for so long.

Graham could respond to this, in a way. He was upset by her distress, he loved her and wanted things to be better between them. Intellectually, he could understand her objections, although he could not share them. In the therapy, we worked with his being "caught" by Elaine: was the unconscious motivation an attack on his partner or a desire to be rescued by her?

In response to this session, Graham agreed to restrict his use of the Internet; Elaine received his gesture gratefully as a loving gift. Silently, I was concerned about this, as I thought we had hardly begun to get to grips with the meaning of the pornography and feared where the need for the stimulation and excitation would be displaced. Could he begin to act out his urges more directly, with Elaine or with others?

Elaine, meanwhile, explored her tendency to "go along with" the other, and related it to some therapeutic work she had done in the past on being a "replacement child". During her birth, her thirteen-month-old sister had died of a cot death. This had left her with a terrible sense of responsibility and she had felt the onerous task of trying to live two lives. She had often felt not good enough as a child, and imagined her mother's silent comparison of her with a perfect lost daughter. Much of the work in this area originated from a self-help group Elaine and Graham had belonged to in the past. Visualisation, re-birthing, and meditation were part of this process, and I thought about how important the visual aspect was to them as artists. Unusually, in my experience, this couple brought no dreams to therapy and I wondered about the link with the more concrete images of pornography and absence of dreams. Was symbolisation difficult?

## *The next phase*

As Graham attempted to give up the Internet pornography, he continued trying to think about what it all meant. Part of his defence was to claim it was "a gender thing", that "lots of blokes liked pornography". I wondered whether he was seeking to reassure himself, Elaine, or me about his masculinity. On the other hand, his concern for Elaine created a quality of shame and embarrassment in him out of being the cause of her distress. I was worried that this seemingly shameful concern may lead to a kind of pseudo moral stance that would mask the fact, to himself as well as to her, that he was still dissociating from his own experience of the pornography. He had no real link between thinking and feeling about what he was doing. The shame he felt was about distressing Elaine's sensibilities, not for his sense of what he was doing.

Alongside this material, there had been discussion and thoughtful work concerning their careers and the identity crisis Graham had initially spoken of. They were able to describe the frustration and disappointment of not being as busy or successful as they had hoped to be, and to mourn the loss of this. The desire to separate had, in part, been an attempt to deny seeing the other as a failure and to avoid being perceived as a failure by the other. This anxiety about seeing and being seen once more brought the visual to my mind, the dynamic between voyeurism and exhibitionism.

Much of this couple's philosophy had included magical thinking and omnipotent ideas, that the right attitude and approach can make anything possible. This left them with an onerous sense that they had only themselves to blame for things not being better. I think this fed into a shared unconscious phantasy that they could not be a creative couple, that theirs was a barren union. As is so often the case, the unconscious phantasy was a striking contrast with the conscious fantasy of creativity expressed in their work. This shared unconscious phantasy had obvious meaning for the childless Elaine, who cast herself in the role of "wicked stepmother", and Graham's gender role-swap of being left with the children. I mention this briefly for two reasons, to identify areas of other work going on in the therapy and also to emphasise the difference in their functioning in the area of pornography. In this material, like that of parenting, they were reflective and needed little help with the process.

My concerns as to the cost of Graham's avoiding the Internet proved irrelevant, as he was caught again in his continued use of online pornography. I saw this as the healthier part of him asking for help from both Elaine and myself. This time he was more thoughtful and curious about the sense of compulsion he was aware of feeling; also of the detachment he felt and the time that went missing. It was as if he had begun to observe himself at the activity, which was a little closer to being inside his own skin. Elaine's reaction was concerned, not judgemental, once again focusing on her feeling excluded. However, with each of what emerged as a pattern of lapses, her anxiety grew. Graham was ceasing to use Elaine's concern as a prompt to help him control his compulsion. Gradually, she was able to voice her concern as to what else he might be hiding, but was unable to give words to her conscious and pressing fantasies. I found I was holding these fantasies and speculations; was he viewing child pornography, violence? What could not be voiced between the couple was now located in me.

As we continued with this work, their sexual relationship developed problems. He found it difficult to orgasm and certain ways Elaine touched him caused him aversion. She was fearful of upsetting him, wanting to comfort him. She tried to avoid what upset him but did not understand why it caused revulsion. However, this interaction between them felt more real and preferable to the manic sexual energy of earlier in the therapy. It was as if Graham's body was finally connecting up some of his experiences and trying to communicate something to him.

Gradually, Graham began to explore whether his identification in the pornography was with the "being done to" and "up for anything" aspect, the recipient, not the perpetrator of the acts. This was a focus of exploration for several sessions, and on one occasion of thinking about whom he identified with in a particular image, he rather abruptly associated to a memory. He described how he had broken his leg and been confined to a wheelchair shortly after his sister's birth. He remembered his mother and father taking them out for a walk, his sister in her pram and he in the wheelchair, both being pushed while in a totally dependent state. He smiled as he recognised how like the baby he had become. He could remember hating and resenting his sister, wishing her dead, but he also remembered loving and playing with her and not being able to make any sense of this. I thought of the split between his loving, compliant, conscious wish to reassure Elaine and the unconscious continued attack on her through the pornographic images he searched for online.

Graham then returned to the previous thought, of being identified with the person who was "up for anything" and "being done to". His identification with the one being penetrated was linked with how this had been incorporated into their sexual relationship, and this led him back to think of, and question, his sexual orientation. Elaine found this as difficult as he did, wondering what meaning it might have for her sexuality. However, his curiosity also offered her the thinking and talking space to admit to some of her own discomfort and confusion around colluding in these specific sexual activities.

### *Trauma*

As Graham questioned his sexual orientation, he began to talk about his first sexual experience. Elaine was aware of this, but he explained it in detail to me. He described how he had entered into a sexual relationship with a fourteen-year-old boy when he was just eleven. I noticed that this would have been shortly after his sister's birth and the accident that had broken his leg, with its association to regression and infantile dependency. He described the relationship as if he were the one to take advantage, as he took money from the other boy. I was struck at how responsible and in control of all this he presented himself as, and I asked Elaine how she viewed the story. Like me, she queried the power differential between a boy of eleven and a fourteen-year-old. Because he had experienced physical pleasure, it had never occurred to Graham that there might be anything seductive or even abusive about the experience. Indeed, he felt *he* was the abuser for taking money. This material, and beginning to think about the theme of abuse, led to an opening up of a wealth of confusion and distress for both of them.

Graham became initially depressed, an uncomfortable and scary experience for a man more familiar with an energised, if on occasion rather manic, mood. This offered Elaine a far more creative role in their mutual struggle, as she could readily empathise with his sense of deprivation and sadness. Through depression, Graham became angry, an expected phase of mourning loss and trauma. He continued to use Internet pornography, but felt increasingly uncomfortable with it. He was angry with Elaine for constraining him, and angry with me for exposing him. I think for the first time, being in the room with two women discussing this material was intensely painful and shaming. He felt judged and belittled. I felt sad and awkward that I could not help more with such difficult feelings being aroused as his dissociation crumbled. Elaine felt powerless to help and felt Graham was pushing her away. Their separate transferences to me, and my countertransference to each of them and to them as a couple, an intimate unit, were complex to handle. Interpretations were difficult: just surviving the conflicting emotions was challenge enough. Their attendance became more erratic; however, they continued to come and seemed to recognise that their anger could be contained in these sessions, even if they struggled to empathise with each other. Slowly, anger became easier to manage and this helped to process the underlying shame. For some time we stuck with this uncomfortable material, and their relationship's history provided them with a belief that this storm could be weathered.

And it was. The depression moved from anger into sadness and mourning. As Graham recognised how angry he still was with his mother, he became more aware of the abusive nature of the images of parts of women he looked at. This was difficult for both of them. Elaine had to review the part of her that could relate to her own denigration and allow this activity, her need to try to be everything, to be the child her mother had lost as well as herself. My countertransference moved from voyeurism to impotence, then to pity for their plight, and on to respect for their courage in exploring these darker aspects of their fantasy worlds.

## *Conclusion*

The therapy drew to a close. The couple initiated ending with a sense that there was still much to work on, but they had the capacity to do this together. Their shared ethos and history of self-help was central to this, and commanded my respect. The relationship was no longer under threat and was functioning again as a secure attachment for both. We agreed a follow-up appointment a few months later as a "safety valve", as they put it. They returned for this session and we said a final farewell. Prior to this meeting, I had expressed my wish to discuss using their case material if anonymously disguised. The session covered this and what had been happening since we last met. They told me that Graham's use of the Internet had gradually reduced and the nature of the pornography softened, though he still very occasionally revisited it—more, they thought, as a kind of bearing in mind the dangers that had passed than the desire to re-engage with it.

Elaine felt happier with this, though she still harboured some concerns. Generally, this seemed manageable between them; they had no expectation of a perfect resolution.

To think of their dilemma more generally, secure attachment between adults is characterised by realism, valuing relationship and cooperation, clear expression of needs, responding sensitively to the needs of a partner, and willingness to work at difficulties rather than walking away. Given their personal relational histories, it is probable that both partners had insecure individual attachment styles. However, they were able to forge a relationship, faced with adversity from the start, which is marked by "earned security". No doubt their spiritual practices and commitment to self-help and other therapies enabled this to happen, but earned security can be undermined by too many stressful and traumatic events. *In extremis*, people tend to revert to old defences and ways of coping. However, secure attachment can also be re-established with time and commitment, and couples therapy can play an important role.

Reflecting on this material, I believe the Internet pornography activity was a communication from Graham's unconscious to his conscious mind in an attempt to process early childhood trauma. This was a large part of the therapy we three engaged in. Without the pornography, what might or might not have happened? The fact that the pornography was online could also have significance. Graham's computer was central to his creativity, was where his unconscious roamed. It was private and secret, factors that also applied to his trauma. While the anonymity of cyberspace facilitated dissociation, being noticed, caught, and fought for (as had not happened in childhood) helped him to confront and process all of this.

I present this case as an example of Internet pornography use being a conduit for an old, repressed trauma—the sexual abuse—to find a way out of the hidden area of a person's mind and into the fresh air. As such, it functioned like a dream where real dreams were absent, sending images, metaphors, and symbols to be decoded. Like a dream, the clues were in the specific content of the pornographic material of choice, but were hard to understand as they meant shame and pain would also have to be faced. At core, this was a healthy and securely attached couple with the courage to face their more fearful and hidden experiences and accept them as part of their narratives as to who they really are.

A final word on the process of writing this paper: as with the therapy itself, many conflicting emotions, feelings, and thoughts have arisen in my mind during the writing. I believe I have revisited my experience of voyeurism that occurred during the therapy. I, too, feel shame and anxiety at turning a real experience into a narrative at best, a fantasy at worst. I, too, feel exploitative and fearful of judgement and doing harm. However, I also feel a tremendous respect for the courage and resilience this couple had, for their tenacity in sticking with painful work. I believe their love and mutual care is worthy of their pride, and I hope I have given it justice.

*CHAPTER FIVE*

# Surviving as a psychotherapist in the twenty-first century

*Linda Cundy*

## *Introduction*

Digital technologies have crept incrementally into our personal and professional lives, creating new pressures and offering new possibilities for counsellors and psychotherapists, and for our clients. These technologies have an impact on the therapeutic process long before it even starts; their presence is felt in the consulting room in both concrete and symbolic ways, and the very nature of the therapeutic relationship is influenced by recent developments in communication media. Psychotherapies have always been embedded in, and responded to, the prevailing social, historical, and cultural context. We cannot ignore the changes and try to live in the past, yet neither should we adopt and adapt unthinkingly to this new technological environment.

In this chapter, I reflect on changes I have noticed in our profession since I trained as a counsellor in the 1980s and as a psychotherapist in the 1990s, highlighting some of the challenges we face in the technological landscape of the early twenty-first century. While some trainings are beginning to address the impact of digital media on the practice of our craft, most of us will have had to think on our feet at times, often under pressure to react; should we include a photograph on a professional website, respond to an enquiry from a potential patient that arrives in the inbox or messaging service late in the evening, agree to conducting sessions via Skype when a client needs to travel for work, challenge a patient who answers a mobile phone call during a session? It might all feel innocuous enough, but with each decision we communicate something of who we are, our capabilities, needs, and anxieties, our ability to contain the client's anxieties, and the nature of the relationship we can offer—whether we can provide a secure or insecure attachment.

My focus in this chapter is on the private practitioner working with adults. Although it is a personal perspective, I imagine many of you will recognise the issues I discuss. The title of the chapter is a reference to *How to Survive as a Psychotherapist*, a delightful book by Nina Coltart, published in 1993, the year before I began my psychotherapy training, and before the world was changed so radically by personal computers, mobile phones, and widespread access to the Internet. I wonder what she would make of life as a psychotherapist in the digital age.

## *Public profile*

The Internet has contributed to changing public attitudes to mental illness and distress. In the National Health Service (NHS), a system of "stepped care" is in operation for people in need of psychological therapies. Patients who are assessed as having mild symptoms of depression or anxiety are offered low-intensity interventions that may include guided self-help, with materials available online, and computerised cognitive–behavioural therapy. For a proportion of the population, this will be the introduction to "therapy". Meanwhile, the Internet gives access to information and support from the NHS and mental health charities for a wide range of psychological problems, available at the click of a mouse, day or night. "Stars" of the stage, screen, and sports arenas blog and tweet about their battles with addiction and obsessive–compulsive or bipolar disorders. All strata of society are better informed as a result, and perhaps this has helped to reduce stigma about these manifestations of suffering, and normalise seeking counselling and psychotherapy.

The drive to help more people, including those who live in remote locations or are otherwise difficult to reach, has led to a plethora of online mental health resources. Organisations that traditionally offered telephone support and information now provide "listening" and counselling via the Internet. There are dedicated chat rooms moderated by trained practitioners to facilitate the sharing of distress within a virtual community, where mutual support reduces isolation and stigma. One particularly creative project is the Big White Wall, partnered by the Tavistock and Portman NHS Trust, which recruits, trains, and supervises the "wall guides" staffing the service. Aimed at helping people with mild to moderate mental health difficulties, it offers individual, group, and art therapies, and an online community as well as information on wellbeing. It is available around the clock, and because of the twenty-four hour nature of the service, the BWW has been commissioned to provide psychological care to armed services personnel and their families, either at home in the UK or posted overseas in different time zones.

"eTherapy" is now a profession in itself: it is possible to train via the Internet, work online, and follow a framework of ethics and practice developed to reflect this new therapeutic environment. Online counsellor Lindsay Dobson writes,

> We now use technology to mimic face-to-face work - for example . . . the use of chat rooms or email messaging. . . Practitioners may introduce the idea of a whiteboard to draw on, sound to work with, webcams so that client and counsellor can see each other, the use of Skype or in the case of virtual worlds such as Second Life, the use of avatars to represent the practitioner and client and to re-create the counselling room. (Dobson, 2010, p. 29)

As well as being a valuable addition to available psychological therapies, this way of working also opens up new possibilities for the practitioner, who is freed from the traditional consulting room to travel the world, take up residence in the Outer Hebrides, or practise from anywhere that boasts a reliable broadband connection.

I applaud the aim of reaching more people in need of help, and I believe that supporting others through dedicated chat rooms—in effect becoming a kind of attachment figure to one's peers—is a valuable and potentially healing experience. Lindsay Hamilton (Chapter

Nine, this volume) writes persuasively about the importance of community; belonging to a community, being "known" and being useful to others confers dignity and builds self-respect. Of course, not everybody who makes use of these online groups has the capacity to give to others, and some might have a more destructive agenda. It is the role of the moderator to contain these aggressive elements.

On the one hand, having tools that help us take responsibility for our own wellbeing is empowering, and people can now access many different online resources to help them connect in a meaningful way with others when support is needed, perhaps—perhaps—reducing the need for traditional psychotherapy. On the other, these relationships are disembodied, virtual, *almost* real. Many will argue that these relationships *are* real, and that *they* are being "real" when they communicate via the Internet. However, no matter how authentic and unambiguous we try to be in our online relating, the scope for projections and transference is inevitably greater than when we occupy the same physical space and breathe the same air. Without the full range of feedback and cues, we tend to fantasise more, fill in the gaps with our imaginings, benign or otherwise, and there is less opportunity for working through transferences and taking back projections. The "other" continues to be more of a construct, a fantasy, than a living, breathing, whole person.

Of course, I also recognise the economic constraints of providing psychotherapy to all in need. We must live in the real world and cut our cloth accordingly. However, we do not have to accept that the minimum input to help us manage our symptoms and ameliorate isolation—valuable though these are—is enough to bring about *change*, a reconfiguration of our relational models and defences. The aim of attachment-informed psychotherapy is "earned security", to become more secure, autonomous, and resilient (Holmes, 1996). Emotional and psychological distress, low self-esteem, and rigid defences originate in the early interactions of an infant or child with his or her attachment figures, and it is only through a transformational relationship that these old ways of being can change. In particular, I suggest, the philosophy of self-reliance and managing one's own symptoms (and even *perceiving* oneself in terms of symptoms) tends to stoke the more avoidant belief systems: the expectation of holding oneself together, not troubling others, not making a fuss or being a burden.

People with a predominantly dismissing attachment style (Main & Goldwyn, 1984; Main, Hesse & Goldwyn, 2008) tend to downplay their distress. Gerhardt refers to them as "low reactors", and suggests that years of disguising their anxiety may have led to the shutting down of some cortisol receptors in the brain (Gerhardt, 2004). They continue to hide their stress from others and take pride in "managing" problems alone. Any symptoms that leak out are rarely florid, other than, perhaps, occasional angry outbursts. I suggest that these individuals are likely to make use of the less "relational" forms of therapy that technology has now made available, such as computerised cognitive–behavioural approaches, mindfulness techniques (perhaps downloadable from the Internet), various forms of "distance therapy". and online forums where they can maintain anonymity or reserve. Conversely, those whose attachment styles are preoccupied or unresolved (disorganised) are "high reactors" and "will produce a lot of cortisol at the least provocation. [They] may be easily depressed, easily panicked and prone to overeating" (Gerhardt, 2004, p. 66). In other words, these kinds of insecure individuals have learnt to make their distress highly visible, to alert attachment figures and demand help in regulating their emotional states. Their distress is often apparent on their bodies—obesity or dramatic fluctuations in weight, extreme agitation, even scars from attacks on their own bodies.

Self-harm is a desperate attempt at managing an over-aroused state of mind, but is also a desperate plea for help to down-regulate stress. Various addictions are also possible as they attempt to self-medicate, and these coping strategies themselves become presenting problems. In times of particular difficulty, there can be a dramatic quality to suffering, and I propose that preoccupied and unresolved (or "borderline") patients are more likely to be offered the high-intensity options within the mental health and stepped care systems, including longer-term individual psychotherapy conducted face to face and, in crisis, even inpatient care. Unlike the dismissing patients, their symptoms demand a relational response. Whatever may be offered by way of online help is rarely adequate, a mere tantalising taste of what is needed.

### *Private practice*

There are simply not the economic resources to provide open-ended psychotherapy to everyone free at the point of delivery through statutory services, or low-fee through charitable organisations. There is still very much a role for the private practitioner, although, inevitably, many people who would benefit remain excluded because of financial constraints. But for those who can choose to embark on private counselling or psychotherapy, it has never been easier to find a practitioner. As with other services—plumbers, solicitors, acupuncturists, and personal trainers—the public searches online for psychotherapists. However, we face an unusual difficulty in our "impossible profession"; if I need a carpenter or a child-minder, I log on to my local community website, where I find details of tradespeople and other services along with recommendations from satisfied customers to help me make an informed choice. But it is not usual practice for satisfied therapy "customers" to post endorsements of their shrinks online! So, how can the resourceful potential client research the best person for the job? Having found a name on a professional register, or a website providing more detail, the next step may well be to "Google" the practitioner.

When did you last "Google" yourself? Do you know what might be in the public domain about you, captured by the Internet? There may be information about your professional credentials and activities, a book you have written, an organisation you are involved with. But it is also possible that there are personal details that you would not choose to publicise to patients: an unintended photograph, reference to your previous career, involvement in a court case, your home address, and who you live with. There may be confusing information, such as details of another person with the same name. There is another Linda Cundy in Edmonton, Canada, who is well known for her work with deaf people. I do not mind sharing a name with her, and most people can fathom that I am a different Linda Cundy, living not too far from Edmonton in North London. However, some namesakes are less desirable, as one supervisee discovered to his dismay when "Googling" himself: all entries on the first page of the search engine concerned someone by the same, rather unusual, name involved in a case of fraud and financial misconduct. Another person I supervise, a woman with impeccable professional boundaries, was careful with the privacy settings on her Facebook account, but forgot that her profile picture was a family holiday snapshot taken with husband and children; she had been puzzled by material emerging in several patients' sessions until the penny dropped that they had looked for her on the social network site.

Information is power, and the Internet is designed to disseminate information. Not all of it is approved, not all is accurate, but it is out there. Individuals arriving at the door of your consulting room for the first time could know quite a bit more about you than you yet know about them. The therapist's anonymity was never really a possibility, and certainly not for Freud, though, in many theoretical paradigms, it is understood that personal information about the practitioner is an intrusion into the treatment. The less that is known about the person of the psychotherapist, the greater the space for fantasy, transference, and the necessary "as if" quality of the relationship. Of course, not all potential clients feel the need to dig so deep, but I believe that having the capability to access personal details about one's therapist, without recourse to actual stalking, has a subtle impact. The therapeutic relationship is one of asymmetry, but the odds have levelled just a little. That is not necessarily a bad thing. Certainly, being able to search for a potential therapist online has also contributed to the demystification of talking therapies.

## *Building a practice*

How does a newly qualified counsellor or psychotherapist get established in private practice? During my training in the 1990s, I remember a psychoanalytic teacher known for his rigour and propriety addressing this question. He recommended the tradition of networking with professionals who may be in a position to refer patients in the time-honoured way. Any attempt to promote oneself directly to the public was, he intimated, if not unethical, then at least distasteful. It would be an expression of the therapist's desperation, unhelpful to the therapeutic process. I hold this person in high esteem, and he had (and has) such a sterling reputation among colleagues that I imagined the couch in his consulting room was always occupied with patients they referred to him. But I rather despaired of filling my own books the same way. Coltart endorsed his view, recommending that trainees should catch the eye of their seminar leaders in the hope of receiving referrals.

> Although there is something unseemly about touting for custom, one cannot just sit back in one's chair and wait for a suffering world to beat

> a path to one's door. One has made a colossal outlay of time and money and emotional effort for many years in order to reach this point . . . (Coltart, 1993, p. 27)

Having paid for a further four years of training (after my counselling course), a further four plus years of personal therapy twice or thrice weekly, supervision, and so on, I needed to make a living. Letters to health centre managers, personnel departments, and the like having failed to produce a crop of referrals, I eventually succumbed to the temptation of having business cards printed to pin on notice boards in various shops, libraries, and other venues. I felt fraudulent, shamed by my analytic superego (Colman, 2006). It took many years for my practice to fill and I do not think the business cards helped at all. Eventually, referrals started to arrive through my teaching and training work (which, thankfully, had helped me to pay the bills in the meantime). Those first years were a struggle, though.

Fifteen years on, recently qualified counsellors and psychotherapists have other options. They can be listed in numerous online directories, and many promote themselves directly through their own websites. It has become acceptable, and many highly reputable practitioners can be located in this way. Although my esteemed psychoanalytic teacher does not appear to have his own website (I have just "Googled" him to check), his name and contact details are listed on several professional registers available on the Internet. Some practitioners have gone one step further, developing their websites into online resources giving information about mental health, suggesting reading material, reviewing books, and providing links to other websites. Some even include a blog, a dedicated Facebook page, or a "notice board" for people to comment and make recommendations—in other words, their websites have become an interactive project.

I observe an increasingly competitive attitude creeping in amongst certain colleagues seeking to develop a client base. It is no longer sufficient to launch a website and wait for it to register on search engines. One can buy a higher position in the listings through linking with Google Maps (I do not—I work mostly from my practice at home and choose not to disclose my address to all and sundry—although I am aware that that information can be easily accessed by anybody with a mind to find it). Paying extra for a premium listing ensures that one's professional profile grabs attention ahead of one's colleagues. With a well designed, informative website and a little financial investment, relative beginners can attract as many or more referrals as seasoned practitioners, even their teachers and supervisors, who might be more resistant to self-promotion. These advertising practices are legitimate; however, I gather that there are shadier techniques for stepping over the competition, for those in the know.

Perhaps I am a little envious that today's trainees will have it easier than my generation; in a paper of 1996, Otto Kernberg suggested, tongue-in-cheek, that psychoanalytic candidates should receive a stultifying training to inhibit their free-thinking and creativity. Implied in his paper is the idea that trainees must suffer the tedium of the same initiative sapping education as their teachers *because the teachers had to put up with it so trainees should, too.* Maybe I feel a little of this "hardship is character-building" attitude myself!

* * *

I recently discussed writing this chapter with my supervisor and saw an expression of confusion pass over her face. In her corner of the psychotherapy world, referrals still arrive the traditional way via colleagues: the daughter or husband of a colleague's patient is thinking about starting in therapy, a friend of a supervisee needs help, the aunt of a neighbour is having difficulties. So, perhaps my experience is not yet ubiquitous, though I believe it is increasingly the norm. However, my supervisor reminded me that websites have multiple functions other than selling one's professional wares. Once she has been recommended to a potential client, she anticipates that he or she will do some preliminary research to find out more about her before making contact or arriving for an assessment. Her website, therefore, is intended to convey a sense of who she is, her approach to understanding people, the kind of language she uses, and something of her values. This can help reduce the anxiety and natural mixed feelings felt by people embarking on psychotherapy. It will also influence the pre-transference (Thomas, 1992).

In attachment language, we all have our own internalised relational models that develop out of interactions with attachment figures and significant others in the formative early months and years of life. We project these relational, or internal, working models (Bowlby, 1969, 1979, 1988) on to later relationships, anticipating that others will conform to our expectations—perhaps by ridiculing us, using us, suffocating, tantalising, shaming, or abandoning us. So, beginning therapy, a patient will unconsciously anticipate that the therapist will be "just like everyone else" and evoke the old familiar feelings. This represents his or her resistance. Alongside this expectation, however, is another feeling, a hope that this time will be different, this relationship will be transformative and healing. Freud understood it in the language of libido and transference: "If someone's need for love is not entirely satisfied by reality, he is bound to approach every new person whom he meets with libidinal anticipatory ideas" (Freud, 1912b, p. 100). Thus, an internal conflict is always present at the start of a therapy, and one function of a website is to fuel the hope of people considering making an appointment, stoking the positive transference and reducing resistance. An online professional presence enables us to do this before first contact has even been made.

Regarding my own website, I have found its greatest value is in providing information about the ways I think and work, the boundaries and expectations, in order to *deter* those who are seeking something else. In the early years, quite a few people enquired about therapy and came for assessment with no familiarity of the process and what is required, resulting in a mismatch between what was asked for and what I could offer. This was painful and frustrating for both parties; I prefer to receive fewer enquiries, and only those from individuals who feel a resonance with my philosophy and approach, and who want what I can provide.

## *Apparent trivia*

Another consideration when promoting one's practice on the Internet is whether or not to include a photograph. A chapter in Coltart's book is entitled "Apparent Trivia", and the question of the photograph is a twenty-first century example of this. I have always resisted using a photo on my website, hoping that my choice of words would be the decisive factor. I understand that some practitioners feel differently. A black colleague spoke of the discomfort of meeting new patients and seeing the expression of surprise on their faces at the door; for her, the online portrait eased that moment. I have heard of others with unusual names preferring to make their gender known this way. Photographs also reveal age, and hint at class and wealth. They invite people to identify, to match themselves with the person in the picture: "She seems a bit unconventional, perhaps a bit feminist—we'd get along well", or "She looks rather scruffy and not very professional; I don't think she would understand the world I live in." "He looks old and wise; I imagine he's heard everything in his life and I could trust him to listen to my painful stories", or "He looks very elderly. The things I need to talk about might be too much for him, could make him ill. Anyway, at his age I imagine he'll retire soon." In selecting a photo for my website, I can imagine worrying about whether I look approachable but not too casual, warm but also contained, youthful enough but not too young (or too desperate to look young). It all begins to feel uncomfortably like a profile picture for an Internet dating site.

Recently, browsing an online register of counsellors and psychotherapists, I realised that, since I had last looked, most of the practitioners listed are now identifiable through photos. My own profile stood out by its anonymity, a dark hole in the photograph album. I found myself imagining the thought process of a potential client, perhaps not even registering my credentials—we are so preprogrammed to respond to a pair of eyes and a mouth. Or perhaps people wondered why I was so elusive; perhaps I am hideously ugly or have something to hide? It then occurred to me that I have not received any enquiries from this site for several years, while colleagues and supervisees seem to fill their practices that way. Feeling competitive, I wondered whether to succumb to peer pressure and, ignoring my troublesome analytic superego, submit a "selfie", too. I have not yet decided; it will take more time and reflection to feel comfortable with whatever choice I make.

## *We have contact*

Another change I have noticed in my own practice over recent years is that most initial contacts and enquiries about psychotherapy now arrive via email more frequently than by telephone. Although some emails include a phone number and a request to speak before arranging an assessment, it is not unusual for new patients to arrive for a first session without us ever hearing each other's voice. As I have already suggested, at the beginning of a therapy it is possible for the client to have more information about the therapist than vice versa, and now we might not even have aural clues to orientate ourselves. Written communication can be very different from the spontaneous interactive language of spoken dialogue.

Should a potential client make first contact by telephone, either in the hope of speaking to the psychotherapist straight away or to leave a message, he or she is likely to observe certain niceties; it is generally understood to be unsociable to call late at night or in the small hours, although weekends seem acceptable. The same is not true for emails or, I gather, text messages. I am amazed at how many people search for a psychotherapist after midnight. This little piece of information about a potential patient can stimulate all kinds of questions and fantasies for the practitioner, the germ of a pre-countertransference.

Online directories make the search for a counsellor or psychotherapist simple, and they offer some protection to the public; practitioners must provide evidence of training, qualifications, and insurance before being listed. Many people who access these resources will note down contact details of a few therapists who seem suitable, and either telephone or email each of them. This is one method of checking out practitioners before committing to a meeting, either choosing one or arranging to meet several before deciding. But sometimes it is more a matter of who replies first, and this can put pressure on the therapist to respond to enquiries quickly, regardless of the time of day or day of the week. For those of us in private practice, the concept of being "off duty" is easily eroded in order to catch hold of a new client, especially if we are starting out or otherwise trying to increase our caseload.

What subliminal message do we give if we respond to enquiries in this way? What might a patient understand about our availability, our boundaries, or the urgency of our need for work? Might we be evoking a fantasy of an idealised attachment figure available on demand? Or perhaps of a "care-giver" whose own life is barren and who might need the patient? It will probably depend on the patient's relational history. Of course, whatever fantasies, hopes, fears, memories, and longings are evoked can be worked with, but only if the therapy "takes", if it becomes viable. These kinds of transferences are difficult to verbalise and explore in the early stages, but if we are able to access the patient's imaginings about, and expectations of, the therapist, they reveal a great deal of useful material.

The patient will also note other information about the practitioner that could provide the seed of a fantasy; significance can be attached to the practice telephone number and whether this is a mobile phone or landline, and to the practitioner's email details. I have occasionally come across email addresses chosen by colleagues that seem frivolous, unprofessional, and, to my mind, improper. I imagine these deter quite a few potential clients who might feel uneasy with the informality and the "alternative" message being conveyed. But perhaps that is the point: just as my website aims to deter enquiries where there would be a mismatch between what I offer and what is sought, maybe these email addresses aim to attract only a certain sector of the population and deter others who have different value systems.

## *Availability, boundaries, and the therapeutic frame*

The greater connectivity of life in the twenty-first century, with its myriad means of communication, can challenge orthodox therapeutic boundaries. I have already touched on the psychotherapist's availability outside of sessions and regular working hours. The general view is that such "extra-therapeutic contact" should be kept to an absolute minimum and, in general, I follow this convention. However, there are exceptions.

Michael Balint, an independent-thinking psychoanalyst and contemporary of John Bowlby, described two sources of anxiety and systems of defence against these anxieties that correspond quite closely with adult attachment categories (Balint, 1959, 1968).

Ocnophils, according to Balint, fear the spaces between "objects"—being alone in a world that feels fraught with dangers without relationship or connection. (I have argued in another chapter in this volume that ocnophils—preoccupied individuals—are likely to use communication technology to deny separation and to feel in constant contact with the people in their lives.) They have difficulty containing themselves or feeling whole and complete, so they need to cling to other people in order to feel "held".

In the therapeutic setting, preoccupied patients can "spill out" and, fearing separation or abandonment, cling on to the therapist; for instance, they might have difficulty ending sessions on time. Ocnophils might ask for contact between sessions, such as responses to email or phone messages and texts. They might send journal extracts, copy the therapist into communications with other people, request extra appointments, including by telephone or Skype, and put the practitioner under pressure to concede. Establishing clear, firm, and predictable boundaries about session length, and not acceding to requests for contact on demand, can ultimately enable preoccupied patients to introject the therapist's containing function. Discovering that they can be separated from an attachment figure (the therapist), but that he or she will be available as promised, reliable, attuned, attentive, and responsive, but boundaried, helps these clients to eventually develop the capacity to contain themselves, soothe themselves when they begin to panic, become more resilient and able to manage in the "spaces between their objects" and the spaces between their sessions; in other words, to be more secure and autonomous.

There are, of course, occasions when exceptions must be made to this stance. One example of this is described in "The ethereal m/other" (Chapter Eight, this volume).

Balint also described people who are made anxious by the intrusive *presence* of objects—others—and whose defence is to seek out a degree of solitude, or at least self-sufficiency and emotional reserve. These he called philobats, and his description rings true of dismissing attachment style. Because philobats are extremely self-contained and private, it is unusual for them to ask for support, and accepting help can feel shameful.

Dismissing patients do not resist ending their sessions on time or complain about breaks. For this reason, I view it as a therapeutic breakthrough if such a person reaches out and risks needing the therapist, and I am more flexible with boundaries where they are concerned. They do not need to learn to be more contained, but to relax the restrictive hold they have on themselves and make a meaningful connection with another human being. The offer of contact in certain situations between sessions—via telephone, email, text, or Skype—is unlikely to be taken up, but it is significant when and if it is.

I do wonder whether philobats might be more likely to request therapy via telephone, Skype, or even online rather than face to face, as a way of managing interpersonal anxiety. They might even choose a practitioner who lives some distance away rather than a local, easily accessible psychotherapist, to ensure that sessions are "remote". If this is the case, I suspect that dismissing patients can gain something useful from distance therapy, perhaps addressing a specific problem, but will not have the opportunity for deep change.

Moving from traditional, face-to-face psychotherapy to sessions on the telephone or Skype is another boundary consideration. This has been explored by Niki Reeves in Chapter Six, so I will address it only briefly here.

Regarding psychotherapy via video-link, I reckon that Freud would have given it a go, but Winnicott would not (although—given Winnicott's use of radio broadcasts to speak to mothers and his many public lectures—he might have blogged or appeared in online seminars). In classical psychoanalysis, the word is king; language is privileged above all else. There is no reason to discount "tele-analysis" or "Skypotherapy" if the focus is on verbal components of communication—listening for resistance, interpreting defences, transference manifestations, or Freudian slips as clues to unconscious processes. The aim of this approach is insight. Winnicott worked at a different level, tapping into barely formed thoughts, elusive feelings, prelinguistic relational ways of being. A major tool, it seems, was countertransference experiencing that informed his transference interpretations. These different styles are eloquently described by Guntrip, recalling his first analysis with Fairbairn (practising "Oedipal analysis"), and his second with Winnicott (practising Winnicott) (Guntrip, 1975). Regardless of how sophisticated and reliable technology becomes, it is difficult to imagine the level of intimacy and attunement required for Winnicott's approach being "remotely" possible.

Some patients, like Guntrip, can make use of interpretative analysis, but find a different benefit from the therapist's sensitive attunement and attention to pre-verbal communication. Other patients are not (yet) able make use of a therapy aimed at insight and meaning-making. Perhaps this indicates something about who can benefit from technology-mediated therapy and who cannot. Killingmo (1989) distinguishes between those whose inner worlds are defined by "conflict" (who can use interpretative analysis), and those whose internal realities are sculpted out of "deficit": that is, a severe dearth of what an infant or child needs to flourish and develop, a deficit of secure attachment. This latter group of patients might not feel contained enough through therapy in cyberspace.

I have used Skype with several individuals after a period of traditional therapy. In one case, I worked with a patient with whom I felt well attuned as a result of a long, face-to-face therapy prior to the shift to Skype requested by her when she needed to travel abroad for several months. It was a frustrating experience. I felt that I was still picking up subtle communications about her internal state but *she was no longer attuned to me*; she was not reading the cues that I had something to say. Attempts to explore this and to understand what kind of attachment figure or transformational object (Bollas, 1987) I had become for her—or she had made me into—came to nothing because I was reduced to an insubstantial, impotent observer. She continued to send out signals but was closed off to receiving anything in return. This was a person who was well functioning and who could operate effectively at the level of language and interpretation, but the shift to Skype had somehow reduced me to a useless blank screen for her, a voyeur. It was as if the geographical distance between us rendered me ineffectual; I could try to say helpful things to reach her but I could not literally be there to give symbolic protection. She needed the three dimensions of my presence to contain her so she could operate with a fair degree of psychological sophistication. Perhaps the added anxiety of working in an unfamiliar culture and context contributed to the change in her. We were able to talk about it usefully on her return, but it was an unsettling countertransference experience at the time, making me question what had seemed "real" between us.

There is one further boundary issue I want to address, and that is the temptation a practitioner may feel to "Google" a patient. Some clients have asked me to do so, and at times my curiosity has been piqued by information I have been given. It might seem harmless, and we may even tell ourselves that it is helpful to know what is in the public domain, especially if the patient has some kind of celebrity status. Yet, it feels wrong to me to know without being told by the person concerned. I have one experience of discovering something that was not at all controversial, yet gave a very different perspective on a patient's life, but knowing that I was not supposed to know—she needed me to be one person who was not influenced by this knowledge. Of course, I wondered about parallels in her life, and about her decision to withhold this information from me, but I felt I had betrayed her through my failure of self-containment. The job of a psychotherapist is relational and participatory. Through my idle online search, I had made her into an object of voyeurism and I regret it.

### *In patients' lives*

Digital and communication technologies have an impact on patients' lives in so many ways. In the consulting room, we might hear explicit stories about relationships conducted in chat rooms and on social network sites, welcome and unwelcome contacts from the past, the distress of hearing that an ex- has married and photos of the happy couple appear to taunt the abandoned partner, competitiveness with a friend—for instance, if he or she posts an announcement about promotion or a pregnancy. They might talk of searching for long-lost relatives, or dating online, or involvement with self-help communities on the Internet. Some develop alter egos and socialise by playing fantasy or war games on role-play websites.

Several of my patients have discovered evidence of a partner's infidelity by checking emails, messages on mobile phones, and the history of Internet access. Other people have found images or links to websites downloaded on their spouse or child's computer that have deeply disturbed them. We might hear of incidents of identity theft, cyberbullying, or cyberstalking. Addiction to online gambling, Internet shopping, even online Scrabble, might be a presenting problem or could be a symptom of other difficulties.

Many clients struggle in their online communication with others. It can be frustrating, anxiety provoking, and even paranoia inducing to send an important message out into the ether and not have it met or responded to. There is so much scope for misunderstanding, especially when those involved have different attachment styles. I have the impression that preoccupied individuals need more contact, with more emotional connection. They often prefer to speak on the telephone or spend quite a lot of time communicating on social network sites. They might interpret email or text messages negatively and begin to feel persecuted by partners, friends, or colleagues whose messages are perceived to be cold, critical, or withholding. They are troubled if other people are less effusive in their messages, or if they do not respond quickly. Meantime, dismissing people can feel harassed by the demands of a "needy" friend, family member, colleague, or partner, and may well withdraw a little to protect themselves from feeling intruded upon. They do not understand that the other person experiences this as abandonment, and that this is likely to result in ever more demands for communication.

Each of us will have numerous examples of the role of technology in clients' or patients' lives, yet I suspect that some stories are not brought into therapy, perhaps because of shame or perhaps because the client senses that the material is incomprehensible to the therapist—especially if the latter is clearly a digital immigrant or appears reluctant to engage in the technological environment as it is now. It may be perceived as a cultural difference, where the client's life is embedded in the digital world and the practitioner is felt to be an alien in this environment. This is particularly the case if the patient is much younger. It can be very useful to enquire at assessment about the place of the digital world in the patient's day-to-day life; how he or she uses technology and what they use it for, how much time is devoted to online surfing or relating, what they might be doing if not sitting at a computer, posting photos, reading "tweets", searching websites, watching video clips, completing transactions, and so on. We may learn a lot about their internal objects, relational style, defences, and fantasies, and also convey that this is suitable material to bring to sessions.

## *In the room*

Digital devices have almost become extensions of ourselves; we seem to need them with us at all times. They keep us connected to people, to information, and often to work. Although some of us may feel persecuted by the bombardment of calls, voicemail messages, and emails, it can be difficult to manage without a smartphone nowadays. It provides an illusion of company when we are out and about alone, and we probably feel safer in unfamiliar environments with an iPhone or whatever in our pocket. These devices seem to function as transitional objects, both representing our attachment figures and linking us to them.

I have conflicting thoughts about the issue of mobile telephones in the therapy room. If a patient's phone rings during the session, there is potentially useful insight to be gained in how he or she responds, whether the call is taken or the device turned off. The difficulty a patient might have in cutting off contact with family, friends, or work, even for fifty minutes, is helpful to explore. On the other hand, this intrusion from the outside world shatters the two-person relating and "as if" quality of the therapy—the illusion that external reality is temporarily suspended while we focus on what happens in internal reality and within the four walls of the consulting room—in a most unhelpful way.

Rather than imposing a non-negotiable rule that the therapeutic hour is "digital detox" time, my compromise is to state on my website that "Generally I recommend turning off mobile devices during sessions—most people are relieved to be free of such intrusions for an hour or so to have space for their own thoughts and feelings". I note that most of my newer clients, those who have begun with me since this addition to the website, have switched off their phones from the start.

But there are also benefits to bringing laptops, tablets, or mobile phones to sessions. I have always welcomed certain kinds of "intrusion" into therapy, in the form of photographs of family or from childhood, or patients' artwork. This might be due to my years working for a bereavement counselling service, where I discovered the usefulness of these "impingements" in evoking memories and emotions, and facilitating grieving. I am particularly moved when rather dismissing patients reveal their personal life to me in this way, showing me family snapshots on their phones or computers or, in one case, playing me a digital recording of herself singing. At one time, a client might have planned to bring a photograph album or portfolio of paintings to show the therapist, but it is now possible to produce these spontaneously if the images are stored on a portable device. Of course, we must wonder whether these revelations are a distraction from dealing with something anxiety-provoking, or if there is a seductive quality to exposing such intimate mementos to the therapist, but generally I enjoy these moments and feel they contribute greatly to the therapeutic process.

## *Professional matters*

There is one more area of the counsellor or psychotherapist's life where digital technology has had a major impact: ongoing training, support, and professional development.

Of particular value to private practitioners is the opportunity to connect with others as a means of staying informed of developments in the field, participating in the decision-making process of our member organisations, and simply being known and held in mind by our peers. This is especially useful for colleagues who live at a distance from major cities and centres of training. As well as professional networking sites, such as LinkedIn, all registering bodies—British Association for Counselling and Psychotherapy, United Kingdom Council for Psychotherapy, British Psychotherapy Foundation, Institute of Psychoanalysis, and so on—have websites disseminating information about the profession, policies, training courses, accreditation, events, and so on. They have dedicated Members' Areas encouraging the exchange of ideas and views, and promoting active participation. Professional bodies have always had these functions, but prior to the advent of the Internet, and email, communicating with disparate members was often a cumbersome procedure.

The relationship with our training "family of origin" is a kind of attachment, and can be secure or insecure. Some individuals choose to stay in close proximity on completing their training by attending conferences, serving on committees, and eventually tutoring, teaching, supervising, and taking the role of therapist to the next generation of trainees. Others may prefer a peripheral role, with more space around them to develop in other directions. In both cases—close involvement with the "family" or remote—communication technologies can mediate these relationships.

As for continuing professional development, there is now a plethora of exciting online options from one-off "pick and mix" talks (podcasts from the Royal College of Psychiatrists, public lectures from Gresham College, and TED Talks, to name but a few), to structured courses. "eLearning" is offered by many universities: there is the eTavi programme run by the Tavistock and Portman NHS Foundation Trust, and themed modules offered by independent training organisations. Some of these courses also have an interactive component so fellow students can connect with each other as a learning community. It might not be possible to meet for a coffee before lectures or discuss the seminar together on the journey home, but relationships are encouraged for the purpose of engaging in learning together. These options for distance learning are of particular benefit to practitioners who complete a training in one country then return to their homeland, or who settle in locations where there are limited possibilities for developing expertise in specific areas of interest.

There is a well-established infant observation seminar group at the Tavistock Clinic, with participants in different countries video-linked with the facilitator in London (Magagna, 2013), and the Chinese–American Psychoanalytic Alliance provides not only academic seminars via Skype from the USA and other countries, but also personal analysis "remotely" for candidates in China (Fishkin & Fishkin, 2011). While there may be deficiencies in offering full professional psychotherapy training in this manner, it is a creative solution to bring talking therapies to the wider world where the infrastructure of experienced senior practitioners to teach, supervise, and offer psychotherapy to trainees does not yet exist.

Another bonus of providing video-linked conferences, lectures, and "webinars" is the matter of environmental impact. Rather than flying internationally renowned speakers across the globe to address a gathering, leaving a significant carbon footprint (and perhaps putting undue strain on those giants of the profession who have reached a venerable age), we can now benefit from seeing them, hearing their presentations, and interacting with them, mediated by digital technology. I feel sure that if this technology had existed during his lifetime, Freud would have delivered his *Introductory Lectures* to a global audience online.

For those of us intent on further study and research, we can access excellent specialist book vendors and libraries of professional journals on the Internet. It is possible to obtain papers and articles any time of the day or night (should we need to check a reference before bedtime!). It is difficult now to recall the time when these resources had to be ordered from a traditional library or bookshop. The spontaneous gesture—or creative moment—was long gone by the time the desired texts were delivered.

Some training institutes are now requiring members to use secure online sites to keep records of continuing professional development, supervision, and even client notes. I accept that details of seminars and conferences attended, books read or written, and the learning gained as a result needs to be monitored for the purpose of maintaining standards, and it is convenient for the training organisation to manage the monitoring process if information is stored and collated in this way. However, I have a resistance to keeping notes from sessions or supervision online, no matter how secure the site. I believe (and perhaps there are research findings to support my hunch) that writing with a pen on paper connects different areas of the brain from those involved in tapping words into a keyboard. I am more engaged with a pen in my hand than sitting at a computer, and I believe that a process occurs when writing by hand that is absent in word processing. My notes might not be legible to others, but then, they are confidential. These very sentences started out as thoughts scribbled on a notepad. (I have a patient who is well embedded in the technological world. Encouraging him to bring dreams to therapy, we discussed the habit of writing them down in the morning. I suggested rather strongly that these should be hand-written, not entered into a smartphone or tablet. I suspect that there is an extra filter applied to the material where technology is involved, a kind of tertiary revision.)

Another option available to the twenty-first century practitioner is supervision via Skype. This can be helpful to those practising in small communities where there are likely to be boundary complications with otherwise suitable local supervisors. There are also highly experienced people who have taught, supervised, or been psychotherapist to very many of the practitioners in the vicinity; receiving consultation or supervision from someone further afield could be the solution. It is now possible to choose a supervisor with a specific area of expertise or from a particular theoretical perspective regardless of geography.

Skype (or FaceTime) technology has improved dramatically over recent years and is quite good enough, in my experience, for supervision purposes. Although I am more reticent about working with patients "remotely", the nature of the supervisory relationship is different. Describing her experience of facilitating an online seminar group, Magagna writes,

> I try to use the whole of my feelings and bodily sensations occurring in the seminar. My observation of my own and other participants' tone of voice, facial expressions, body posture, velocity of reading material and emotional responsiveness or flatness in receiving and delivering comments informs my countertransference. This facilitates my awareness of being an emotional receptor of all that is occurring . . . (2013, p. 286)

I think these same processes happen well enough in the supervisory relationship when working on Skype.

When the time comes for semi-retirement, I might choose to leave the cosmopolitan delights of north London for a more rural existence.

If that becomes a reality, I believe I would happily embrace the possibilities offered by communication technologies to continue my supervision practice "remotely". And, who knows, by then the technology may have been perfected, with no more loss of connection, frozen frames, or poorly synchronised sound and vision. Should that moment arrive, I might also become more wholeheartedly committed to working as a therapist on Skype, for those who are able to benefit.

## *Conclusion*

Nineteenth-century biologist Herbert Spencer first published the term "survival of the fittest", which was later taken up by Darwin. It refers not to the healthiest members of a species, but to species that best fit—are adapted to—their environment. As counsellors and psychotherapists, we need to adapt to the realities of twenty-first century life, but without losing what makes our profession valuable. We are trained to be patient, to wait for clarity, to contain anxiety rather than react. We look for complexity rather than split experiences, processes, and "objects" into good and bad. If we are informed by attachment theory, we must be sensitive to the attachment needs, the need for both intimacy and autonomy, of our clients. Their relationships with digital technology, and our own, can either promote secure attachment or entrench alienation.

> Even the most reticent of our colleagues have to acknowledge that our changing world affects how we ultimately relate to our patients and our peers, and they to us. Technology can and does create expected as well unexpected possibilities. (Zalusky Blum, 2013, p. 49)

A person who has internalised a secure base can explore the world, welcome new experiences and opportunities, be curious about difference rather than feel threatened by it. So, let us thoughtfully embrace the possibilities presented by technology in the twenty-first century.

## *References*

Balint, M. (1959). *Thrills and Regressions.* London: Maresfield Library [reprinted 1987].

Balint, M. (1968). *The Basic Fault: Therapeutic Aspects of Regression*. London: Tavistock.

Bollas, C. (1987). *The Shadow of the Object: Psychoanalysis of the Unthought Known*. London: Free Association Books [reprinted 1994].

Bowlby, J. (1969). *Attachment and Loss: Vol. 1: Attachment*. London: Hogarth Press.

Bowlby, J. (1979). *The Making and Breaking of Affectional Bonds*. London: Tavistock.

Bowlby, J. (1988). *A Secure Base: Clinical Applications of Attachment Theory*. London: Routledge.

Colman, W. (2006). The analytic super-ego. *Journal of the British Association of Psychotherapists, 44*(2): 1–16.

Coltart, N. (1993). *How to Survive as a Psychotherapist*. London: Sheldon Press.

Dobson, L. (2010). The net generation. *Therapy Today, 21*(4): 29–31.

Fishkin, R. & Fishkin, L. (2011). The electronic couch: some observations about Skype treatment. In: S. Akhtar (Ed.), *The Electrified Mind: Development, Psychopathology, and Treatment in the Era of Cell Phones and the Internet* (pp. 99–111). Lanham, MD: Jason Aronson.

Freud, S. (1912b). The dynamics of transference. *S.E., 12*: 97–108. London: Hogarth.

Gerhardt, S. (2004). *Why Love Matters: How Affection Shapes a Baby's Brain*. Hove: Brunner-Routledge.

Guntrip, H. (1975). My experience of analysis with Fairbairn and Winnicott: (how complete a result does psycho-analytic therapy achieve?). *International Review of Psycho-Analysis, 2*: 145–156.

Holmes, J. (1996). *Attachment, Intimacy, Autonomy: Using Attachment Theory in Adult Psychotherapy*. Northvale, NJ: Jason Aronson.

Kernberg, O. F. (1996). Thirty methods to destroy the creativity of psychoanalytic candidates. *International Journal of Psychoanalysis, 77*(5): 1031–1040.

Killingmo, B. (1989). Conflict and deficit: implications for technique. *International Journal of Psychoanalysis, 70*: 65–79.

Magagna, J. (2013). Being present for each other: long-distance video-linked seminars. *Psychoanalytic Psychotherapy: Applications, Theory and Research, 27*(4): 280–295.

Main, M., & Goldwyn, R. (1984). Adult attachment scoring and classification system. Unpublished manuscript, University of California, Berkeley.

Main, M., Hesse, E., & Goldwyn, R. (2008). Studying differences in language usage in recounting attachment history: an introduction to the AAI. In: H. Steele & M. Steele (Eds.), *Clinical Applications of the Adult Attachment Interview* (pp. 31–68). New York: Guilford Press.

Thomas, L. (1992). Racism and psychotherapy: working with racism in the consulting room – an analytical view. In: J. Kareem & R. Littlewood (Eds.), *Intercultural Therapy: Themes, Interpretations and Practice* (pp. 133–145). Oxford: Blackwell Science.

Zalusky Blum, S. (2013). Musings on therapy and technology. In: J. S. Scharff (Ed.), *Psychoanalysis Online: Mental Health, Teletherapy, and Training* (pp. 49–57). London: Karnac.

CHAPTER SIX

# The use of telephone and Skype in psychotherapy: reflections of an attachment therapist

*Niki Reeves*

## *Introduction*

Some practitioners train as telephone counsellors or study online as "e-therapists", and there are now ethical guidelines for these professions. However, this paper addresses those whose training prepares them for working with the client in the consulting room. The traditional mode of psychotherapy is face to face and it appears to be optimum, so why would we consider working with media such as the telephone or Skype?

There is a growing emphasis placed on inclusion and therapy for all, and we are increasingly considering client groups that in the past have been unable to access psychotherapy. These groups include the homeless, those with limited mobility and disability, psychological issues that make leaving the home difficult, including anxiety and agoraphobia, cultural restrictions, and the need to care for a relative. In addition, we live in a world where people increasingly travel greater distances to work, have longer working hours, and might be out of the country for extended periods or with a frequency that would interrupt the psychotherapeutic flow too often for a productive therapy to be undertaken. This can restrict the ability to commit to face-to-face psychotherapeutic work, where regular time and place are prerequisites. With the advent of the phone and digital technologies such as Skype and FaceTime, these restraints need no longer be a bar to getting the help that is needed.

However, psychotherapy on the phone or with Skype raises questions around how working without sight of the client—or with restricted view through a computer screen—affects the therapeutic relationship, and whether therapy done in this way is really "as good" as the therapy we conduct face to face. When considering work from a distance, questions are raised concerning boundaries, the effects of location and proximity, and the impact on transference and countertransference. With our experience of the other person limited, will we miss the subtle dissociations and shifts in the work, as described by Bayles (2012), who, in her very thoughtful article, queries whether the use of Skype can at times work against the psychoanalytic process. She asks the important question: "is seeing the physical presence of the patient/analyst different from *being* in their physical presence? Or, is actual physical presence an intrinsic element of the analytic process?" (p. 572). Will enactments still occur? Do they occur in the same way they would in face-to-face work? Is it possible to be aware of interoception and proprioception, the senses of our own bodies and where they are in the space they inhabit, and the relational interaction of those feelings as a result of sensations and affects felt in the body of another?

Some "traditional" therapists will only work in the consulting room. I have not yet met one who would opt for working on the phone or with Skype rather than in person, although I am sure they exist. Yet, when it is necessary to use another medium, some therapists prefer the phone to working with Skype, and some prefer Skype to the phone. I think that the preference between these media might be akin to the preference for working with clients sitting opposite us, or lying on the couch. Those who prefer working with their client on the couch experience limited visual cues, but they feel more effective when they hear the client's voice and simultaneously have their own private space in which to think and consider, as would occur in telephone therapy. The freedom to limit the visual sensory information is seen as a way of enabling work at a deeper level. Those therapists who prefer to see their clients face to face rather than on the couch will perhaps feel a loss of connection when they cannot receive visual information and prefer to include the visual cues in the way enabled by Skype.

Perhaps the reticence about using phone- or Internet-mediated modes partly lies in unfamiliarity with the technology, the complex legal and confidential issues, our wanting to give the best service we can, and concerns about our ability to maintain an element of control. Some therapists like to focus their attention on the content of the work, and blur out what they see as external interference. For instance, when supervising counsellors and psychotherapists, my queries about such matters as payment of fees and time boundaries are often met with hesitation. Some practitioners tell me they find talking about these things with the client intrusive, thinking it is outside the therapeutic work. I believe the opposite is true; these frame issues allow access to underlying conflicts and transference material. And so, in cases where the therapy involves telephone or Skype, concern that some of the therapist's thought and attention might be expended in monitoring the effects of a possibly changing environment evokes anxiety and raises questions about the capacity to give one's best. However, just as boundary violations give us a window into the psyche of the client and the relationship between us, the issues that arise through the use of telephone and Skype give us a window into the client's and our own ability to be close, to be in the presence of another, and to feel safe.

As a relational therapist, I have reflected a great deal on how these communication technologies affect the work, and, as an attachment therapist, I have given thought to the attachment style of the clients I see and questioned whether technology has been a help or hindrance to the therapy. Does attachment style influence the choice of media? How does the matter of proximity and distance assist or hamper the work?

Therapy traditionally takes place in the practitioner's environment. The therapist chooses the contents of the room, controls how sessions are conducted, and decides how interruptions and anxiety-inducing events are managed. Clients are required to hand themselves over to, and put trust in, the person who "owns" the space. For the majority, this is a small consideration, but for those who have traumatic attachment histories, whose earliest experience of a carer was unpredictable and maybe even frightening, this can be a huge undertaking. They are unlikely to feel safe in an unfamiliar environment, with a therapist in a position of power who might be experienced as frightening.

For those who have no alternative, improving our familiarity with these tools, and a better understanding of the attachment style of self and client, can enable us to help them withstand any difficulties that may emerge.

Traditionally, we can observe how clients walk into the room at the start of a session, what they bring with them, how they seat themselves. They also register a flood of information about us from the way we greet them, how we walk, and how we seat ourselves. This is an important exchange, a ritual marking the transition from ordinary relating that takes place "out there in the world" to the special kind of relating that takes place "in here during sessions", and it enables a reacquainting with each other before the work begins. When working "remotely", there is a loss of this visual and contextual information that can affect our sense of each other and our settling into the therapeutic mode. This important ritual needs to be present in some form before the client can feel safe enough to engage, and we need to bear this in mind when conducting therapy on the phone and through the screen in order to be effective.

## *Therapy by phone*

In face-to-face therapy, we meet in the same place each session. If something occurs in that setting, we experience it together at the same time and a sense of "our space" is created. The client's presence changes the atmosphere, as do we: the space between us is a felt experience, warm, hostile, cold, or safe. When on the phone, there is a duality to our presence that is akin to magic. We are at the same time in our own practice and in the location that the client inhabits; *the client experiences the therapist in the client's environment, sharing it with him or her*. It is easy to forget this because we cannot see the other's location, but the client experiences us, and the effects of the work on their emotional state in "their space". When face to face, our practice room becomes a safe space over time in which the client feels held because the memories of what has happened there affect their expectation of what will happen there again. For this reason, work done on the phone can be very powerful. Once a feeling has been experienced in their own environment through the use of the phone, that space has been changed. In our consulting room, they experience and leave, returning to their own space, their reality. When therapy is conducted on the phone, they leave *a* reality, but something of it remains in *their* reality.

The loss of observable cues will have a significant effect on the therapeutic process. Consideration needs to be given to the absence of visual information and how this affects both parties. When I began clinical practice during my training, sitting across from my first clients many years ago, I took considerable time in thinking about how to hold my hands, how to sit and be still, ensuring clear sight of a clock, and so on. It took time before I found "my way" to be in the room. Telephone therapy required the same trial and error to find how I work best, with my focus and attention placed where it is needed. When conducting therapy on the phone, I ensure I sit in my usual therapist's chair and look across the room as though the client is present in my room. At the same time, I imagine him or her in their space, where they might be, how it might look. In my early work, I have been tempted to "get more comfortable", to take off my shoes, to move about, to look out of the window. When this has happened, I found my thinking drifting, that sense of "me the therapist" melting away, and I felt the discourse tend towards a conversational style.

When therapists are familiar with their own way of working, they get a sense of what they feel and whether it originates internally or in the other. If they find themselves distracted, they consider whether it is due to something of their own, something happening in the work, or because the client is distracted. Why has the connection been broken? Recognising this takes time and comes with experience. Perhaps those who are hesitant to work in other media have not considered that we must begin again to build up our expertise in another medium in order to be able to sense and recognise this phenomenon there, too. Just as someone who loses their sight takes time to reacquaint themselves with their world and learn to see it anew, the therapist has to take time to learn how to see the therapeutic landscape from this different vantage point.

In face-to-face therapy, visual signals often enable us to orientate ourselves, and reorientate ourselves when the client changes subject or is hesitant. Clients also rely on visual stimuli and peripheral sight to reassure themselves, and to resettle when there is a break in the flow. Without these cues, in telephone therapy we are deprived of one sense, but, as we become more familiar with this way of working, we find other routes to achieve and maintain connection. As human beings intent on communication and attunement, we are primed to find ways of being heard, recognised, and felt.

We use many tools and cues to connect and disconnect from one another. As far back as 1979, Thomas and Malone described how we give and receive clues in order to manage our internal states in a process of mutual attunement. Our understanding of the connection between therapist and client has soared because of work in this area: we experience attunement in the way we unconsciously match the feeling state of the client. Lachmann (Beebe & Lachmann, 1998) writes about a client he calls Karen and describes the way he dampened down his sense of presence when he says,

> In treating Karen, I (Lachmann) responded to her constriction by partially constricting myself, narrowing my own expansiveness in order to more closely match her range. Partially out of awareness, her facial, vocal, visual, and orientational behavior created a resonant emotional state in me. (p. 493)

This emotional state of which he speaks was felt through many senses, not only visual, and it demonstrates the multitude of ways in which we continuously give and receive important prompts. Vital information that we wish to be recognised is sent, and, in turn, received and felt by the therapist and client alike. We come to find a way together where we tune in to what is being transmitted.

I experienced the power of this process with a client with whom I had been working on the phone for almost two years. The client was visiting the UK and was able to come to my practice. We spent some time talking about the possibility of having a face-to-face session and preparing to finally meet in person. I experienced the one-off, in-person session in a very strange way; I had the sense of being in an underpass, with a train shooting past overhead. After the session, my head was buzzing. It did not feel comfortable. At our next session, once again returning to the phone, I was able to talk with my client about *her* experience of our meeting. She said it felt somehow wrong; it was a rush, there was too much to take in. She quickly changed the subject—it was perhaps too much to process all at once—but over the next six months we returned to reflect on that session often, working through the experience piece by piece. At first, the mere mention of it brought back a sense of being overwhelmed, something we had both experienced. I believe that through our work on the phone, we had been able to tune into each other in a measured way, but the face-to-face meeting had literally been "too much" to take for our refined senses of each other, and of what occurred when we met.

With this client, when on the phone, I became aware that she could hear—or, rather, sense—my shifts in attention or posture, just as I could in her. In this way, when working on the phone, my movement has an effect on the clients' sense of my presence, and for me, their movement affects my sense of them being present, comfortable, and alert. Once we have established a relationship, I become attuned to their stirring and stillness, to their breath, their spaces, and their resonance as signals of certain feelings—anxiety or shame, for example.

It is easy to be seduced into thinking we are special when a client chooses to work with us via phone or Skype, rather than begin the process face to face with another therapist who might live within a manageable distance. But we should also consider whether the choice of phone therapy might be a defence against discomfort in being seen, or in seeing the other, or of making a connection. Just as when working face to face, we reflect on all that is said and all that is not said when taking on a piece of work that will be conducted by phone; I consider all that can be felt, and all that cannot be seen. It might be that the client who has chosen this medium is acutely prone to shame, and for that reason I am particularly careful to avoid evoking shame and ensure I do not use brevity or humour in the work until the therapeutic relationship is well established.

## *The voice*

When working on the phone, I give extra consideration to my voice. In the first sessions, before we are accustomed to each other, I remind myself that my voice might be my only presence for the client, and, as such, I place importance on every aspect of it. Practising face to face, we can see how the client dresses, walks, and smiles, and we notice changes from week to week. As my normal way of working is face to face or through Skype, I rely on visual cues when I have them. How the client sits down, compared to previous sessions, tells me a great deal before a word is uttered. In the room, a movement of the head or a flick of the eyes is picked up by both therapist and client. So, on the phone the timbre, the speed of speech, and the inflection all matter a great deal. Just as texts can be misinterpreted when read, so the voice can be misinterpreted when the visual cues are missing, and we are unfamiliar with each other.

I am aware I have a different "voice" when working with clients on the phone: in comparison to the calm, quiet, even tone I use in the room, my speech becomes more animated, I use the up and down vocal flow to carry meaning and emotional content in a way I would not when I can see my clients and, more importantly, when they can see me. Only when we have built a therapeutic relationship in which the clients trust that I know them and in which they know me well enough that the possibility of misunderstandings is reduced (or will not be irreparable) will my vocal pattern become more like the one I use in the room. By this time, we have become tuned in to each other and our voices transmit information that we are both able to receive.

The voice is a tool, and over time in telephone therapy, mine becomes more like the one I use in the room, but there are still important differences. Without being able to use my gaze or the visual impact of my body to assist in holding the client, my voice must convey extra meaning and needs to be experienced as containing in a way that would not happen in in-person sessions. To understand the way in which this information is experienced, we can learn from what Stern (1998) has to tell us about vitality affects in the infant. Vitality affects are the qualities of feeling expressed by words such as "surging", "fleeting", or "gushing". He explains that the infant can experience vitality affects through cross-modal capacities (the ability to experience in one sense and connect it to another, for example, to touch something and be able to identify the object by sight).

> [I]n trying to soothe the infant the parent could say, "There, there, there . . .", giving more stress and amplitude on the first part of the word and trailing off towards the end of the word. Alternatively, the parent could silently stroke the baby's back or head with a stroke analogous to the "There, there" sequence, applying more pressure at the onset of the stroke and lightening or trailing it off toward the end. If the duration of the contoured stroke and the pauses between strokes

> were of the same absolute and relative durations as the vocalization–pause pattern, the infant would experience similar activation contours no matter which soothing technique was performed. The two soothings would feel the same (beyond their sensory specificity) and would result in the same vitality affect experience. (p. 58)

## *Silence*

The absence of sound holds extra importance on the phone where the visual cues are not present to reassure the client. In face-to-face work, the therapist's silence may be experienced by the client as a calm soothing space, but on the phone might be felt more readily as desertion, a black hole, where the therapist is simply gone. An anxious "are you still there?" indicates a sense of abandonment. If the client feels the need to check your presence too often, the sense of a safe place will be compromised, and this is not conducive to therapeutic work. For this reason, when working on the phone, I will raise this in the assessment session, explore how the client might experience silences, and how he or she would prefer to be held. I make sure to ask, "I wonder how it would feel if neither of us were talking", or "Sometimes there is silence in work such as this, and I wonder how that would feel for you?" If the client's history includes experiences of abandonment, I might ask, "If we are on the phone and you are not okay, how would I know?" In the first few sessions, after short silences I would check with the client what was going on for them, and how the silence felt, until I was familiar with their ability to withstand those spaces.

I revisit the question of silence and holding as the work progresses and the client's sense of my presence at the end of the telephone is more robust. As an attachment therapist, I am careful not to leave my clients feeling abandoned: the making of a trusting relationship is vital, but it is also important to gauge the individual's need for quiet contemplation in the presence of another. Some people experience silence as a safe space in which to think, and will often use it in the same way babies do when they look away from the face of their mother to self-regulate, as described by Beebe (2005). Words may create intimacy and closeness, and silence helps to regulate emotional space—a demonstration of the dance of proximity and distance in our relationship. I discovered with one client that when he reconnected following a silence of maybe fifteen seconds, his voice was always lighter. I was reminded each time of the face of the child when his care-giver walks into the bedroom first thing in the morning—refreshed and eager to engage in a new day. During phone therapy, as in sessions using the couch, we are removed from the client's gaze and have the opportunity for reverie, allowing such images to enter one's mind. This is often a bonus, providing additional information evoked by our engagement with the client, an extra dimension of unconscious communication.

## *Rhythms*

In my experience, it is not long before the client and I, the therapist, find our dance, a rhythm to the sessions. I am more keenly aware of this in the absence of visual cues. A client with whom I worked for some time on the phone lived very close to a railway line and, on the fourteenth, twenty-second, and thirty-eighth minute of our sessions, I could hear trains pass by. Although never aware of waiting for this soundtrack, our sessions began to take on a pattern. The first fourteen minutes were used to reconnect with each other when the client would talk about her week and there was more "to and fro" than I would normally experience in face-to-face therapy. This was the client's way of enabling a re-acquaintance through engaging me and hearing my voice; she would use this time to settle and feel safe in our familiarity. From the fourteenth minute to the thirty-eighth, we would work at a deeper level; I would spend more time silent, and the client used this space to let me hear her. From the thirty-eighth minute, we would begin to resurface, enabling her to return to her world. Patterns of this nature occur in all our work, but with this client, the audible rhythm of passing trains became the cue to move from one phase of the session to the next.

Once aware of this pattern, I began to pay attention to the cadence of other phone sessions where the train timetable was not a feature. Indeed, I found that the timbre of my voice would change at certain times. For anxious clients this was more apparent, with greater emphasis than with others. But in all cases, my voice played a major part in giving information to boundary the work, such as indicating that the end of the session was approaching.

This ability to experience affect and to communicate without vision is further demonstrated by Trevarthen (1999), when he talks of a film produced by Gunilla Preisler in Stockholm. A five-month-old girl, blind from birth, is the subject of the film. Trevarthen describes the expressive precision of the infant's hand gestures as her mother sings nursery rhymes to her:

> Her gesturing is recounting the message in non-verbal mimesis. She is dancing dramatic moments and the progress of the adventure in these little 'myths'. We see that she does so with the 'right' moves, even as a trained conductor might. She accentuates the flow of feeling in the 'story', pointing up high notes, spreading to the side to follow the surges of energy, closing her fingers and/or dropping her hand eloquently at the close of a phrase. Her sense of pitch space seems to be aligned with the axis of her body while she lies on her back, higher pitch being accompanied by a move headwards, lowest pitch being below the waist. As her gestures occasionally anticipate the mother's melodic and rhythmic change by a fraction of a second, we know she is recognizing the songs and performing them, at least partly, from memory. We have evidence now that this is perfectly natural infant behaviour. Babies dance to the pulse and expression of music. This case is just so astonishing because the baby cannot see her movements. She just 'feels' the music in her, and has learned them that way. (p. 103)

Conducting therapy on the telephone can have something of this quality. It has greatly increased my awareness of my voice and how I use it. This, and sensitivity to the client's voice, has enabled me to have a more "delicate" touch in sessions, in all media. But the voice is not used in isolation; the ability to hear, to sense, and to consider the presence and the feelings of the other, and to be sensitive to the form and shape of sessions are intrinsic aspects of this work that can be learnt, practised, and improved upon with experience.

The remainder of this chapter will address the use of Skype, as a form of communication and a vehicle for therapy.

## *Skype*

Skype, a system of using a computer with a webcam, microphone, and speakers, allows people in different locations to see each other on the computer screen. While therapy—or at least counselling—via telephone has a long history, with helplines such as ChildLine, the Samaritans, and Parentline offering a range of easily accessible support, including listening, information-giving, and formalised counselling sessions, Skype is still a relatively novel medium in which to work psychotherapeutically. (For further information on this digital technology, equipment, and specifications I suggest you consult Scharff (2013).) At the time of writing, communication via Skype has been available for over ten years, but it is relatively recent that the initial technical difficulties have been more or less overcome; the early irritations of unsynchronised sound and picture, fragmented speech, image freezing, and broken connections are pretty much behind us, happening rarely, if at all, nowadays. In my experience, only when Skyping to certain countries, such as China and South Korea, will these difficulties mean that it might not be a feasible or reliable method of "meeting" for the purpose of therapy. That the medium is currently rarely used is not, I believe, because clients hesitate to engage with it; on the contrary, clients seem to enquire about this more and more often. However, I think its rarity is due to the resistance of *therapists* in embracing it. Most therapists, after all, grew up before digital technology was widespread and have needed to "catch up" with the younger generation. They may justify their wariness of the novel as a reluctance to flout the traditional tried and trusted methods of conducting therapy.

Carlino (2011), referring to face-to-face psychoanalysis, writes,

> [The] distance between the interlocutors should not always be the decisive point which makes the treatment possible or impossible. In analytic dialogue, there should be an encounter between the material contributed by the patient and the catching of that material, using the free-floating attention of the analyst for its specific elaboration. (p. 67)

In my experience, those therapists who find it easier to work using Skype are those who have considerable familiarity with the medium, contacting relatives abroad on a regular basis, or using it as a way of maintaining relationships with friends and colleagues who live far away. With familiarity and repetition, the screen becomes more a window than a door to their relating. "Digital natives" (Prensky, 2001), those born after 1980 and, as such, brought up with digital technology, are in the habit of spanning distance using FaceTime and Skype. They use digital technology as a way of "bridging" rather than "being separated" by distance. It is not uncommon for digital natives to watch television together using this medium, cook together, and just spend time together through Skype while living in different locations. Laptops are positioned in such a way that each can see the other as well as one television screen. The use of digital technology in this way means that distance does not have to mean being alone. Watching television, commenting as thoughts occur, and laughing together, enhance the experience of watching and doing, and increase a sense of togetherness. I know of a grandmother who, since her son and his family moved to Australia, has a weekly appointment with her granddaughter to watch a children's television programme. The granddaughter comes home from school and sits in front of the television with a glass of milk and biscuits, while the grandmother, an early riser, gets up and watches with her breakfast. The granddaughter laughs and comments to her grandmother, who can feel close, join in, and make sense of what is being seen on the television screen. They have a shared experience that is their own. The grandmother's only complaint is that she cannot cuddle her granddaughter when they laugh together.

When using the phone, both parties have to understand the other to attune to the rhythm of the other. Each silence, each pause, may be felt as a tiny rupture. When we have visual contact, the sight of the other repairs these tiny ruptures; a small reassurance, like a bridge, connects both sides. On the phone talking with friends, silence can be experienced as awkward, a sign that the conversation has dried up and it is time to end. The new way of being together via Skype gives an opportunity to be present together without the pressure to speak for periods of time. Unlike telephone contact, the experience is about companionship and time spent in each other's company rather than the dissemination of information. Perhaps this is why it is a favourite of the young, who enjoy just "hanging out". It uses visual cues as reassurance of presence. While proximity on the phone is enhanced by interjections and the sounds of the other's presence, on Skype, it is the knowledge of a shared experience that is its appeal.

Working with clients in the room remains my preference and is, I believe, optimal for many reasons. However, just as experience and the development of "my position" has enabled me to successfully make the transition to telephone therapy, a different set of "positions" has enabled me to feel comfortable and confident when working via Skype with clients who cannot be in the room with me.

## *Distance and proximity*

Skype clients, or those who begin therapy in person and then change to Skype, are making a significant choice. Even those who have had to move away for their careers—a situation that appears to be out of their control—and can no longer come to the practice do have the option to begin with another therapist in the new location. But they are choosing not to and we must consider the reasons behind this decision. It may be that the level of trust and familiarity has become very important at a crucial time, and as a relational therapist I see this as an important component of a successful therapy, but could the newly created distance actually enable a *greater* sense of safety for some clients? Are some of those who choose therapy via Skype *more* comfortable when there is a distance (and a screen) between themselves and the therapist?

Bowlby asserted that, unlike animals that run *away* to a place of safety when alarmed (a tree, burrow, or den), the human, when alarmed, runs *to* a "person of safety": the attachment figure. With this in mind, imagine a situation where the source of fear *is* the attachment figure. The infant has no place to run; he cannot leave and he is afraid to stay. This results in "fright without solution" (Hesse & Main, 2000). In the Strange Situation Test, the security of attachment between a parent and child of twelve to fifteen months is categorised as secure (B), avoidant (A), or resistant/ambivalent (C) (Main & Morgan, 1996), based on observation of the toddler's reaction to certain stressors and how he or she uses the parent to alleviate anxiety. Some toddlers, however, exhibit unexpected behaviours, including contradictory, misdirected, incomplete, or interrupted movements and expressions, freezing, stilling, slowed movements and expressions, and confusion *in the presence of the parent*. It is now understood that these behaviours demonstrate the absence of coherent strategies for dealing with stressful situations. Rather than situations where a carer or parent may assist the child in finding resolution to difficult affect, these behaviours result from experiences of "fright without solution".

As the infant grows, there is evidence that this dilemma is partially resolved by the child finding a "zone of proximal distance", far enough away to feel autonomous, yet close enough to remain within safety from external threat. A client who we might consider to have an "unresolved" or "disorganised" attachment style would display similar behaviours in their approach to therapy. I suggest such a client would feel a great deal safer in a situation where they are at home and at distance from the therapist, but can still see the therapist and, thus, feel close. With such a client, there is a threat to their sense of safety when the process elicits a sense of intimacy or closeness. When this occurs, might the client have an urge to end the work, to run, to click the mouse and cut off the contact, before the anxiety evoking contradiction of fear of closeness and fear of distance is inevitable? Is it possible that through the work new strategies can be evolved for managing such stressful situations, resulting in the client feeling prepared to attempt face-to-face therapy?

The answers to these questions are, unsurprisingly, "yes" and "no". I have no doubt that there are clients who choose this medium because it enables them to keep emotional distance and, therefore, maintain some of their defences, but it is not by any means the main or the only reason for this choice. For those who do feel safer with "remote therapy", I think, with time, the gap can be bridged. Just as some clients begin by requesting only six sessions in order to sample the experience before committing to the work, so others might find the therapist's presence too much to handle: for example, those clients who suffer from intense anxiety.

## *The space*

In traditional therapy, the client comes into a unique, customised setting. The environment in which we work is designed to facilitate creation of a different "headspace", a little like the experience of being at school, or at work. Each time the visual cues occur, we access a part of brain functioning and thinking that is used for that specific activity—state-dependent memory. There is a subliminal recognition that what happens here is a different from other activities: in this location, certain processes and rituals of therapy take place. The more familiar the setting becomes, the quicker we access the state of mind associated with that location. This predictable, boundaried space itself provides holding over time. When working in a GP surgery, or other facility, counsellors are taught to guard their space keenly, informing the surgery that, from the beginning of the work, the therapy room must be fixed and agreed upon. As therapists, we know the importance of providing a private space protected from intrusions.

However, for clients who have therapy via Skype, their own "space" might not be consistent. Appointments could be held in an impersonal hotel room, or a succession of hotel rooms. This is an unfamiliar and possibly unpredictable environment, for both the client and the therapist, with background noise that they have no control over; this can create tension that distracts the client, or the therapy might feel more formal, like a business meeting.

Meanwhile, clients Skyping from home might be using an office space, a bedroom, a living room, or a spare room. The therapist is invited into the client's environment and something is communicated in the location chosen for sessions. It might help to consider what recent and historical events took place in the room; was the client's last experience there an argument, or tenderness? Are there memories of people loved and lost connected with these surroundings? If a bedroom is used, might the client be communicating something important about intimacy to the therapist?

Working with this medium, the therapist can no longer guard the therapeutic space. Although the family may have been informed that the client is "off limits" for the next hour, privacy cannot always be guaranteed. If children are present at home, even if another person is child-minding, the sound of crying or arguing can take the client away in spirit and thought, if not in person, as can the ringing of a telephone or doorbell. Therapists can also be dysregulated by interruptions, or by a change in the client's environment. These things can and will influence the work and need to be explored in supervision, and with the client, if appropriate.

In addition to the points made earlier about settling in, reacquainting, and proximity, there is another consideration when working "remotely". In traditional therapy, the time taken to travel to and from the consulting room is a valuable aspect of the routine, an opportunity for the client to prepare for the therapy and then to prepare for re-engaging in daily life. The individual who leaves their session on Skype and within a few seconds walks back into the family or work situation does not have the use of an important transitional space. If this is the case for a client, I ensure that the last five to ten minutes, dependent on needs, are used for some form of "resurfacing".

On the positive side, just as the telephone client experiences the therapist as simultaneously in the consulting room and with the client in his or her space, this also occurs through the computer screen, with the Skype client feeling the therapist's presence in their own home, office, or hotel. Kudiyarova writes,

> My patient from another country, smiling, said: "I notice that now you always are with us in our house." At first, I could not understand what she meant. She used to have her sessions at her office computer. Then she got the internet at home . . . (2013, p. 187)

### *Clients who work face to face and use Skype intermittently*

The biggest group of Skype users in my practice are clients who start therapy in the traditional way, but who must intermittently travel because of work commitments. Within this category, there is a split, with some finding it easier than others to transfer to a new medium. For these, the relationship we have established "in person" enables the work to continue well, and they are grateful for maintaining the connection when they have to be elsewhere. The work of therapy continues despite changes of location, with sessions sometimes in my practice and at other times via Skype. These are clients who have established a secure attachment to me, for whom my office has come to be sufficiently experienced as a secure base to maintain that sense of safety and connection when the location changes. This sense of a secure base is aided by the ability to see that I, and the office, remain intact in their absence.

Other clients can find it takes a little while to settle into Skype sessions, but once the to and fro of our discourse begins, they are reminded of the relationship we have in the practice and they find that place in their mind that is "our therapeutic space". With this subgroup, I experience some disorientation each time and ensure I make space at the beginning of each Skype session to check in with them, talking a little about where they are, how comfortable they feel in their unfamiliar surroundings, and such like. In this way, I allow them the opportunity to hear my voice, to reacquaint themselves with our relationship, and to settle into the session in their own time.

I observe that preoccupied clients, unable to manage their sometimes overwhelming affect effectively, are shaken by the unfamiliarity and only when they see that I am calm and unperturbed can they settle. I am reminded of an anxious child looking to a parent for reassurance that all is well, and the adult's demeanour conferring confidence.

In the experience of secure infants, stress has been encountered in the presence of a carer who can respond not only to the stressor, but also to the experience of the infant. The carer recognises and attunes to the feelings of the infant, and reassures and soothes appropriately. Over time, the infant learns that stress can be borne. Initially, the infant looks to the carer for assistance in this, but gradually builds the necessary capacity to bear stress and frustration without overwhelming distress. Unfortunately for those infants whose attachment style in the Strange Situation Test is categorised as ambivalent, this containing and managing experience with the care-giver has not occurred. The infant has experienced anxiety without a capable attachment figure to help make sense of the event or soothe the resulting affect. As such, each stressful event is experienced as beyond the capacity of the infant to bear.

As the infant reaches adulthood, this attachment style, now termed "preoccupied", results in any perceived stress being experienced as completely overwhelming. The clients seem overwhelmed by feelings and much of the therapy is taken up with affect regulation and the building of structures in order to assist in this. Slade (1999) describes how the client might be experienced in therapy:

> Therapeutic insights, instead of paving the way toward the development of real structure, take on a hollow, unintegrated feel. Within the session, these patients are so "driven" by feeling that they jump from one issue to the next, without any sense of an inner purpose. (p. 586)

These clients begin with a flood of affect and it is my task, as it would be in the room, to let them know that I attune to them and can hear their discomfort, with all the force with which it is transmitted. As in our sessions, they need the joint experience of a "capacity to bear" anxiety before they can contain themselves and dare to bear it alone.

### *Clients who begin with face-to-face work and use Skype due to a permanent relocation*

With the group of clients who begin in the office and then move to another location, continuing the work using Skype, my experience is that the relationship created in person can transfer well. The initial awkwardness and settling in might take three or four sessions, but clients are soon able to create a space in the new location in which the boundaries they experienced in my practice can be maintained. Because they are familiar with occupying a space that is just for therapeutic work, they can more easily create the setting and access the necessary state of mind. On occasion, intrusions such as family noise or problems with connectivity do occur, and are felt as keenly by us both. We work through these, talking about how the rupture felt, and the impact it had on our space. We are then able to move forward.

With one such client, our work together culminated in the resignation of his post, a move some four hundred miles away, and the start of his own business. It was important to him that, throughout the transitional phase of setting up his new home and beginning his new enterprise, I was available to him and we could continue working on the anxieties that had brought him to therapy to ensure they did not return in the new circumstance. We maintained the therapy for a further ten months, at which point the client felt confident that he could go it alone. He had experienced me as responsive to his need for a secure base, and he was able to develop his autonomy knowing that the therapeutic relationship could still be accessed to help him manage should he need further support.

### *Clients who begin and end the work using Skype*

Many clients approach me via my website because they particularly wish to address relational difficulties and feel drawn to working with a therapist trained in attachment. Some prefer to work with me even when they are geographically distant, and there are other, more local, options not necessitating the use of Skype. It would be flattering to think that my training, or the way I present myself on my website is such a powerful draw, but other reasons may well influence their choice.

When I first considered this group, I assumed that the clients who prefer to use Skype might have a primarily dismissing attachment style. Bowlby writes about certain kinds of patient who are uncomfortable with intimacy (Bowlby, 1993[1988]). He cites several reasons for their specific defences, including the expectation—based on early relational experiences—of being hurt, shamed, or rejected by others, or the fear of being ensnared in a relationship intended to serve the other person's needs. This makes the client evasive and distrustful:

> Evidence shows that these states of mind occur especially in those who, having developed an anxiously avoidant pattern of attachment during early years, have striven ever since to be emotionally self-contained and insulated against intimate contact with other people. These patients . . . avoid therapy as long as they can and, should they undertake it, keep the therapist at arm's length. (1993, p. 143)

However, when I examined the clients who have requested to work via Skype, I found they do not fall into one attachment style alone. Of those I would categorise as primarily dismissing, I notice that when I consider the subject of the difficulties of the medium with them, there is a dismissal that the technology makes any difference at all, and so I hold the knowledge that using Skype enables a further distance to exist between us. I consider how much this affects my ability to feel connected to the client, and how much of this difficulty is because the client prefers distance at this stage.

I have noticed that of clients who begin and end using Skype, those I experience as primarily preoccupied appear not to notice that they are not in the room with me. There is much more emphasis on the use of my mind as a container for their unprocessed affect than on the location of the therapy. My reflection on the possible difficulties experienced in our relationship due to the medium is quickly agreed with and experienced as a rupture, without real consideration.

Only once have I had an assessment session for Skype-only therapy with a client I would regard as having a primarily disorganised attachment style. The work lasted for three months, was sporadic, and the client disappeared. It is possible that the reduced sense of my presence via Skype was insufficient to hold her, but perhaps I would have been unable to hold her even if the work had been conducted in my practice. Individuals with disorganised attachment strategies are considered to be "unresolved in respect of trauma or loss", and often their internal and external worlds are chaotic and unpredictable. As noted earlier, this client might have felt a sense of closeness developing that began to awaken anxiety, evoking the contradictory needs for both proximity and distance. Had I noticed this and named it in the sessions, perhaps the dilemma could have been resolved: I will never know for certain.

## *Clients who start on Skype and end face to face*

At the time of writing, I have experienced this only once, and I do not believe this is sufficient to make a generalisation. This therapy lasted twenty-seven months, eight months on Skype and the rest face to face. The sessions were begun as the client was moving to my area from a distance of some 200 miles, the move having been planned for six weeks after the beginning of the therapy. My suggestion that we should begin after the move was turned down, as the client wished to address the closure of some complex relationships at her current workplace. As it transpired, the relocation was delayed by some six months. This experience is very interesting to me because of how the therapeutic work deepened noticeably when the client was able to visit my practice. There is little doubt that if the client had not been relocating, the therapist chosen would have been one who lived within travelling distance. For me this raises a question: was the deepening of the work due to the move to the consulting room adding something integral to the therapy, or because the client experienced the fulfilment of the original plan?

## *Boundary setting and practicalities*

When contemplating working with Skype, it is important to consider effective boundary setting to enable both therapist and client to feel more comfortable in the work together. Each therapist, with time and experience, will find a way that works for them. I give some information on my way of working, not because I believe it to be the "right" way, but in order that therapists may consider their own choices more creatively.

Before I begin the work, I discuss in detail what will happen and where I believe the work may be compromised. We discuss how the client experiences this technology and its possible effects. We talk about the difficulties that might occur with connection problems and the like. I always make it clear that the client must call me, rather than I connecting to them; in this way, they come to the sessions as they would if they came to my practice. This allows for acting out such as turning up late for an appointment. I also arrange with the client that if, for any reason, we are unable to use Skype, or it disconnects and we are unable to reconnect, the client is to call me on the phone. This avoids the desperate situation of either one of us being engaged because we are calling each other. Having to end the session by phone has happened on a few occasions and, as would be expected, we talked about the rupture and worked towards its repair.

I inform my clients that Skype is owned by Microsoft and, as such, is accessible by them. In this regard it is not a 100% confidential medium, and the client needs to be informed of this. Although I have never heard of a Skype conversation being recorded or hacked, or even taped, it is possible that this could happen. Unless the client is well known, or has a high profile, the value of hacking or recording a Skype conversation is questionable, but the client needs to begin the therapy process having had a space to think about these implications.

In order to maintain boundaries, a separate professional Skype account can be set up. There is no cost, and maintaining a presence that is purely professional, where only clients can contact you, enables the therapist to access that mental place when using the computer for this work. This also prevents the disturbance to you and your client by the familiar ping when a member of your family or a friend comes online. It would be distracting to receive messages from others, asking to join your call. I would suggest, for the same reason, that you close your email and any other applications or programmes, rather than just collapsing them. The "ping" when an email is received can be an annoyance. Also, it is important that you adjust your settings so that other clients are unaware that you are online. The feelings evoked in a client can be akin to those of the client arriving early to your practice and seeing your last client leaving. Unlike when a client arrives for a session in person, without this setting adjustment, a client could be getting notification of you being online many times a week.

Consider where the computer is placed and what it is the client will view when they see you. What is the visual background? I ensure that the angle is one that would be as close to level as possible, and that the client can see me from the waist up. My computer is set up in such a way that it is in the consulting room and the client will be seeing me sitting in the chair in which I sit when I see face-to-face clients. Using a television table on which the computer or laptop can be placed, a few feet from me, enables this without too much trouble. I try to ensure that clients seen via Skype have, as much as possible, the same view of me as do my face-to-face clients. I suggest you have someone you know check out how you will be seen by your client before beginning the work. Ensure that the session is as close to face-to-face work for you as possible. Once you set up a position you are happy with, that is easy to repeat, the sessions become more about the work and less about the environment. The client is then able to reacquaint him or herself with the familiar view of you seated in your practice.

How we sit, what we wear, and how we make space for our clients indicates that this is not a social situation, but a very particular kind of relational therapeutic engagement. These details are important to note, especially if you are familiar with Skype through spending time with friends and family. Although becoming familiar with the technology through social use is helpful, when working with clients it is important to remember this encounter is not conversational, it is not spending time with friends, where you may be sprawled on the sofa, or bed. This is therapy, and there needs to be a distinction in your mind and in the mind of the client. When the client comes to see you in the same place, with the same demeanour, this becomes the "safe space", the "secure base" in which the work can be done. If the client is making a Skype call from a place where he or she habitually also Skypes friends and family, this distinction is especially important, as your demeanour may be the only trigger to the "therapeutic space" in the mind of the client.

## *Assessment*

Assessment via Skype is different from assessment in person. It gives the opportunity for both therapist and client to consider not only if working together is the right thing, but also whether working in this medium will be beneficial. Frequently, the client has not considered all the aspects of using Skype, only the ease of access, so the assessment and initial sessions are an important place in which to bring up these points for consideration by you both.

Following a face to face "consultation session", I give the client paperwork that includes the basic housekeeping information, such as the complaints procedure, payment for missed sessions, and so on. I also include a sheet that I ask them to sign and date, saying they have seen that document and have had the opportunity to discuss with me anything they felt they wanted to consider further. When working with Skype, I send the paperwork via email, and give the client the opportunity to ask questions at the "consultation session". Then I ask that they sign the relevant parts and return them to me.

## *The frozen screen*

Very often, therapists who are anxious about working using Skype cite as the reason for their reticence the difficulty in maintaining the therapeutic space due to possible interference from technical issues, specifically the Wi-Fi dropping out either on the side of the therapist or on the side of the client. Just as therapists occasionally experience someone knocking on the door of their practice, or roadworks outside causing disturbance, these difficulties are usually rare. The client's experience of the interference becomes part of the work. One of these disturbances is worth discussing a little further, however.

When working with Skype, the Wi-Fi dropping out can result in the visual frame freezing mid-sentence. The frozen face remains on the screen, the other cannot hear you, or see you. This can be dysregulating, and the affects can replicate the emotional disturbance observed in the "still-face paradigm" devised by Tronick and colleagues (1978). Mothers are filmed engaging with their three-month-old infants in face-to-face play. After two minutes, they are asked to maintain a still face, not responding, not speaking, and not smiling for a further two minutes, and then to interact as normally for the final two minutes of the test. The infants "attempted to solicit the mother's attention and when their efforts failed they looked away, withdrew, and expressed sad and angry affect" (Tronick, 2007, p. 11). Some infants become confused and have difficulty re-engaging after the still-face phase.

When working with Skype, I myself have experienced this disturbance and it has left me temporarily dysregulated. My concern quickly transferred to my client, and to regaining our connection. Discussing this with the client, either within the minute or so it takes to reconnect, or on the phone if connection is lost, often they will laugh, their relief at reconnection clear. Our work then is the vital repair that follows the rupture and strengthens our relationship. To demonstrate this strengthening, I quote from Tronick (2007) again:

> . . . [we] found that infants who experience frequent repairs of minor interactive errors (e.g., misreading of cues) during mother–infant face-to-face play were likely to elicit their mothers' attention using smiles and vocalizations during the still face. Infants who experienced fewer repairs were more likely to become distressed. (p. 312)

Far from being destructive, "[they] concluded that infants who routinely experience repairs have a representation of themselves as effective and of their mother as responsive and sensitive" (p. 313). The important point to note here is that the interruption itself will not be the damaging event over which therapists express anxiety. On the contrary, the effective working through of such a disturbance can strengthen the therapeutic alliance and increase the clients' sense of a strong and effective self.

## *Conclusion*

We are trained and skilled in conducting therapy face to face. We perfect our skills and our senses through extensive training and experience over many sessions with many clients. Then we consider conducting a therapy over the telephone, or via Skype. It is different, and we can fear that we are losing something important in the new medium that does not have the same feel. There is no surprise, then, that our instinct is to return to the arena where we have more confidence, in which we have been trained and supervised. However, with practice, with thought, with consideration, and with appropriate training, we can work as well and as effectively with other media as we can in person. As the British Association for Counselling and Psychotherapy notes, "Online provision is a specialist area, requiring a level of competence at least as high as that for face-to-face work. Competence as a therapist in one medium does not necessarily translate into another medium" (Anthony & Goss, 2009, p. 5) The benefit of this extra time and effort is the ability to engage with, and to help, groups of clients that at the present time are excluded from the beneficial work that is done in therapy.

When practising therapy with clients face to face, we consider, among many things, the effects of their attachment style on our experience of them, and their experience of the therapist, the therapy, and the world around them. That consideration helps us understand them better and attune to them more effectively. This is also the case when using the phone or Skype. These factors are not the only, or even the deciding, factors in the clients' choice (if, indeed, they have one), to approach us with a request for "distance therapy", but we are aided by our understanding of the relational aspects of the encounter.

I have no doubt that some of my telephone and Skype clients could have been helped more rapidly, or with greater ease, had we been able to work face to face, just as I am sure that there are clients who were unable to stay in therapy with me as long as may have been in their best interest, had they been able to proceed from the safety of their home or from the safe distance that the new media would enable.

My final thought is that for the majority of the clients with whom I work using the phone or Skype, these media have allowed important therapy to be continued when there has been no other choice and a break in the work would have been detrimental. Far from losing something of our relationship or the effectiveness of the therapy, these media have given us the opportunity to better understand our relationship and the way in which we relate to each other. For those who had no choice and have conducted a therapy that would otherwise not have happened, an opportunity for therapy has been taken, the results of which have changed the lives of people who otherwise would not have had that opportunity. In the engagement with these clients, we have experienced rupture and repair, we have discussed the effects of distance and the clients' sense of instant access to me the therapist, and we have felt each other and experienced real depth that in no way seems less to me than the experience of connectedness I feel with my face-to-face clients.

## *References*

Anthony, K., & Goss, S. (2009). *Guidelines for Online Counselling and Psychotherapy* (3rd edn). Lutterworth: British Association for Counselling and Psychotherapy.

Bayles, M. (2012). Is physical proximity essential to the psychoanalytic process? An exploration through the lens of Skype. *Psychoanalytic Dialogues, 22*: 569–585.

Beebe, B. (2005). Mother–infant research informs mother–infant treatment. *Psychoanalytic Study of the Child, 60*: 7–46.

Beebe, B., & Lachmann, F. M. (1998). Co-constructing inner and relational processes: self- and mutual regulation in infant research and adult treatment. *Psychoanalytic Psychology, 15*: 480–516.

Bowlby, J. (1988). *A Secure Base: Clinical Applications of Attachment Theory*. London: Routledge [reprinted 1993].

Carlino, R. (2011). *Distance Psychoanalysis: The Theory and Practice of Using Communication Technology in the Clinic*. London: Karnac.

Hesse, E., & Main, M. (2000). Disorganized infant, child, and adult attachment: collapse in behavioural and attentional strategies. *Journal of the American Psychoanalytic Association, 48*: 1097–1127

Kudiyarova, A. (2013). Psychoanalysis using Skype. In: J. Savege Scharff (Ed.), *Psychoanalysis Online: Mental Health, Teletherapy, and Training* (pp. 183–193). London: Karnac.

Main, M., & Morgan, H. (1996). Disorganization and disorientation in infant Strange Situation behavior: phenotypic resemblance to dissociative states? In: L. Michelson & W. Ray. (Eds.), *Handbook of Dissociation: Theoretical, Empirical and Clinical Perspectives* (pp. 107–138). New York: Plenum.

Prensky, M. (2001). Digital natives, digital immigrants. *On the Horizon, 9*(5): 1–6.

Scharff, J. S. (Ed.) (2013). *Psycoanalysis Online: Mental Health, Teletherapy, and Training*. London: Karnac.

Slade, A. (1999). Attachment theory and research: implications for the theory and practice of individual psychotherapy with adults. In: J. Cassidy & P. R. Shaver (Eds.), *Handbook of Attachment: Theory, Research, and Clinical Applications* (pp. 575–594). New York: Guilford Press.

Stern, D. N. (1985). *The Interpersonal World of the Infant: A View from Psychoanalysis and Developmental Psychology*. London: Karnac.

Thomas, E. A. C., & Malone, T. (1979). On the dynamics of two-person interactions. *Psychological Review, 86*: 331–360.

Trevarthen, C. (1999). Language development: mechanisms in the brain. In: G. Adelman & B. H. Smith (Eds.), *Encyclopedia of Neuroscience* (2nd edn). Amsterdam: Elsevier.

Tronick, E. (2007). *The Neurobehavioral and Social-Emotional Development of Infants and Children.* New York: W. W. Norton.

Tronick, E. Z., Als, H., Adamson, L., Wise, S., & Brazelton, T. B. (1978). The infant's response to entrapment between contradictory messages in face-to-face interaction. *Journal of the American Academy of Child and Adolescent Psychiatry, 17*: 1–13.

*CHAPTER SEVEN*

# Finding words: the use of email in psychotherapy with a disorganised and dissociating client

*Tony Hanford*

## *Introduction*

The following is a true story, based on my recollection of various events in the therapy. The name and identifying characteristics of my client have been changed in order to protect her anonymity, and I have rearranged and/or compressed events and time periods in service of the narrative. Extracts from the client's emails have been reproduced here without alteration, in her own words, as has a poem she wrote early in the therapy.

As an attachment-based psychoanalytic psychotherapist and experienced mental health practitioner, I am sensitive to issues of attachment, separation, and loss. I also have a clear understanding of severe disturbance and the therapeutic needs of clients with unresolved traumatic histories. My approach is grounded in the creation of an empathic therapeutic relationship where I recognise the powerful effects of unconscious, preverbal, and non-verbal dimensions of communication. I am committed to practising psychotherapy within the clarity and containment of the psychoanalytic frame, and the management of boundaries was of central importance in this therapy, undertaken while I was a trainee.

I am grateful to my client for her consent to publish this account of our work together.

## *My client: Ava*

One of my first training clients, whom I will call Ava, had a chaotic inner world mirrored by a troubled, anxiety-evoking life situation. When referred, she was an attractive twenty-eight-year-old married woman without children, working with the public in a large organisation. Struggling in a difficult long-term relationship, she told me that she had been in one relationship or another since adolescence with few gaps in between. She sought out therapy with me to try to understand her low self-esteem and her battles with intrusive thoughts and feelings. These frequently led her to self-harm by cutting and burning her skin, a compulsion she constantly struggled to stay in control of. Her attachment style was somewhat avoidant within our sessions and—I was to discover—preoccupied in our contact between. She was highly disorganised in relation to trauma and prone to frequent bouts of dissociation.

My first task in therapy was to engage Ava, set boundaries for the work, and create the basis for a safe therapeutic relationship. As the work progressed, she frequently contacted me between sessions via email. I soon found myself in a position of holding disturbing information (for instance, about her self-harming and other risk-taking behaviour) but being unable to intervene. However, by making decisions about clear boundaries and keeping to them, despite the anxiety this entailed for me, I was able to provide her with a sense of safety. I also encouraged her to engage with local mental health services for further containment, enabling our work together to continue. At this early stage in training, my style of working was to acknowledge the presence and power of transference, but to make transference interpretations only occasionally. Likewise, I rarely made direct use of the countertransference, but instead used the responses she evoked in me to carefully direct my empathy and attunement.

## *Disorganised attachment and dissociation*

Davies and Frawley (1994) posited that the major psychic damage done by abuse or neglect is not caused by the actions or events themselves, but, rather, by the interrelationship between the experiences and the client's attachment system. They describe the clinical presentation of sexually abused clients as characterised by an inconsistent combination of primitive and disruptive symptoms and alternate high functioning. Such clients can present as highly emotional and reactive (showing an extreme degree of affect dysregulation), or emotionally cold and split-off.

Wallin (2007) describes dissociation as a kind of disintegration that includes "the self-protective splitting off of an unbearable state of mind . . . from other states of mind that are more tolerable" (p. 247). Dissociation, argues Wallin, also refers to a "defensively altered, trance-like state of consciousness" (p. 247) into which the client may fall when the trauma resurfaces in the mind. He stresses that both kinds of dissociation play a central role in the psychotherapy of unresolved clients.

> Unresolved patients, by making reality less real, by spacing out, by becoming drowsy, and so on, have been able to blunt the impact of experiences they feared would overwhelm them. Yet, the same altered state that keeps painful realities at bay also makes it impossible for those realities to be confronted effectively. (Wallin, 2007, p. 248)

## *Establishment, development, and pattern of email contact*

From the beginning, Ava felt unsafe in my consulting room. She found eye contact difficult to manage and became shy and withdrawn as sessions progressed. Defending against this, she often assured me that she was usually confident and sociable with friends or work clients. She struggled with having the focus of therapy on her, and sometimes said that she would rather be the therapist than the client, as this seemed less frightening. Ava talked about the difficulty of expressing her feelings verbally and suggested that she might sometimes write things down and send them to me. I told her that she could email me between sessions if she wished, and although I might not respond straight away, I would always read the email and would then invite her to talk it through with me in the next session.

As the therapy progressed, Ava started to send me long emails repeating what we had discussed in previous sessions, but her state of mind seemed more open and communicative, and she was more in touch with painful feelings in these written messages. Back in the therapy room, she found my attempts to instigate conversation about her emails difficult and she was resistant to discussing them with me. She was often passive in her responses, saying she no longer felt connected to the material emotionally, although she could relate to what I was saying intellectually. She often deliberately changed the subject, and this became established between us as a cue that she no longer felt able to discuss the material today. In retrospect, I can see how I was trying to help Ava gradually "titrate" her unintegrated experience. By gradually exposing her to small amounts of her distress at a time, in the context of a secure attachment relationship, I found that she began to develop the tolerance and capacity to manage her difficult emotions, to regulate affect.

Writing things down had multiple functions for my client: it was a coping strategy between sessions, a method of keeping both connection with, and distance from, me, a way of letting go of feelings and of remembering what might otherwise be dissociated. Ava talked about using email to record and hold on to her thoughts and feelings, saying that she needed to do this straight away or else they would be lost. She described her fear of this information being found and used against her by other people in her life. In sending something to me and then deleting it on her own computer, she was keeping it safe and protecting it from discovery: splitting and projecting on to me, a good object, and keeping herself safe from the bad object(s) in her internal world. She was effectively trusting me as the caretaker of her distress, sending me parts of herself that she was currently experiencing as unmanageable to hold on to, to contain them for her for a while.

The conflictual functions of Ava's email messages (to simultaneously remember and forget) were evidence of splits in her self-states. Davies and Frawley (1994) argue that, with traumatised clients, a minimum of two different selves form and are likely to appear in therapy. Recognising and interacting with these selves is difficult, as some might be non-verbal and only initially available in a language of "disembodied images, dreamlike states, somatic memories and physiological states of hyper-arousal and disorganization" (p. 55). They believe that it is essential to build up a relationship based on containing and holding the client's overwhelming states and affects.

Recovering and verbalising traumatic memories is a precondition for integrating the splits in the client's self- and object-representations.

> I have been thinking about the sessions and that I seem to find it difficult to talk and recall feelings when I am in that room. I think it's probably a combination of the focus being all on me, and also that sometimes in situations I seem to at the time experience and feel them, and then afterwards only remember what happened and the feelings associated seem to disappear somewhere. I quite often find it easier to write about feelings than to talk about them, so I decided when I wasn't feeling that great that I would start to write stuff down so that I could let go of how I felt which makes it easier to cope, and also it would help me remember it which might be helpful at some point to look back on. (Ava, email)

### *First phase: establishing safety*

Ava's attacks on herself induced strong feelings of concern and protectiveness in me. I had to work hard to contain and process my countertransference anxieties while creating a safe therapeutic environment in which useful therapy could take place. Boundary issues (such as how to respond to out-of-session email communication) required careful thought: I needed to reflect on the meaning behind her challenges to the therapeutic frame, as well as deciding on the most useful way to respond. I used supervision to consider the emotions, sensations, and thoughts evoked in me, and attempt to separate what I brought to the situation from what were unconscious communications from the client.

Herman (1992) describes how the psychotherapist experiences (to a lesser degree) the same terror, rage, and shame as the traumatised client, and this can be emotionally overwhelming for the therapist. She argues that the therapist's adverse reactions must be understood and contained, or else they will lead to disruptions in the therapeutic alliance. Herman describes how the "patient's symptoms simultaneously call attention to the existence of an unspeakable secret and deflect attention from that secret" (p. 146), and that "the first apprehension that there may be a traumatic history often comes from the therapist's countertransference reactions" while "rapid fluctuations in the patient's cognitive state may leave the therapist with sense of unreality" (p. 146). This was certainly my experience as Ava's psychotherapist.

Before Ava was able to talk about the issues underlying her low self-esteem, we had first to spend a long period of time establishing safety. The great majority of the literature on trauma has developed this theme. There is a major focus on the importance of this first stage, working towards safety, structure, and the ability to self-regulate (Davies & Frawley, 1994; Herman, 1992; van der Hart, Nijenhuis, & Steele, 2006; Wallin, 2007). Some authors argue that, for complex patients, it might not always be necessary or appropriate to move on to further stages, and that the decision to progress beyond stage one should always be the client's. The first of Bowlby's (1988) five therapeutic tasks was to provide clients with a secure enough base to enable them to access painful thoughts and feelings from the past or present. Similarly, Wallin (2007) describes how creating a relationship in which the client can actually feel safe is difficult, yet essential. "It should be seen as both the ultimate goal of therapy and a precondition for beginning to resolve the patient's trauma" (p. 245).

For Ava, establishing safety meant facilitating her gradual reduction of self-harming behaviours and their replacement with alternative strategies for affect regulation in response to the triggers in her life. It also meant supporting and encouraging her to engage with other sources of support external to the therapy. On my suggestion, she met several times with her general practitioner, who eventually referred her to the Community Mental Health Team (CMHT). Ava found these meetings with her doctor difficult, as she felt that all the responsibility was put back on her, without the offer of practical advice to keep her safe from self-harm. My supervisor suggested that some of the frustration she was expressing might also relate to her sessions with me: she might be telling me that I was also failing to offer her anything practical or useful that would keep her safe from herself, and that I was also putting all the responsibility back on to her.

Her early relationship with the CMHT was also fraught with problems. In one instance, she described being shocked when the social worker assessing her asked to see the scars from her self-harming. I saw this as a coded communication to me—the social worker had crossed a boundary, and Ava was warning *me* against a similar intrusion in the future. She decided to write to the CMHT asking for a different social worker and emailed me a copy of the letter. It was firm, acknowledging, and polite. It clearly stated her needs and the way in which she wanted the CMHT to work to help her address her problems: the high-functioning aspect of her personality was evident. Again, I saw this as communicative. What Ava was requesting from the CMHT very much linked to the way she had asked me to work with her; to first make it safe enough for her to think and feel before asking her to talk.

As therapy progressed, Ava's negative obsessive thoughts worsened and her attacks on herself escalated as we began to talk about self-harm. We discussed the difficulty of establishing safety in her life without cutting or burning her skin—for Ava, attacks on her body had the function of keeping her *mind* safe. Wallin (2007) describes how the bodies of clients who dissociate "can thus become a battleground on which psychological issues are fought out" (p. 249). He describes how

> patients who dissociate may wind up in a panic when they begin to feel cut off from themselves and from their bodies—necessitating dramatic measures to reconnect. Self-mutilation in the form of cutting, burning, or beating themselves enables such patients to feel more embodied again. (p. 249)

Mollon also conveys how precarious therapy with a self-harming client can be:

> Self harm, violent self-stimulation or other forms of distracting action may be resorted to in order to keep away threatening mental contents. The therapist need do no more than listen attentively in order for the patient to be traumatised by what is in his/her mind. (Mollon, 1996, p. 69)

Ava and I acknowledged the difficulty of talking about self-harm directly in the therapy room. Her emails functioned as an extension and development of the therapy, and she would use them to make links to the feelings of anger, sadness, frustration, and guilt that often followed the sessions.

> . . . I feel as though I'm going to explode. All my feelings, memories and thoughts are building up inside me and I have to get rid of them. I have to get them out of my body before they infect the rest of me . . . As I lower the blade into my skin and let it glide freely, I can feel

> the freedom enter me . . . I am in control of my thoughts and my pain. I feel strengthened as the pain drains from me . . . It is not this pain that I loathe, it is the pain that I have no control over that I hate, the pain that other people force upon me. It is this that I cannot live with, it pollutes my body and I can only get rid of it by creating pain that I can control . . . (Ava, email)

These messages were also used as a form of avoidance at times. I received some email messages telling me in explicit detail that she had done something she was ashamed of, such as taking an overdose, and making it clear that she was informing me about it in this way in order to side-step having to talk about it with me face to face.

Ava always found self-harming far easier to write about in an email than to talk about directly with me. For a long while, although she initially felt contained when she managed to talk briefly about it in the room with me, she would be overcome with panic when she was alone later, and would often then self-harm once again in an attempt to regulate the horrendous thoughts and feelings that threatened to overwhelm her. However, over time, she gradually came to feel safe enough to begin to explore it tentatively in the room with me, at least to the extent that she did not then feel as if she was falling apart once she was alone later. Around six months into the therapy, her self-harming had reduced to about once weekly and was less severe when it did occur. I also noticed her emails becoming increasingly coherent when talking about difficult feelings and behaviours compared to even a few months earlier.

## *Middle phase: uncovering past abuse*

As we began to touch on more difficult experiences, thoughts, and feelings in our sessions, transference and communicative material was increasingly evoked. Ava continued to use email to communicate aspects of herself that were split off or shameful, involving me in a complex dynamic where I found myself cast in the role of a protective, intimate care-giver and confidant, as well as a helpless onlooker as she acted out her distress. By using supervision to constantly reflect on how I was being "used" in my work with her, I was gradually able to respond with greater sensitivity and clarity.

Wallin (2007) argues that the client's defences play a role in evoking the therapist's countertransference and, "because that which is evoked in the therapist is often enacted with the patient, these defences exert considerable influence in shaping the therapeutic relationship" (p. 247). He describes a process of defensive projective identification whereby "In the process of relocating dissociated experience in us, the patient treats us in such a way as to evoke in us what he cannot bear in himself and we come to identify with it" (p. 249). The therapist feels this non-verbal communication, often viscerally, and comes to identify with it.

Throughout our work together, I was functioning as a container for the feelings and anxieties Ava put into me, holding them for a while before finding words to make sense of her distress, and then returning her experiences to her in a more manageable form. At the time, I was unable to fully recognise my function and its importance, as I was too focused on trying to hold my boundaries in the face of a barrage of distressed and overwhelming messages. Looking back through her emails and my responses, I am struck by how boundaried, sometimes cold, my responses were, as I repeatedly invited her to bring things back into the session, back into the room. Perhaps this apparent coolness reflected my own struggle to contain two sets of anxiety, Ava's and my own.

> To sit with a patient, I have to be willing to explore my own pain and the defences I used to protect myself from the pain. What this means is containing both their and my feelings and experiences. The containing function I perform I see as the most basic and most important thing I do throughout the therapy. Being able to explore and contain my own feelings precedes being able to contain the feelings of my patients. (Stevens, 1996, p. 194)

The breakthrough moment came after the first long summer break, during which Ava discovered she was pregnant with her first child. After resuming our work together for a few weeks, she emailed me between sessions, apparently in a dissociated state, implying that a significant traumatic event had happened to her in the past that was still affecting her. At this stage in our work together, I did not know that the trauma she was hinting at was a rape, although, based on her clinical presentation and my countertransference responses to her, I was almost certain that she had experienced some kind of sexual abuse in her past. She had hinted about this in a number of previous emails, but this was her first direct acknowledgment to me (and, indeed, to herself) that perhaps she did finally need to talk about it with someone.

> Sometimes i feel like you're helping me to piece together a jigsaw. But i know inside that there are some big pieces missing ... Recently i think those things, big pieces have moved up nearer to the surface, and i am finding them really difficult to cope with ... I guess i have two choices: bury them again and hope they don't resurface (but ultimately i know that they will) or face them, and hope that i get through it. The thing is i know that they are significant reasons as to why i hate myself and that filters down and affects so many other things; therefore i know that it would probably, maybe, help to talk about them but i am scared of letting the words out into the open. (Ava, email)

The impact of telling me about the trauma was initially too much for her. She was overwhelmed, feeling unstable and out of control, and frequently dissociated by self-harming. Despite this, she did not give up, and I felt that her pregnancy was an important factor in Ava's determination to finally begin dealing with what she experienced as the pollution inside of herself. She quickly came to feel increasingly protective of the "baby inside", both of the physical baby growing inside her and also in its potent symbolism for the childlike part of herself she had not, thus far, been able to protect. She wanted to try talking about it in her sessions with me, not just in her emails, but first she needed my help to stay safe while coping with the feelings that were inevitably stirred up for her afterwards. Over the coming months, we continued to work on the trauma, both in sessions and via email. Ava struggled with the difficulty of talking about the past, the seeming futility of it, the impossibility of changing what had happened. She wanted to bury it again, but knew it would come back to the surface. The good work, the progress we were making in sessions, was repeatedly attacked by her internalised aggressor.

> ... my head is throwing all the memories at me, I feel disgusting, I feel like my skin is crawling with disgusting dirty infestations which are eating away at me and making me all putrid and stagnant. I want the smells to go away and the noises. Why is my mind doing this to me? I can't do the things I need to do because I feel too guilty now, and too

> much like I want to look after this baby inside me. But I don't know how else to make it go away or at least numb it down a bit. I don't feel safe, in myself, from myself, from life, from memories, from my mind . . . (Ava, email)

Main (1995) and Hesse (1999) propose that the client's apparent shifts in states of consciousness, detached tones of voice, present tense descriptions of the past, and lengthy pauses can be understood to reflect the disorganising and disorientating return of the dissociated. Similarly, Wallin (2007) describes how "the internal world of unresolved patients is built to a greater or lesser degree on working models and states of mind that have to be defensively dissociated from one another" (p. 248) and that "Such a history leaves radical discontinuities in the internal world of the adult, resulting in a vulnerability to sudden shifts from ordinary to overwhelming states of mind" (p. 248). "Round after round of attunement, misattunement, and interactive repair are usually necessary before the unresolved patient can begin to trust in the emotionally regulating potential of the new relationship" (Wallin, 2007, p. 252).

* * *

Initially, I gave only brief, boundaried responses to Ava's emails, but I now began working more actively with her via email itself, summarising the content of her messages, empathising and encouraging her, even making interpretations. In my replies, I reflected that she no longer felt able to access any of her coping strategies, and that she felt under pressure to get better. I said I was aware that a double bind was being set up in her therapy, whereby she wanted to face up to the difficult feelings inside herself, but became scared and backed away from them. She then felt like a failure and feared I would get fed up with her because she was not getting better quickly enough. I repeatedly told her that psychotherapy took as long as it took. I stressed that she was working on painful automatic feelings and that a lot of emotional edging forward and backwards was normal in this work and did not mean she was a failure.

We continued together in this way until therapy was interrupted by the impending birth of her child. Ava struggled in the first few months after having her baby. Her social worker referred her to the Crisis Team and she had regular contact with them as well. She felt that they were holding her, but that she was only treading water. She tried a few different kinds of medication, but her psychiatrist felt that changing medication would not necessarily help, as her feelings were linked to past issues and ongoing conflict with her partner. Ava later reported that the relationship between herself and her partner had improved since the Crisis Team and her psychiatrist met with him individually. These meetings seemed to have helped him better understand and relate to her situation. This was also an extra source of support for him that, although unacknowledged, was probably much needed.

## *Final phase: beginning to heal trauma*

A few months after the birth of her son, Ava resumed email contact. She had started to experience flashbacks in the form of nightmares and visions, and had reached a point where she realised once again that burying her difficulties did not work. For the first time, she had written down detailed memories of rape that evoked shame for her. She was beginning to realise that this was where much of her self-hatred and low self-esteem originated. Ava said that, although it might not seem like it from the outside, she felt I had helped her come a long way in her own mind. She would never have been able to write these details down or use the "r" word before. I felt incredibly proud of her and emailed her back to tell her how brave I thought she had been and what a big step forward this was.

> I want to highlight the importance with most unresolved patients of recalling experiences of traumatic events and putting them into words, rather than simply re-experiencing trauma related feelings in a relationship with the therapist . . . When old traumatic experiences can be revisited without the patient feeling re-traumatized, the memories of trauma are changed. (Wallin, 2007, p. 253)

Over the next month, we communicated via email in preparation for her return for a brief period of twice-weekly sessions, with the focus on talking about her rape and the trauma she had experienced afterwards. The explicitness with which she was able to reveal these memories in her emails fluctuated constantly, something she found very frustrating. Clearly, she was struggling with dissociation and needed to manage potentially dysregulating thoughts and feelings, especially because she now had a baby to care for. I assured her I would try my best to make sessions safe for her, and that we could proceed at whatever pace she needed. After a number of weeks working together, and as we were approaching the end of the agreed period, Ava sent me a long email where she finally told me everything that had happened in a coherent, sequential way.

She described how, from early in her childhood, she had found herself used as an object by others, always needing to be liked, and finding it impossible to set boundaries or to say no. She talked about feeling good and powerful when she felt in control, crushed and powerless when she did not. She told me all the details of the rape, what happened, when, and how. She talked of her disgust and her belief that her life was ruined forever. In my reply to her email, I acknowledged how difficult it must have been for her to finally put all of this into words, and simply said that she was not disgusting, that she deserved to be loved and cared for. When we met for the final session, we were able to talk through everything she had told me, but not in as much detail or with the same passion and connectedness as in her email. Some time later she sent me the following:

> I wanted to say thank you for helping me start to talk about things. I think you would see quite a difference in me now in how I am able to talk about things that have happened in the past and what's happening in the present . . . It's a shame I struggled so much to do it in the past sessions with you, I guess it was the first time that I'd tried; but if I hadn't have tried with you and if you hadn't have been so supportive and patient, I wouldn't be able to talk about things now. So thank you. (Ava, email)

## *Post therapy: continuing to work through the trauma*

Since our work together ended over two years ago, Ava has communicated with me from time to time by email up to the present day. She has continued to have periods of support from the CMHT and Crisis Team, and has gone on to have a second child with her partner. She has also completed a course of one-to-one cognitive–behavioural therapy and has recently started attending a large psychodynamic therapy group. In other words, she is continuing the difficult work she started with me in our sessions together and via her emails.

### *Little person inside (a poem by Ava)*

I don't mean to make you not feel wanted, I don't mean to make you feel like i don't care. I think it was a shock to find that you were living in there.

I hope that it's comfortable, i hope that it's cosy, i hope that you can relax and know that you are safe.

Things are just a bit tough at the moment—through no fault of your own. I thought these things were sorted, I thought some things would never resurface, but they have and i am trying to do the right thing and sort them out now. If i can.

When i cut i'm not cutting to hurt you, when i burn i'm hoping it doesn't reach you. It's no reflection on you, it's me that i hate not you. When i think about killing myself, at those times i've lost focus on you. It's me i'm trying to end, not a life with you. Since i found out you were there so far i've resisted doing things that i know will hurt you inside, i hope i manage to be strong because i know you don't deserve that.

I know i sound selfish and like i don't care, but when i'm down it's hard to explain, i'm just too tired to carry on. But i need to remember that what affects me will affect you and i know that's just not fair. I promise to try that bit harder, and say no to those pills that sit and stare. They coax me and taunt me but i need to remember that you are in my care.

I'm just scared at the moment, this is all very unknown to me, but we're going to get through it, i promise, you'll see.

No matter what i think about myself, no matter what i put us through, please remember that you are wanted, and i love you

(Written early on in the therapy in response to discovering that she was pregnant.)

## *Conclusion*

Ava had a disorganised attachment style and often dissociated in relation to memories of past abuse. Starting from very early on in the therapy, she communicated with me via email between appointments: these messages were often lengthy and contained a lot of material that she was unable to bring into the session directly. They often seemed to have been written while she was dissociated, and were also a form *of* dissociation. Over time, the emails effectively became a concurrent, but separate, therapy. A major part of our work together involved containment of intense affects while gradually trying to bring these fragmented self-states together in the consulting room.

Theoretically, I have considered attachment perspectives on trauma, dissociation, and use of the countertransference in learning to work effectively with a client with an unresolved attachment style, drawing especially on the work of Davies and Frawley (1994), Herman (1992), and Wallin (2007). In retrospect, I recognise that this therapy closely followed Herman's (1992) model for therapy with victims of trauma. Her three stages of recovery (establishing safety, remembering and mourning, reconnecting) seem to fit well with the shape of this therapy.

While I found theory useful in informing my clinical decisions and in helping me to think in stressful, complicated situations, theoretical constructs cannot be imposed on a live therapy. For a large part of the time I was working with Ava, I attended a weekly clinical supervision group at the Bowlby Centre. This group, along with my individual supervision, was invaluable in helping me contain the anxiety evoked by the client's self-harming behaviours, reflect on the meaning of her communications, consider the role of boundaries in the work, and formulate therapeutic decisions.

As an attachment based psychoanalytic psychotherapist, I am well aware of the impact of intergenerational trauma. Disorganised attachment in adults is also termed "unresolved trauma", and most often results from being parented by a traumatised attachment figure. In the therapy reported here, we did not reach material about the relational histories of Ava's parents, but it is my hope that this therapy may have helped, to some extent, to protect Ava's children from the potential damage of having a traumatised parent. The quality of attachment—secure, insecure, or disorganised and disorganising—that a parent can offer a child is shaped by the extent to which traumatic events have been resolved and integrated.

I want to end by highlighting how everything I have written about email illustrates the vital role that technology played in this therapy. As a contemporary form of the written word, an email is concrete, a permanent record of fleeting self-states. Telephone messages would not have the same function for Ava as the written word, and, indeed, she refused to consider the possibility of holding extra sessions on the phone in a crisis. Likewise, writing a diary and bringing it to me (rather than instantly sending it to me) may not have provided enough holding. Indeed, when Ava did occasionally bring written material into my room with her, she found herself unable to look at it with me during the session. Without email, perhaps Ava could not have made the progress she did.

## *References*

Bowlby, J. (1988). *A Secure Base: Clinical Applications of Attachment Theory.* Hove: Brunner-Routledge.

Davies, J. M., & Frawley, M. G. (1994). *Treating the Adult Survivor of Childhood Sexual Abuse: A Psychoanalytic Perspective.* New York: Basic Books.

Herman, J. L. (1992). *Trauma and Recovery: From Domestic Abuse to Political Terror.* London: Pandora.

Hesse, E. (1999). The adult attachment interview: historical and current perspectives. In: J. Cassidy & P. R. Shaver (Eds.), *Handbook of Attachment: Theory, Research and Clinical Applications* (pp. 395–433). New York: Guilford Press.

Main, M. (1995). Attachment: overview, with implications for clinical work. In: S. Goldberg, R. Muir, & J. Kerr (Eds.), *Attachment Theory: Social, Developmental, and Clinical Perspectives* (pp. 407–474). New York: Guilford Press.

Mollon, P. (1996). *Multiple Selves, Multiple Voices: Working with Trauma, Violation and Dissociation.* Chichester: Wiley.

Stevens, B. F. (1996). The effects of sexual trauma on the self in clinical work. In: B. Gerson (Ed.), *The Therapist as a Person: Life Crises, Life Choices, Life Experiences, and Their Effects on Treatment* (pp. 183–206), Analytic Press.

Van der Hart, O., Nijenhuis, E. R. S., & Steele, K. (2006). *The Haunted Self: Structural Dissociation and the Treatment of Chronic Traumatization.* New York: Norton.

Wallin, D. J. (2007). *Attachment in Psychotherapy.* New York: Guilford Press.

CHAPTER EIGHT

# The ethereal m/other

*Linda Cundy*

"I'm inclined to think that we're all ghosts"

(Ibsen, 1964)

## *Introduction*

Computers, smartphones, and tablets are portals into parallel universes. We invest the devices themselves with significance, often taking their wizardry for granted, yet depending on them utterly. The meaning a patient ascribes to the device and its many functions is significant and may reflect something of his or her personal "aesthetic" (Bollas, 1987). How these relationships with technology play out in the therapy can provide insights into the inner world of the patient.

## *Julie*

"Attachment disorder" is an extremely unusual diagnosis for an adult, yet an astute psychiatrist had recognised the features in Julie and recommended twice-weekly attachment-focused psychotherapy. Julie herself searched the Internet for suitable therapists, found my website, and made an initial approach via email requesting a meeting.

In her fifties, divorced, and with adult children, Julie worked in an office environment and was popular with her colleagues. However, she suffered from chronic depression that could not be treated with medication due to a physiological intolerance of antidepressants. When I first met her, she described a feeling of profound inner emptiness and a sense of not knowing who she was. Indeed, there seemed to be two Julies—one who drove to work each morning and chatted in a friendly if superficial way to people around her, and a different person who emerged from the depths when she was alone. This was an angry, frightened, and despairing woman who felt alienated from everybody, even her children, whom she dearly loved. In fact, this character seemed more like a child herself. It became clear that she longed to feel intimacy and connection, yet it took an act of will to be with people.

Human contact was problematic for Julie. She felt ashamed about her clinging, demanding, needy behaviour that was evident in many previous relationships. The first of these began at school with a female teacher when she was eleven or twelve years old and continued until recently. They were intense attachments she formed to people whom she could not bear to be separated from. She would stalk them, wait outside their doors, and telephone them repeatedly at all hours. Some were social relationships, others professional, but the one feature they had in common was that these individuals had shown kindness to her, and this opened up an intolerable longing to be loved and physically held. On one occasion, the husband of her object of affection eventually intervened to prevent further intrusion into his wife's life—Julie had been too much for her. While in therapy with me, she was also receiving some complementary treatment that was due to end. Feeling rejected by the impending termination, she acted out with furious tirades, directing numerous telephone calls and emails of complaint, peppered with expletives, to the practitioner and his manager. She forwarded this correspondence to me. I had been warned.

Julie's need for symbiotic closeness overwhelmed her and drove other people away. She was afraid of this pattern repeating, especially at work, so she developed an effective false self to keep an emotional distance from those who showed her warmth. But the façade dissolved once she was alone and she ruminated over all the interactions of the day. By night-time she would be frantic, angry with those who had taunted her with kindness, terrified that she had responded inappropriately, yearning for love and security. This is when she turned to the Internet.

My patient frequented chat rooms and self-help forums. She communicated with individuals around the world who also suffered with depression and who had established a virtual self-help community. She solicited their concern, encouragement, and prayers, and offered the same in return. Her connection with disembodied others crossed temporal and geographical boundaries, a disembodied experience of timelessness that rekindled unconscious memories and states. She gave herself over to remote, ethereal others to provide her with emotional containment.

Meanwhile, Julie had found other strategies to prevent her fragile sense of self from disintegrating. She was a prolific diarist, charting the subtle shifts from depression to desperation and despair that swept over her in the early hours, tapping her inner world into the containing memory of her smartphone. When she finally slept, she dreamed profusely. Her dream landscapes were usually monochrome with just one object rendered in colour (one colourful internal object), recalling a famous scene from Spielberg's film, *Schindler's List*. These inner worlds were populated with starving, neglected babies with haunted eyes, and ghostly figures in gloomy houses. The environments were reminiscent of her childhood in post-war London.

Julie was the second child born to a depressed mother and sentimental but violent father in the East End. The family struggled financially. She remembered a "loving" mother, albeit one who did not hold her or delight in her. Several times during her infancy, mother was confined to a psychiatric hospital; on at least one of these occasions this followed a suicide attempt. The children were sent away to stay with a relative during each hospital admission. Then mother was diagnosed with cancer and eventually died when Julie was eleven or twelve, leaving her adrift and afraid, with only the memory of an enigmatic maternal presence. This led to her first obsessive relationship with a schoolteacher.

Julie seemed to live in a world of ghosts. She described paranormal experiences and the sense of a "presence" near her at times. She took this to be her mother watching over her, yet it rarely comforted her. She demanded a real substantial mother to cradle her, stroke her hair, and whisper loving words. Both of these features—the insubstantial maternal object and the demand for an embodied attachment figure—found expression in the therapy.

Julie had an extreme form of preoccupied attachment characterised by intense hunger for love and reassurance, desperate fear of abandonment, and furious protest when she felt rejected. Longitudinal research has highlighted inconsistent responsiveness to the child's needs as a key feature in the early lives of preoccupied people—parents sometimes recognise and respond to their child's fears and distress, but at other times they are distracted, wrapped up in their own troubles, or even punitive when the child needs reassurance. There is enough love to tantalise and evoke a craving, but it cannot be counted on. This certainly fitted with the picture of childhood painted by my patient.

### *Therapy*

Early on in therapy, Julie began to send me occasional emails between sessions. Her preoccupied attachment style alerted me to her need for a reliable, predictable relationship and I decided not to respond to these messages. As there would be occasions when I might be away or busy, I decided it was better not to tantalise her by acknowledging some of her communications—her calls for attachment—and not others. I explained this to her, invoking the early memories of a small child seeking out her mother's lap and submerging herself in intimate connection only to be pushed away the next time. However, I understood that this would be experienced as a rejection or abandonment to somebody with an extreme preoccupied attachment style, so I agreed that Julie could continue to send her emails if it helped her, and I would do my best to read them before the next session. These messages were written at night in a liminal, other-worldly space when she was able to access states of mind that were unavailable in our daytime sessions, attended during her lunch-breaks from work. I believed it would be valuable to read these communications in advance of the therapy appointment, where possible.

However, Julie began to attach ever-longer excerpts from her journal, which she also printed out and brought to sessions to read aloud to me. But by the time we were sitting together in the consulting room,

Julie was no longer connected to the content or feeling states of her diary entries. Rather than aiding communication, this reading of a text seemed to block the connection between us—it sapped the life from the relationship and created a gulf, which I sometimes despaired of bridging.

I started to feel the pressure of this relationship as the emails became ever more frequent and I could not keep up with her hunger for my time and attention, the insistent starving baby greedy for life-giving contact. I was being stalked through the ether. On one occasion, a Monday appointment, I had not yet read the weekend's messages. Julie was furious, accusing me of being cold and heartless. She left the session early in protest. Two days later, she returned for the next appointment with a peace offering, a Christmas cactus covered in pink buds. I accepted her reparative gift as a symbol. We agreed that the plant represented Julie herself. It was to live in my consulting room, to be watered, fed, and re-potted by me. She would have a symbolic presence near me and I would nurture her through my care of the plant. It was my intention to take cuttings and eventually present the new plant to Julie to care for and enjoy herself.

With clear, predictable boundaries, the initial intense attachment did not become obsessive: it gradually evolved into something safe that she could enjoy and absorb. In one later journal entry, she commented that this felt like a very ordinary relationship, and that was a great relief to her.

Over time, Julie's use of chat rooms declined. This seemed to be in parallel with a gradual "letting go" of her mother as we made her into a more substantial object. Through exploring their relationship, creating a narrative of it, imagining who mother was in her own context, we gradually put her into perspective. One session, she brought a poem written by her mother, who, like Julie, had a gift for evocative words. Julie's journal keeping also changed as she started to document the good things she was creating in her life as well as her darker moments, and she felt less need to send these entries to me or read from them during her sessions. I began to understand that her email messages had been an ethereal intrusion into the therapy, used to turn me into an unreachable, insubstantial mother, a mother who could not be a transformational object (Bollas, 1987). Her dreams were changing, too—the babies were more robust now, still unkempt but no longer neglected or close to death.

A few days before Christmas, two and a half years into the therapy and at the start of our winter break, I received another email message from Julie. She had been experiencing abdominal pain and wanted me to know the results of the latest medical tests. She had received shocking news; the consultant had given the diagnosis of a rare form of inoperable cancer. With no support as yet in place from her hospital over Christmas and my absence until the New Year, this was one message I had to respond to.

### *Ghosts*

During the first months of cancer treatment, Julie was in shock, fear, and pain, and often nauseous from chemotherapy. She turned again to Internet chat rooms for comfort, contacting spiritualists to give her guidance, and Christian Scientists, who prayed for her. I felt she was reaching out into the void in anticipation of her death, trying to connect again with her mother in the hope that maternal arms would be there to greet her "on the other side" when her time came. The online presences, available day or night, were the disembodied comforting arms and soothing voice of the dead mother once more watching over her. They were *almost* real. Julie also resumed the virtual dimension of her relationship with me, regularly forwarding wise words, spiritual messages, and evocative photographs that she found on the Internet. I received these, but did not reply.

However, for a few brief months she finally found peace. Her family rallied around her, caring for her tenderly. Even her ex-husband proved himself a reliable and affectionate companion. In the moments when her pain was under control, and while treatment still held out some hope, she could finally relax into the very real embrace of her loved ones to be stroked and held.

By summer, the pain returned—the tumour was not responding to treatment. We maintained erratic contact via email over the break, and when I next saw her she was tired and breathless. Regular sessions were now disrupted by medical appointments and often by her exhaustion. Where possible, I re-scheduled, but when that could not be arranged we maintained our connection through telephone sessions.

In autumn, I received a message from Julie to tell me she was in hospital. She was frightened, believing death was close. Her smartphone was both her transitional object and umbilical cord, linking her to me, to the outside world, and to the living. She asked if I would visit her. I agreed, and we spent our fifty minutes together on the ward. It was now clear that her breathing difficulties were the result of new tumours in her lungs. In her weakened state, she was no longer considered suitable to take part in a trial of new drugs, which might have prolonged her life. Her situation was hopeless. However, she was to be discharged and provided with oxygen to help her manage at home. As I left, she hugged me—something we had always refrained from—and I became an embodied maternal figure to her.

The following week, during a telephone session, we talked about how her therapy might continue. She hoped that there would still be some face-to-face meetings and was making enquiries about a portable oxygen tank to facilitate this. We also considered sessions via Skype for the future. Perhaps we were colluding in denying the inevitable.

The next telephone session, she was tired and could not manage the full fifty minutes. I told her I was sorry not to see her. The Christmas cactus she had once given me was in full flower and I had hoped she would see it in its perfection in my consulting room. As we ended early, I used the remaining time to photograph the plant and sent the image directly to her mobile phone. She used it as her screen-saver.

The day prior to our next scheduled appointment, I took the initiative to email Julie—something I would never do under ordinary circumstances. I wondered whether the portable oxygen tank had arrived, but assured her that we could talk on the telephone again if it had not. She did not arrive for the appointment, and neither did she call. Unwilling to disturb her rest, I waited several hours before texting to make contact. She replied, just "Hello Linda". The following day, I received a telephone message from her daughter, who told me that Julie had died in the night.

## *Conclusion*

Julie had introjected a non-corporeal mother, one who did not hold or touch her, who could not transform her anxiety into comfort. She remained attached to an *idea* of a mother—a ghostly presence—for most of her life. Like me, Julie was a "digital immigrant" (Prensky,

2001), born before the advent of personal computers and mobile telephones. She became computer-literate at work and, I believe, found particular qualities of online relationships evoked primitive memories and self-states that were otherwise inaccessible and that seemed to connect her to an ethereal mother.

Initially, in attachment-focused psychotherapy, she communicated with me, too, through the ether, thus turning me into a disembodied maternal object. In sessions, she read to me from her diary rather than looking at me and taking me in with her eyes, as if my physical reality was too much for her. Eventually, however, I became more substantial in her internal world. Her relationships with people in the real world began to take precedence over her contact with strangers on the Internet. Her cancer, eerily replicating her mother's, revealed an unexpected strength. The love, warmth, and care she had bestowed on her children and ex-husband were repaid: they held her physically and I held her in my mind, enabling Julie to let go of life and embrace whatever she believed would come next.

* * *

The Christmas cactus continues to flower every year.

## Acknowledgement

I would like to thank Julie's family for granting permission to publish this paper.

## References

Bollas, C. (1987). *The Shadow of the Object: Psychoanalysis of the Unthought Known* (reprinted 1994). London: Free Association Books.

Ibsen, H. (1964). *Ghosts: A Domestic Drama in Three Acts*. Harmondsworth: Penguin.

Prensky, M. (2001). Digital natives, digital immigrants. *On the Horizon*, *9*(5): 1–6.

*CHAPTER NINE*

# It takes a village: co-creation of community in the digital age

*Lindsay Hamilton*

> "Facebook allows you to share the funny things and the things that make you angry and every once in a while the things that mean a lot to you . . ."
>
> (A Facebook user, 2013)

## *Introduction*

My focus in this chapter is on the potential role of the Internet in building communities through the facilitation of relational bonding; love in its wider sense. I aim to look at the use of the Internet in interpersonal relationships, for social networking, as a medium with the potential to be, to build, and to enhance community living. My interest in this arises from my participation in social networking for my personal use, from hearing my clients' stories of social networking experiences, and simply from living in an era in which social networking has become the norm for many of us.

Concerning the "inner" and the "outer" realms, Chodorow (1999) describes herself as situated

> right on the cusp, where both exist together and neither can be thought or experienced without the other. I read psychoanalysis as precisely the theory that describes in detail how the individual mediates and creates inner and outer at the same time. (p. 8)

Finding myself similarly "on the cusp", I am approaching Internet based social networking from the psychoanalytic, attachment, and social science orientated blend of perspectives. This chapter is based on subjective experience, that is, participant observation, and is a rumination on the possibilities.

I have been intrigued by the ways in which use of sites such as Facebook and Twitter has influenced my own sense of connection with others, and this sense of its significance has been echoed in feedback from clients and varied reports from colleagues and others, including other Facebook users, about their experiences of social networking of one kind or another. Social networking online has provided opportunities for relating and entertainment, which, for many, does seem to supplement daily offline engagement with others. As a psychotherapist working from home and, at times, missing a team of colleagues, I have certainly come to rely on my regular social networking exchanges to have a sense of something akin to the "work place chat" I have enjoyed in previous roles. This helps to maintain my "buoyancy" while working in a difficult and demanding profession.

Online, I have had dialogues with people which have been full of mirth, hope, and wit, sad, supportive, and meaningful exchanges with those experiencing loss; I have encountered artwork, poetry, and incredible prose, enjoyed discussions on—among other subjects—media related, political, and spiritual matters. Occasionally, when feeling stretched, I have asked for advice from other mothers about parenting teenage children (and received wise and supportive guidance of a kind which might, once upon a time, have been provided by an extended family member), rekindled relationships with college friends from thirty years ago, and have been invited to events of several kinds: poetry performances, art shows, spiritual retreats, attendance at which has been deeply enjoyable, enriching, and above all, *connecting*.

As a psychotherapist trained within the relational, attachment based, and psychoanalytic orientation, I am always interested in that which promotes our connections with others significantly, and I take note of the kinds of communications engaged with by users I have encountered on the social networking sites Facebook and Twitter. I observe the differences between the form and content of interactions on these sites, and how the medium shapes the message.

In preparation for writing this, in addition to my usual social networking, I solicited feedback online. I asked people to respond regarding their use of Facebook to connect with others, and its impact on their lives, their relationships, and their sense of wellbeing (or otherwise). I received numerous interesting responses, some of which I will share here. I also attended a high level panel discussion at the House of Lords on child protection challenges in both the real and digital worlds, during the relaunch of CATS—the Centre for Abuse and Trauma Studies.

## *Community and social networking*

During my years of learning and teaching about psychoanalysis, psychotherapy, and attachment, I have observed that, although we speak of attachment, of relating, and perhaps above all of the transmuting aspects of the right kind of relationship, we do not always think and debate enough about the deep significance of *community*. A community is special kind of social group, a network of interrelatedness, that which is most essential to human wellbeing, providing context, enrichment, and holding. In this chapter, my aim is to open up a dialogue about community, and, more particularly, about the ways in which relating via the Internet may facilitate the maintenance and development of social networks and create online communities, often out of a combination of people known offline and those who are purely Facebook or Twitter associates. I also raise questions in the hope of stimulating solid research.

My background in social anthropology, sociology, developmental and social psychology, and feminism has informed my approach to psychotherapy and, thus, to this chapter. From this perspective, understanding human development and relating in terms of the dyad, the self–other "gestalt", or "interweaving", while deeply meaningful, enriching, and illuminating, leaves me wondering about the role of the overarching "container", the "vessel" which is the community within which we live, or hope to live.

Working daily with the subtle nuances of relating within the consulting room, I find myself wondering about my own and, I believe, *our*, deep need for living-in-community, and feeling aware all too often of the multifarious obstacles to real community based living in twenty-first century Britain. I am aware that I think, relate, and write as a (more or less) middle-class, English, Caucasian woman and that my experiences of community *might* be very different if my ethnicity, regional, or class background differed. However, as a species, we humans are all "social beings" with a deep need for an interconnected network of relationships of one kind or another to provide us with our sense of purpose, place, and meaningful life, or the desire for a social environment in which such emergent possibilities might flourish. As psychotherapists, we often experience a working life which might not supply the social context we may prefer to inhabit, particularly with the current reduction of National Health Service posts and voluntary sector services, and we are challenged by the question of how to ensure that our "working community" needs are met. This is true of many in contemporary Britain, where the global economy has changed employment opportunities and conditions fundamentally. Thus, in considering the theme of "love in the age of the Internet", my interest is in the potential for relating, in addition to the barriers or obstructions to connecting, within the social networking domain.

In a society in which fragmentation, lack of community, and social isolation have become the norm for many, social networking connects us with others. Our sense of agency is developed through our engagement with others, particularly when we are able to make significant choices and have a real sense of participation. If we subscribe to Bowlby's (1988) view that we are innately predisposed towards attachment, towards linking with others, towards being-in-relationship, then surely it follows that we can only develop fully and thrive in a rich social context.

Winnicott (Discussion at a scientific meeting of the British Psychoanalytical Society, ca 1940) stated, "There is no such thing as an infant", and he elaborated: ". . . meaning, of course, that whenever one finds an infant one finds maternal care, and without maternal care there would be no infant" (Winnicott, 1960, p. 586, fn). We might add, in order to acknowledge the significance of the wider community, that "it takes a village to raise a child" (an axiom variously attributed to

African and Native American cultures but source unknown). We need community in which to relate with each other, including the very particular relating involved in raising children. It takes a "village" of one kind or another for us to be truly in-relationship.

Gilda Morelli, Paula Ivey Henry, and Steffen Foerster collected data during months of fieldwork among the Efe hunter-gatherers of the Ituri Forest in the Congo Basin in Africa, focusing on the social relationships of infants and toddlers in the bands they observed. One of the findings is summarised by Peter Gray on his online blog "Freedom to learn" (in *Psychology Today*):

> Not all hunter-gatherers engage in communal nursing of infants, as the Efe do, but all such cultures are apparently far more communal than we are in their care of children. Child abuse is nearly impossible in hunter-gatherer bands. If a mother or father gets irritable and acts harshly toward a child, others in the band will immediately step in and calm the parent while also gently taking the child. Because childcare is public, every person, including young children, can witness all of the childcare in the band. Nobody becomes a parent without having had lots of experience holding and caring for others' children and witnessing many others doing so. No adult is left alone to care for a child unassisted. (Gray, 2013)

It seems pertinent to consider the following questions while remaining mindful that there is probably no single definitive answer to each one.

*What is community?* Peck states: ". . . there can be no vulnerability without risk; and there can be no community without vulnerability; and there can be no peace—ultimately no life—without community" (1990, p. 233). In this chapter, I am using the concept of community to imply a linked group of people, as in "online community", and also to imply a group, or groups, of people with whom we each interact in real life. Our community, or communities, may include work colleagues, family, friends, acquaintances, teachers, club members, leisure activity associates, shopkeepers, medical professionals, hairdressers, police officers, and so on. It is not within the scope of this paper to provide an in-depth examination of the nature of community; however, my assumption is that many in contemporary Britain exist not within one small homogenous social group in which work and home community are one and the same—as was common during the pre-industrial era—but within a variety of communities which may, or may not, be connected.

*What makes a community "healthy"?* I posted the following questions on Facebook: "Do you belong to a community? What makes your community work well?" A friend within my Facebook community replied (in her own words):

> I live in a semi community in the X flats in S . . . we have our own private flats but share some duties and meetings on a formal level, we share a car (although some have their own too) a laundry. I think what makes it work is regular communication, respect for each other's differences, good organisation (of rotas, car club payments etc.) and weekly meetings, plus some shared social engagements. We are all very different people and some don't participate at all whereas others are very active. Tolerance and understanding go a long way. (Facebook user, 2014)

*Does social networking promote healthy community?* In addition to creating opportunities for linking up online through regular Facebook or Twitter exchanges, social networking provides "wall space" for the promotion of meetings and other social gatherings, much like the notice boards we find in some cafes, shops, libraries, and community centres. Of course, joining together to support a cause unites a community for good or ill. The riots and looting in London, Birmingham, Manchester, Merseyside, Bristol, and the West Midlands in August 2001 were allegedly coordinated via social networking, including BBM (BlackBerry Messenger), a mobile phone messaging service on a secure server which does not allow public access and which enables single messages to be shared instantly with an entire contact list. Much of the current anti-fracking movement across Britain is also being coordinated across social networking sites.

In *Dreams from My Father: A Story of Race and Inheritance,* Barack Obama writes of his time as a community organiser in the Altgeld Gardens Housing Project on the South Side of Chicago in the mid 1980s. In order to bring a community together, he and his colleagues identified a cause that mattered to the residents and helped them to coordinate a campaign. Working alongside each other to take action, the local residents were engaging together for a common cause and this enhanced community feeling that outlasted the campaign itself. The multiplicity of causes on social networking sites that can unite diverse people might be an aspect of what makes the sites attractive to so many, and what *may* enable them to facilitate wider community cohesion.

*If real offline community is inaccessible due to isolation through disability/language/cultural barriers and so on, can social networking suffice as community in itself?* My expectation here is that the usefulness of social networking in these circumstances is strong if the user is already a reasonably sociable individual who can negotiate the challenges of interacting in the virtual space. Again, further research would be useful to fully explore this, and it might be possible to use social networking sites to carry out at least some of the research.

*If community is accessible to some extent but insufficient, can social networking compensate enough or increase community involvement?* For those, for example, with disabilities who can interact online but for whom travelling, financing social and other activities, negotiating the physical environment, and so on can be huge challenges, social networking can provide social contact, a forum for activism, opportunities to make arrangements for offline contact, mutual support, information about suitable venues, notifications of events, and so forth. This is not to say that social networking is the answer to social isolation, but is a beginning point to link up, to find a social network, a place to be, and can open doors to a wider world of social relating offline, as well as online.

*Might social networking provide us merely with an illusion of community, a panacea for loneliness, and thereby reduce our impetus to engage more fully in offline community?* It is my impression that we are engaging online in real relationships, with real people, within a virtual space. (This is not to say that there are not those who abuse the medium in order to represent themselves entirely falsely, as the television programme *Catfish* (Schulman, Schulman, & Joseph, 2012) investigates, or some who are unable to experience other people as real and substantial.) This extends our community beyond our immediate locale, workplace, friends, and family, and may keep us more regularly connected with those within our offline community. This appears to be conducive to community engagement, *unless* we spend so much time in the virtual space that we neglect our real offline community, or we lose, or fail to develop, the impetus and skills needed to socialise effectively.

## *Social networking: the medium is the message*

Explanation of some of the social networking terminology will be helpful here: "posting" is the name for the way in which our statements, or "status updates", are communicated on Facebook. The Facebook "wall" is the virtual "space" in which we each post about what we are doing, where we have been, how we are feeling, and so on, in addition to perhaps uploading a photograph, video, or hyperlink, or sharing a quote that means something to us. A "post" may be accompanied by an "emoticon", which is an image of a face expressing a feeling, and a statement such as "feeling sad". Your "post" will show up on the "wall" accompanied by your profile photograph and name so that you are identified as the "status updater". Subsequent dialogue, which occurs as others "like" the post, and/or comment on it, is widely visible to Facebook "friends", and to the public if privacy settings are not set to allow access to "friends" only.

A Twitter user "tweets" a statement, limited to a certain number of words, and/or a photograph, YouTube video, or hyperlink, and subsequent dialogue in response to the tweet seems harder to access and view than on the Facebook site. Twitter, therefore, appears to present far less opportunity for meaningful engagement or sense of group participation. However, it can be useful for publicity purposes, disseminating information, and is, perhaps, more attractive to those who prefer less intimacy (who might be more avoidant or dismissing in their attachment style).

The form taken by a social networking site has quite an impact on the shape taken by dialogue within that forum. I found that Facebook was initially more conducive to meaningful dialogue when all communications from "friends" would appear in real time (at the moment of "posting") and consecutively. This seemed to encourage greater spontaneity, frequency and depth of interaction. Eventually, the format was altered and the "posts" on the wall could be "sorted" to show either "Top stories" or "Most recent" ones. The Facebook default is "Top stories", which inhibits the user's ability to view "friends'" "posts" regularly and in sequence. The fragmentation and distortion created by this change has, in my opinion, been most unfortunate, as it has had an impact on conversational style, so that users are either less liable to share personal information, or the information is less readily accessible. It is unclear exactly how the prioritisation of "stories" is achieved (presumably through programming code that enables automatic assessment), but this clearly creates a filter and, in my experience at times, uncomfortably fragments communication.

### *Social networking and community ritual*

I write this shortly after the death of Nelson Mandela. On hearing of this, I shed own my tears for the passing of the man who was imprisoned throughout my youth, released on 11 February 1990, after over twenty-seven years of incarceration on Robben Island, became president of South Africa in 1994, and proceeded to dismantle the apartheid system. Mandela was a very human leader, universally loved and admired, and sometimes idealised. Facebook and Twitter, I soon discovered, were awash with "posts" and "tweets" marking Mandela's death in moving ways (quotes from the great man himself, photographs, memories, tributes), giving a very real sense of world-wide commemoration of the life and times of a truly significant figure. I was struck by how heartening it was to feel part of a national and global community who were sharing this moment in meaningful ways. It felt very different to the passivity of watching it on the television news. It felt *participatory*.

Rituals—of birth, of entering into, or consolidating, partnership, of achievement, of death—are part of community living and are often absent or insufficiently present in our increasingly secular and fragmented world. I propose that through the widespread use of social networking sites, we co-create healthy ritual anew and this can feed back into our daily offline lives in new and exciting ways. However, although Mandela's death was marked and honoured in this way, what was less in evidence was meaningful discussion or debate about it online.

Online relating can be akin to office chat, or a group of strangers sitting in a station waiting room who pass the occasional comment about the weather but do not yet feel safe enough to reveal too much more of themselves, satisfying enough in its own way, though, at times, the very anonymity of the encounter can enable sharers to reveal more than they would to a friend or acquaintance.

On the whole, there is a narcissism built in to the medium of online social networking in which a "profile" is created (already a carefully chosen presentation) and occasional "sound bites", "tweets", or "posts" are dropped into the networking space that may or may not be responded to or initiate dialogue. The strangers in the station waiting room are making utterances while others are either making their own disconnected utterances, or remaining silent, or are unable to hear, or are now responding to an original communicator who has since disappeared to make a cup of tea . . . However, despite these drawbacks, engagement and dialogue can and do occur. Among the necessary ephemera, conversational gauntlets are thrown down and a dialogue unfolds in the moment, sometimes continued over several hours or, occasionally, days.

Social networking sites enable us to find out what is happening and where (meetings, gatherings, social events, talks, art shows, book launches, and so on), facilitating communications that enable people to meet in the real world, to explore their spiritual or secular inclinations, and create a healthy ritual of relevance to our contemporary life. Shared ritual binds communities, bringing people together to participate in activities and celebrations, marking significant events, and giving meaning and shape to our "rites of passage".

## *Attachment and the use of social networking*

Subsequent to my request on Facebook for feedback about the experience of social networking, a former schoolteacher wrote:

> The reason I joined FB to start with was because I had been told by several of my ex-pupils that they would love to "chat" to me and to stay in touch by this method. It was such an attractive idea that I decided to do it. I now have very many past pupils as "friends" and feel that is brilliant as I can continue to see their development and successes and help with advice when called for (which happens very regularly). I consider these aspects of being a FB member to be of great benefit, making me feel still to be of use to people for whom I feel a great deal of affection and also allowing me access to their lives.
>
> I also enjoy using Facebook for keeping in touch with old friends all over the world and for the very many new friends I have made. It's like a club where one can mingle with like-minded (and also not so like-minded) people knowing that you're bound to find a really interesting conversation to "drop in" on or a beautiful piece of art work to comment on or a brilliant joke to share: all with people it would be impossible to meet up with at the same time! Many live quite a long way away in different parts of the UK and I'm also in regular contact with people on just about every continent!

> Those of us who work from or, for whatever reason, stay at home, benefit greatly from the pleasures of Facebook. Personally it's opened so many doors—apart from that of friendship—the main one being a chance to show my photography to the public and to receive encouragement and positive criticism from others. I have benefited hugely from this and also from eventually getting the courage to, once more, allow others to read my pieces of creative writing. Of course I also see a variety of others' creative work too and get great pleasure from this.
>
> Listening to various points of view is extremely stimulating as well as having discussions and arguments. It keeps me on the ball and opens my mind to so many more possibilities and the stimulus for research is a daily constant. (Facebook user, 2012)

While we can see the dangers inherent in the concept of teachers staying in touch with present and past pupils in this way, we can also understand that social networking provides the means, for individuals whose motives are benevolent, to keep in touch with those to whom they have been significant. There can be a continuity of attachment that may have been present when communities were smaller and less dispersed, and each village had its elders.

The focus of another paper might be on the need for, and potential shape of, monitoring and regulation of this sphere. This is in the wake of, for example, our increasing awareness of abuse perpetrated by too many public figures who have used their standing and access to the vulnerable to exploit others.

What has really impressed, and intrigued, me about social networking is the ways in which people share of themselves. Of course, there are gender differences and attachment style variations in the ways and extent to which people do this. Some are comfortable with more personal sharing and some with less; often, there is a mixture of "ordinary" sharing of petitions, photographs, jokes, inspirational sayings, YouTube videos of various kinds, and every day "postings" of the "just got up and made a coffee" type, and the more intimate posts. An English woman in Europe, whose baby is in hospital because she is having frequent seizures, "posts" daily for a while about her struggle to get her baby the care she needs and survive emotionally within an unfamiliar hospital environment with insufficient food, language skills, support, agency, and information. We all send back messages of support, of love, of concern, and we hope that this makes a difference to the mother–baby dyad that so clearly requires our community "holding".

A former college friend, with whom I would not have had the opportunity to reconnect without online social networking, developed a serious illness and wrote, movingly,

> . . . in 2007 I began subscribing to Facebook. In the beginning I was using it maybe for a half an hour or so a day and sometimes not bothering for up to a week. As I became more adept at the whole Facebook thing I noted that my time on it was increasing. I cut back and only used it for a short time per day again. I was contacted by a few old friends and I found this, in the main, pleasurable.
>
> Facebook was not only offering me an opportunity to renew old acquaintances but to also rekindle an old flame which was for me a beautiful experience. Sadly that relationship petered out but I had made many new friends as well.
>
> I was still spending around a half an hour or so daily when I was, in the spring of 2012, diagnosed with cancer. The bottom dropped out of my world for a few days until the "Chill pills" the doctor gave me kicked in and calmed me down. I was, because of the debilitating side effects, confined to my apartment and at a loss as to how to pass time.
>
> I read books, listened to the radio and watched DVDs. Never a fan of TV I began increasing my Facebook account [*sic*] more and more. I was confined to my apartment for the best part of a year as the chemotherapy continued . . . I was using Facebook for anything up to 8 and even 10 hours a day. It quite literally became a lifeline for me and I was very grateful for its existence. Now that I have been given the all clear and I have returned to work I have cut my usage back down to around the half an hour to one hour mark.
>
> When I am away for any length of time I find that I do not miss the social networking and find more positive things to do in the "Real world". That said and as noted above, my gratitude for the existence of a social networking tool, and Facebook in particular was incalculably beneficial during my illness. (A Facebook user, 2013)

This individual, as a result of his use of social networking, had a great deal of gentle emotional support from Facebook friends during his illness: they entertained him, organised home visits, and generally kept his spirits up during a frightening and gruelling time. Those who knew him in the offline and online spheres were able to keep abreast of his progress and stay alongside his journey in non-intrusive ways. We were also alongside *each other* while supporting, or simply linking up with him, within this virtual social space.

When status updates move the readers, there may be an outpouring of loving responses—virtual hugs (()) and kisses {{{}}}—and words of encouragement and support. When news of a bereavement is posted, messages of condolence pour in. It takes courage to reveal such deeply personal experiences online, and the sharing and responses to this kind of message are, at times, breathtakingly moving.

Sometimes, we are alongside those experiencing other kinds of loss, whether it is separating from a spouse, children leaving home, or even just the end of a much loved television series. Some of the heartfelt condolences and other messages are from those who have no relationship with the one experiencing loss other than through the social networking site. The person who is grieving, experiencing loss or other hardship, genuinely seems to experience holding, containment, and connection with others.

It seems apparent that, for many individuals, Facebook makes a difference on a daily basis. It is not perhaps the *real* community many would prefer, but, as an online social network, it does (or can) provide context and support, an arena for healthy competing, a space for flirting, and for the relaxing "chat over the garden fence". So much of the real community life that provided these necessary daily opportunities for social interaction is missing for so many of us now, it was inevitable that a means was found to recreate something of this kind of experience. It is alienating to live without enough real-world group experience and I hope that the appetite for social connecting manifested online might give impetus to many of us to seek out or create a more satisfying social environment in our villages, towns, and cities.

A Facebook user writes:

> ... on fb we give out support, comfort, encouragement & love to people who need those, and can ask for them in return. This is unique in my experience. It's much harder to actually ask for emotional support & words of cheer in front of people. We get self-conscious/shy/ashamed even (ridiculously), but society despises openness in suffering. We are expected to maintain decorum & be "brave" or risk

> heavy criticism if we fail to keep up appearances—chop chop, chin chin, never say die, etc. So fb offers a huge opportunity for people to "be real" and feel freer to both give & ask for practical help, new ideas & advice, and emotional support around illness, death, loneliness, depression, etc. Besides sharing joy, fun & sheer glee in as unseemly a way as one likes too! If one can't afford "therapy" or "counselling", fb can be a lifeline—metaphorically & even literally. (Facebook user, 2014)

For some individuals, particularly those with a dismissing attachment style, asking for help or reassurance in the "real world" can feel shameful, but those who seek emotional support on social networking sites initially may find that being "met" online increases a sense of safety around judicious opening up offline.

## *Virtual communication and fantasy*

During a recent debate around adolescents and their use of the Internet, it was clear that many participants imagined most young people are spending vast amounts of time masturbating to extremely misogynist hardcore online pornography, accessed in various ways. An assumption appeared to be made that this (supposed) consumption had terrifying consequences. So, I had to ask myself, "What is happening here? Why do people in the caring professions seem to think that the Internet is, for young people, largely a portal to a world of illicit and extreme sexual adventure, and that this is inevitably corrupting and dangerous?"

The discussion concerning adolescent access to pornography seemed to be tinged with a little excitement and a degree of alarmism. In fact, casual research among the teenagers of my acquaintance (hardly scientific, but perhaps meaningful) suggests that they monitor each other and frown upon Internet porn, particularly extreme porn. They are largely too busy trying to get to grips with keeping in with their peer groups, fathoming their own desires, fumbling about in real (or imagined!) erotic embraces, negotiating the delights and drawbacks of drugs and alcohol, and experimenting with identity of one kind or another, to be drawn into a world of extreme sadistic hardcore pornography online. Just *sex* itself is discomfiting enough to many adolescents—venturing off into the darkly taboo is a step too far for many of those who are furtively finding out just what sexual relating means to them.

So, my hypothesis is that it is the adults, the parental generation, who are equating adolescence with sexual experimentation and the Internet, and coming up with a supposition that most teenagers are entering the darkest of possible online worlds. My impression is that this is because this older generation are not themselves familiar with the norms and peer group pressures of online relating, and that their own fantasies around what the Internet represents, teenage sexuality, and what adventures teenagers might be on, are coming to the fore.

There are, of course, some teenagers who use the Internet in dissociated and highly disturbed ways, as highlighted by Peter Spindler, the former Scotland Yard Commander who headed the Savile enquiry and spoke at the CATS debate. However, in his role within the police force, we could imagine that the youths he has encountered are those whose disturbances have brought them to the attention of the legal system and are not representative of "ordinary" adolescent culture. This fear that adolescents are on a twisted and dangerous sexual path in cyberspace seems, as stated, to be linked to adult fantasies about Internet use as a kind of voyage into untrammelled shadowlands of the darkest unconscious without boundary or self/peer circumscription.

What I observe on social networking sites where the online community invites us to interact—to hug, to compliment, to debate, to discuss, to support, to argue, to be politically active, to offer up comment without face to face or vocal interaction—is that many exchanges can become over-intensified through the lack of the usual non-verbal mediating cues and responses, or the usual negotiated, or imposed, social group boundaries (fascinating material here for further research and thought). Hence, the widespread use of emoticons, the clever keyboard representations of emotion through depiction of features smiling, frowning, showing surprise and amazement, and so on:

:-) smiling
:-( displeasure/sadness/anger
:-/ irony/self-mocking/slight displeasure
;-) winking
<3 (heart) love.

Another aspect of non-verbal communication and text-based relating is "voice modulation" using capitals and lower case. Capitals give emphasis and more "loudness" and are equivalent to a raised voice, or even a shout. Punctuation, of course, also has its role: the ellipsis (. . .) for creating suspense, suggestion, insinuation; exclamation marks—single or multiple for gentle or stronger emphasis; the question mark, again single or multiple, like a slightly raised or hugely raised, eyebrow. Punctuation, emoticons (or emojis), and capitalisation breathe life into text allowing us to bring the more subtle hues of emotional colour to our written words. However, these do not, of course, compensate enough for the absence of vocal intonation, the touch on the arm, the warmth in the eyes, the look of disapproval, the glower of hate or defiance, the smile of empathy—they are approximations of non-verbal gestures. Professor Robin Dunbar (quoted in Shah's *Thought Economics* blog) states,

> A lot of our response in conversation picks up facial expressions, tone of voice and so forth. Emoticons simply do not substitute for this and cannot pick up these nuances. The other end of this dimension is where you see people declaring "undying love" after only a few email exchanges. In real life, it can be a figment of their imagination; you would never do that as you pick up on many more non-verbal signals. The removal of these signals, which make us cautious, is part of the problem. (Shah, 2009)

In some situations, this can lead to what Kleinians might understand as an increase in operating from the paranoid-schizoid position during dialogue (Klein, 1935, 1946). Relational practitioners might describe it as inhibited interactive attunement due to the limited cues, which can provide fertile ground for intensely fantasy-based interaction and polarisation—battling rather than measured discourse. A Facebook user writes,

> I do use my social network as a means of communicating with my friends, more so than the telephone (which I loathe . . . don't like speaking on the phone as I never know what to say!!). However, I feel much more eloquent in the written form, which is why I like places like Facebook. Though, the written word can be misconstrued and is open to interpretation, unless one explains clearly and precisely what one means in the words one types . . . It has enabled me to maintain contact with many good friends. (Facebook user, 2014)

This tendency towards polarisation can, of course, be rather interesting and exciting, in that much emerges from the vividness of the "paranoid-schizoid" place, rather than the subtler hues of the "depressive" arena. A bit of a spat draws an interested crowd, whereas murmured discourse does not. "Exciting" in a way perhaps, but counterproductive, in that consolidation of polarised positions might tend to take place rather than genuine dialogue. However, I have noticed the following: that "bystanders" tend to step in to "keep the peace" when spats online begin to gain heat, that older Facebook users will step in when younger ones are beginning to argue, that those who are battling will sometimes stop, pause, draw breath, and move the discussion to a different, sometimes less heated and more measured level, because the online discourse is often, by its nature, interrupted and slowed down by the demands of offline life and the vagaries of technology. Slowing down, taking a pause, having space to think, cooling, and emotionally regulating, allow fresh perspective and enable listening and reflecting. These are, perhaps, the hallmarks of relating from the measuredness of the unfortunately named "depressive position" (a concept I would very much like to rename the "balanced position'", or perhaps the "centred orientation").

An aspect of fantasy-based relating on social networking sites is revealed when a member states that they are about to undertake a "cull". This is a pruning of one's friends' list for a variety of reasons and, as we can see, the verb is revealing and anxiety-provoking. To casually announce to all of one's associates that they are about to be selected or deselected according to random, unidentified criteria, without a say in the matter, suggests that they are experienced as objects, not subjects; they are viewed as there to be disposed of at will. The cull instigator is omnipotent and able to wipe people out at the press of a button, with no consequences, protest, or challenge from those *real* people who are possibly experiencing loss.

One of the biggest drawbacks of social networking is its potential for enhancing fantasies of omnipotence or persecution. We need evidence that we have an impact on others, and they on us, in order to engage in a mature way in the social environment. I propose that is neither healthy nor helpful for the majority of our social interactions throughout life to take place online: family life, schooling, socialising, and so on must take place normally and predominantly in the real world, entailing interactions between real embodied people in order for online interactions to enhance and extend, rather than distort, our development as social beings.

Interacting via the Internet has encouraged us to develop online means of indicating the "non-verbal", through the use of emoticons, so that we can interact through the equivalent of multiple channels of communication almost as we do in real life. Almost, but not quite enough. The quality, the tone of the interactions may feel more shadowy, more paper-thin, more insubstantial, than that of offline contact, yet can still feel deeply significant.

## *What is the potential of social networking?*

Tumblr is a site used largely by teenagers for the purposes of sharing photographs and other information, and shared interest groups tend to emerge. There exists, for example, a "community" of self-harmers, young people for whom dissociation has become a way to manage unbearable feelings. By posting photos of their bodily wounds on Tumblr's self-harm spaces, they cannot viscerally experience the real pain in the eyes, or hurt in the mind of the other—they are exacerbating and representing the dissociations which are being created and depicted there. The images, and the distress behind them, are shocking.

This raises questions such as: does this community help because it provides context and human contact and a sense of "being-like", or does it hinder because it makes a norm of that which is profoundly self-destructive, encouraging competition that escalates self-harming behaviours and perpetuates trauma?

And is the healing potential of social connecting and dialogue *per se* enough? Is the mutual shaping and creating of narrative sufficient for wellbeing? If we were all so securely attached that connecting with others was largely intrinsically helpful and healing, psychotherapy, and other forms of treatment, might be less widely needed. Having secure attachment in relating to others implies trust, warmth, and openness, a greater capacity to nurture and be nurtured, along with more autonomy—we explore further and more comfortably from a secure base. With insecure attachment, arising when early relationship has been insufficiently secure and containing (and not remedied by later secure relationship), connecting with others will be more of a challenge. Even the relating and nurturing on offer will be not perceived, or spurned, perhaps responded to erratically, or clung to so hard that the other will feel suffocated and turn away.

Here, perhaps, lies both the rub *and* the balm. Communicating and connecting, whether on- or offline, is necessary for our wellbeing because we are social beings—created socially, developing socially, finding our self-expression socially. Whether we are seeking and finding that which nourishes, sustains, and enriches us online, or sourcing that which maintains and exacerbates our problematic attachment styles, our dissociations, our uncomfortable internal object relations and internal working models, the opportunities are there through social networking sites and media, chat rooms, and other Internet-based spaces for relating, and we will use them.

We might find these opportunities somewhat compulsive, as described by Dr Aaron Balick, because that which is never entirely satisfying can be seductive, delivering a tantalising taste of what is more deeply desired (Balick, 2013). So, we may embrace social networking if we feel drawn to it, while being mindful that that which is not quite enriching enough, not quite *real* community, can be addictive, and require us to exercise self-discipline at times. And let us be gentle in our compassion and understanding of those we work and socialise with who either eschew Internet-based connecting as "too trivial", or embrace it because it enables them to "bootstrap" into relating and a form of community belonging.

Let us ask these further questions: what does social networking offer us that we did not have before? How might we, through these and other Internet-based routes, give and receive more love, be more loveing, in the age of the Internet than previously? What is the potential of social networking, and does it offer us a kind of "village" in which we can participate in a new and exciting way, across social, national, and economic boundaries, creating links and challenging norms around social interaction, eliding some of the fragmentation that characterises our society? And what kind of regulation, boundary setting, and monitoring might be needed to make social networking safer for us to use?

## *Conclusion*

We are primarily such social creatures, we human beings, that we roll, sloosh, wallow, and emerge within our connections with others, whether they are on- or offline. We have the capacity to thrive within the social milieu, whatever milieu it is, as long as we are able to engage with others wholeheartedly. Of course, this capacity to relate with balance and verve is linked to our work as psychotherapists, as we facilitate the emerging capacity to engage within those whose experiences have impaired this ability, or stifled its unfolding.

As we find our former lovers again, meet with old friends and find new ones, connect with family members, read poetry, and delight at artwork timidly shared, our old familiar attachment styles shape our connecting: projections and transference can be overblown due to the lack of a real, embodied other holding, metabolising, and mirroring our communications to counterbalance the inventions of our imaginations. Yet, we also have the opportunity to play, to explore, to try things out, and experience our social being in a virtual "in between"—Winnicott's "transitional" or "potential space" (Winnicott, 1971), or Buber's "das Zwiscehenmenschliche" (Buber, 1965).

## *References*


Balick, A. (2013). *The Psychodynamics of Social Networking: Connected Up Instantaneous Culture and the Self*. London: Karnac.

Bowlby, J. (1988). *A Secure Base: Clinical Applications of Attachment Theory*. London: Routledge.

Buber, M. (1965). *Between Man and Man*. New York: Macmillan.

Chodorow, N. J. (1999). *The Power of Feelings*. New Haven, CT: Yale University Press.

Gray, P. (2013). Beyond attachment to parents: children need community. *Psychology Today*, 20 July. Available at: www.psychologytoday.com. Accessed 12 February 2014.

Klein, M. (1935). A contribution to the psychogenesis of manic-depressive states. In: J. Mitchell (Ed.), *The Selected Melanie Klein* (pp. 115–145). London: Penguin, 1986.

Klein, M. (1946). Notes on some schizoid mechanisms. In: J. Mitchell (Ed.), *The Selected Melanie Klein* (pp. 175–200). London: Penguin, 1986.

Obama, B. (1995). *Dreams from My Father: A Story of Race and Inheritance*. New York: Times Books.

Peck, M. S. (1987). *The Different Drum: Community-Making and Peace*. New York: Simon & Schuster [reprinted New York: Touchstone, 1990].

Schulman, N., Schulman, A., & Joseph, M. (2012–ongoing). *Catfish: The TV Show*. Original Channel MTV).

Shah, V. (2009). The psychology and anthropology of social networking. *Thought Economics*, 22 April. Available at: www.thoughteconomics.blogspot.co.uk. Accessed 12 February 2014.

Winnicott, D. W. (1960). The theory of the parent–infant relationship. *International Journal of Psychoanalysis*, *41*: 585–595.

Winnicott, D. W. (1971). *Playing and Reality*. London: Tavistock.

# INDEX